JUMPING THE CURB

BY

GAIL DESBERG

In Memory of Edith and Daniel Desberg

1. THE LAST HOLIDAY: Labor Day, 1996

Once again it was Labor Day, and once again it came with a sense of foreboding. For some it was the end of a blissful season, for others, the drumbeat of school grew closer. For those who loved the beach it was the most stirring time of the year. Yet for us, the blue skies of Labor Day had the pallor of gray. As I walked along the Atlantic City Boardwalk watching the gulls and plovers skip at the shoreline, I thought back to the day when the color of our world changed.

It was 1996, and the summer had brought with it a culmination of heat, prostrating temperatures that only an ocean breeze could stifle. Yet on September first, there was more than an ocean breeze. Hurricane Edouard was roaring through the offshore waters and the southern shores of New Jersey. Rain and 135 mph winds pummeled the beaches from Cape May to Atlantic City. The rip currents and undertow made it far too dangerous for anyone to enter the ocean. The surfers were thrilled at the notion that a storm was passing through. This was the ultimate board time. Storm season was the perfect opportunity to fly on water.

Sunday evening, my husband, Alex, and I had the traditional Labor Day Weekend BBQ. Twenty of our closest friends gathered to celebrate the end of the summer. Alex was at the grill with chicken

3

that had been marinating in a homemade teriyaki. He took a swig of Corona, looked at his friend Michael and said, " The secret to tender chicken is to cook it in the oven first. Then you finish it up on the grill." Michelle had brought appetizers. Margie had brought one of her famous salads with homemade dressing. Christina had brought dessert—pies from Hackett's, a farmer's market with the best freshly baked , homemade fruit pies. Val and Jeff were in charge of the liquor, and the list went on. Everyone's kids were in the backyard chasing Pepe, our little Chihuahua. She was blonde, ambitiously fast, and pretty uncatchable for our kids Adam, three, and Danielle, one-and-a-half.

Hurricane Edouard had been hovering off the coast like an alien aircraft. At around midnight the weather channel said he was beginning to follow the predicted course and move up the coast. Our town, Linwood, was left with the remnants of fallen tree branches and whipping winds. It would later turn out that this storm would be the worst storm of the Atlantic Hurricane Season of 1996—not as newsworthy or as deadly and destructive as Katrina, but to our family it would uproot and destroy the life that we knew forever.

September second, a bright and beautiful day, was burgeoning on the horizon.

Alex got up early and took Danielle in the baby jogger for a run on the boardwalk. Our good friends Harry and Amy, who had been visiting from New York, headed back to the city. The aftermath of the storm was evident up and down the tree-lined street where leaves and loose branches lay scattered on the lawns. But the winds from Edouard's wrath had calmed considerably and it was a bright and beautiful day.

A perfect day for the beach.

By the time we got to the beach it was noon, and packed like the mall on Black Friday. Alex dropped us off at the bulkhead where we unloaded the kids, the striped beach chairs with our names on the backs, a cooler filled with snacks, and two bags, one with diapers and spare clothes and another with towels. We were glorified mules, on our way to find a spot in the sand as Alex began to hunt for a parking space.

With a bag over each shoulder, Danielle in one arm and Adam holding my hand, I found my way to a space where all our friends were sitting. It was in front of the Rumson Avenue bulkhead and today the rough waves were crashing closer in than usual.

Whitecaps formed and ripped away from their crests; the surf looked ominous even as it edged on shore. We sat amongst our friends, many of whom had joined us the night before, and I began to lay out the towels for the kids. Alex came walking down with the chairs, his bright green eyes sparkling with excitement.

"How did you find a parking space so fast?" I asked.

"It's all about maneuverability," he answered. He already had ants in his pants, and as usual he couldn't sit still. "I think I'm going in."

Our eyes locked and for a second I felt uneasy. More than uneasy—it was a flash of panic. But it was ridiculous. I pushed it out of my mind and kissed him. After all, he wasn't going in by himself; a group of guys would be going with him. He had lived here his whole life and knew the temperament of the water better than I. Besides, the beach was open, it was Labor Day, and preschool would start on Tuesday. The summer was taking its final bow.

As Alex walked away I decided to take Danielle down to the water to do some wave jumping. She had an easy spirit and loved motion. I asked our friends Sharon and Craig to watch Adam as he played in the sand with his resin animals, and took Danielle down to the shoreline.

"OK, Danielle, time to jump the waves." I lifted her little body with my hands, grasping her arms as she faced the expansive ocean. The first wave came and I lifted her over it as it hit me. "Whee!" I screamed. She giggled with delight. "Here comes another one!" We waited and I lifted her again, then again, and again.

After 10 minutes or so I was getting a little weary, but her joy was so obvious and contagious that I kept going. The next wave took me by surprise with its sheer force. It almost knocked us over. My feet clenched the dissipating sand and I clamped down on Danielle's arms as the undertow pulled on my legs and the lower half of her body. I felt the raw strength of the ocean in a way I had never known. I could feel her trying to steal my baby. There was no mercy in her strength, and I knew that if I didn't keep my hands wrapped and sealed around Danielle's arms, she would be torn from me forever. Finally the undertow receded and we were free from the ocean's grip.

"That's enough for us today, sweetie," I said to Danielle. My heart was racing, but she seemed none the wiser as I held her close.

As we were walking back to our chairs, I could see a large circle of people gathering down the beach. They seemed to be in a huddle, but I had two kids to watch and had no real interest in seeing what it was about.

I sat down with Danielle and began to strip her of her suit and change her diaper. "There you go, baby girl. Nice and dry."

Adam, by this time, had dug a hole so deep he began to disappear in it.

"Did he give you any trouble?" I asked Sharon and Craig

"Piece of cake," Sharon responded.

Just then, I looked up to see Debbie, the sister of one of Alex's best friends, standing over me. She looked down at me. "Gail, Alex has been hurt. Do you want me to watch the kids?"

I looked at Sharon. "We'll watch them," she said immediately.

"OK." I stood up and followed Debbie towards the crowd. As we got closer to the outer edges of what felt like a sea of people, a buzzing began to ring in my ears, bringing with it a sense of trepidation that I had never felt before.

"Excuse me, please," I said to the backs of people in the crowd. They weren't listening.

"Excuse me please," I said louder, and began to force my way towards the center. Finally, I found my way through. Alex lay there, his body splayed out on the sand. His eyes were open. Uniformed police stood around him.

I started kneeling next to him when a policeman thrust his arm out to block me and yelled, " Stand back!" in my face.

I screamed back, "He's my husband!" forced his arm to the side, and knelt next to Alex.

He had a pleading look in his eyes. "I'm sorry," he said.

"Sorry for what?"

Never had a crowd of people felt so insignificant. They had been muted by the buzzing in my ears. Then the chorus of bees grew louder, I looked up to see that a couple of EMTs had begun to come down with a stretcher. Our friend Gary Lowenstein was nearby, he was an electrical engineer who moonlighted as an EMT.

The police officers started to lift Alex.

"No, no," Gary said. "You have to stabilize him before you move him."

Why didn't they know that?

"Why don't you wait for the EMTs before you put him on the board?" he continued.

The officer on duty seemed nervous. People right and left were on their cell phones. Smart phones didn't exist then, just bulky devices that made only phone calls. *Who were they calling?*

The EMTs arrived and I stepped back. They lifted Alex onto the board, and we began a slow painful trudge across the sand towards the bulkhead.

Then I remembered the kids, and turned around to look for them. Sharon and Christina were there, handing me my beach bag.

"We'll watch the kids," Christina said. "Don't worry about them."

I pulled out my keys and handed them over. "Use my car. The car seats are in there."

I kissed the kids goodbye and followed the line to the ambulance, behind a policeman and the EMTs carrying Alex on a wooden board.

Waiting at the ambulance was a man I had never met before. He introduced himself, saying that he was a doctor and would ride with us to the hospital, to make sure everything went smoothly. He had a kind face. I can no longer remember his name, but I will never forget that a total stranger had accompanied us to the hospital to make things easier.

I had never ridden inside an ambulance with the sirens blaring and the lights blazing. It was as if the Red Sea itself was parting, although admittedly there wasn't much traffic on this Labor Day. Everyone was still at the beach.

2. 911

As we entered the emergency room, a nurse asked me to stop at the front desk while they whisked Alex into the back for a CT scan. I had to give them my insurance card and show identification.

"This will only take a minute," said the woman behind the desk. The waiting room was crowded and a nurse came up to me and asked if I would like to be seated someplace a little quieter. Stunned, I nodded and followed her to a room around the corner. We passed a drunk man who was shouting gibberish as he lay on a gurney in the hallway.

I was taken to a peach-colored waiting room. Everything was peach - the chairs, walls, even the tables. Within minutes, I was joined by Craig, one of Alex's closest friends. This was the most unnerved I had ever seen him. He sat down across from me, still wearing his swim trunks and T-shirt. I wore a white cover-up over my bathing suit. I could still smell the suntan lotion on my body. My hair was pulled back into a ponytail and I could see goose bumps on my arms. The air was blowing on the back of my neck, and in any other circumstances I would have felt it. My body registered the cold, but my head was somewhere else.

"Have you heard anything?" Craig asked.

9

"No."

We both sat there quietly, waiting, as we listened to the man wail in the hallway.

Then an obscenely handsome man in a white coat walked in. He was tall with dark curly hair and bright blue eyes. Apparently I wasn't in too much shock to notice and feign a smile.

He looked at me and asked, "Are you Mr. Kiejdan's wife?

"Yes," I said.

He stuck out his hand. "My name is Dr. Lowe." He sat across from Craig and I and said, "There is no good way to tell you this. I am sorry, but Alex has a fractured vertebrae. And from the looks of it, it involves C6 and C7, which are in the cervical part of the spine, or the neck. He has a spinal cord injury and frankly, it's one of the most serious injuries you can sustain. We won't know much more until we get him to the Atlantic City Mainland Division where they have an MRI."

In laymen's terms, Alex's neck was broken. Once again I was stunned into silence.

"I am really so sorry," the doctor repeated. "Right now they are putting a catheter in Mr. Kiejdan. I will be back if I have any more information." Then he stood up, shook my hand, then Craig's, and left the room.

Craig looked at me. "Shit."

I did not cry. I felt nothing. I didn't know if or when I would ever feel again. I didn't know if it was a protective mechanism or it was the shock, but not only couldn't I feel anything, my brain and its capacity to function as a smart, intuitive, organ had ceased as well..

Just then, Michael Grossman walked in. He was one of Alex's other closest friends. Michael looked at Craig and nodded hello, then he turned to me, kissed me on the cheek, and asked me how I was doing.

I couldn't reply. Craig took over and reiterated what the doctor had said. Michael sat down and I could see the familiar stunned expression.

"How did you hear about what happened?" I asked.

"My mom called me from the beach. She told me Alex was hurt and that you were on the way to the hospital, so I left the store and drove right here." He crossed his legs, his fingers drumming on the arm of the chair. The three of us stared off into space.

I felt the pull of gravity lead me as I floated far from the chair I was sitting in. But as I seemed to gravitate further and further away, Alex's mother Molly walked in, along with his brother Michael and Michael's wife, Jodi. Molly was crying and they sat her down. Then Michael and Jodi left to see if they could find out anything else about Alex's condition.

Molly was a little woman, no taller than four foot ten. She was round in the face, and her body followed suit. Her accent was from Lithuania, and as a Holocaust survivor she had seen more than her share of tragedy. She had been witness to some of the greatest organized horrors brought about by mankind.

She began to cry as she rocked herself back and forth. "Vy did this happen?" she asked. "Vy?"

I knelt in front of her. "I don't know."

"He shouldn't have been in the vater. Vy is this happening to me?" she cried. "First I lose my husband, and now this."

I tried to console her. Her husband, Pinky had passed away three years earlier. He was the patriarch of the family, and together they had four boys and two girls. His parents had lost most of their family during the Holocaust. Having six children was their way of beginning to rebuild the family name.

Alex was the second to youngest, and he was the wildest one in the family. He was athletic, and strong, and had a twisted sense of humor. And most importantly, he didn't mesh with the family line-up in the traditional sense. He was more immune to the guilt that was served up daily with a cup of tea. He had defied the odds of becoming a product of his environment.

Malka, or Molly and Pinchus, or Pinky had known each other since they were children. Malka Avidon had been born to a farming family near the river. Her village dwelled on the outskirts of Vilnius, Poland which eventually became Vilnius, Lithuania. She had four brothers and the whole family worked to make ends meet, rising before dawn to milk the cows and get the fresh eggs from the chicken coop. Her parents struggled to put food on the table and keep the animals fed. The hardships of the 1930s had weighed heavily on her father's mind. They could no longer feed all of their children.

One day, while Malka and her father Rufca were visiting her uncle in town, her uncle had an idea. Her uncle had a beautiful store filled with handmade porcelain dolls. She loved to visit this particular uncle, so she could play with the dolls in his store. His name was Rachmiel and he and his wife, Hanna could not have children. They had offered to take care of Malka in such difficult times.

Her father had always said no until this day, when he had a change of heart. So, at the age of five, Malka was given to her aunt and uncle, severing her ties with her brothers, whom she loved dearly. "Please papa, please, please let me come back with you," she pleaded. He kissed her keppe with a tear in his eye, turned around and left Malka with uncle Rachmiel.

She would spend several years living in a better world but the footsteps of war were not that far away, and her life would turn into a fight for survival.

It was after three in the afternoon and Alex's brother Michael and his wife, Jodi had returned to the waiting area. Jodi was an internist and knew the ins and outs of the trauma unit from working as an ER doctor. She had done her residency at Jefferson Hospital in Philadelphia, and told me that there were twelve spinal cord centers in the country, Jefferson being one of them.

"I think you need to get him out of here," Jodi said. "He needs to go up to Jeff. They have a heliport, and I'm going to see if I can arrange for him to fly out of here."

My breathing started to get shallower and I felt as though I were part of an audience, watching, unable to move and unable to think. Everyone was looking at me and I had no idea why.

"I need to make a phone call," I said.

I stood up, went into the waiting room, found a pay phone and dialed. It was Labor Day, that much I remembered, and my mother was at my brother's house in Lyndhurst, a suburb of Cleveland, Ohio..

My brother answered the phone, Gary's voice was warm and cheery as he said hello. "How are you doing?"

"I'm at the hospital," I said. "Alex had an accident and they just told me he has a fractured vertebrae."

Dead silence. The shock wave continued its ripple effect as he said, "Oh God. You'd better talk to Mom."

He handed her the phone and she said, "Gail, what happened?"

When I finished talking her only response was "Get him out of there. Go to Philadelphia. Let me call the airlines and I will be there as soon as I can. I love you."

13

"I love you too, Mom." I hung up the phone.

I turned around to walk back down the corridor and found out that Alex had been moved to a waiting area, behind pale blue curtains, with the head of the bed slightly raised. It was the first time I had seen him since they'd taken him back for testing. He had an IV in his arm and a catheter with a bag hooked on to the bed, as well as a pulse oximeter on his finger.

I looked at him, and all I could register was the sorrow on his face. I kissed him on the mouth and his lips were warm and sweet.

He looked at me earnestly. "Gail, I am so sorry. I am really so sorry."

"It's OK," I responded. "Don't worry, everything will be OK. Jodi is going to get you out of here. She's going to try and put you on a helicopter to take you up to Jefferson. It's one of the top spinal cord centers in the country. We'll know more when you get there. "

"How are the kids?" he asked.

"They're fine, they're at home. Tina, Gary, and Sharon are watching them."

"I'm sorry," he said again. "I screwed everything up."

"Alex, you didn't do it on purpose. It's OK."

"I was trying to get out of the water because it was so rough, and I could feel the pull of the undercurrent. I decided to use a wave to help me get back in, when the wave broke I was thrown down and my head was slammed into the bottom of the ocean floor. I ruined everything."

"Shh. It's OK. I love you," I said, trying to reassure him.

"No, you don't understand. I have no feelings from my nipples down."

Once again, I was stunned. Then I heard the bustling of people around me. A nurse had come in to speak to us.

14

"Mr. Kiejdan, you are being moved," she said. "We have an order to fly you to Jefferson Hospital in Philadelphia. You will ride on a helicopter. It will be landing here in about half an hour and will take you directly to Jefferson. Mrs. Kiejdan, I need you to sign some release forms. If you could follow me I would really appreciate it. Mrs. Kiejdan, you should probably say goodbye to Mr. Kiejdan because they are going to be right down to take him upstairs."

"OK, thank you," I said. I looked at Alex. "I will see you in Philly."

With that, more nurses arrived to take him to the roof where he would be airlifted to Jefferson. I kissed him again, told him I loved him again, and walked into the corridor.

There, I saw Craig. He was going to take me to Michael Grossman's parents' house, where I could shower and pick up a change of clothes. Then Mark Dannenbaum would drive me up to Jefferson. Since my brain had left my body and I had no idea what I was doing, it was important that other people were thinking for me.

Our friends were incredible. They were communicating with each other and doing the thinking for us. I couldn't see past the goose bumps on my arms, let alone plan the next 15 minutes. Shock had taken over and wrapped itself around me like a cocoon, protecting me from my own emotions and muting the world around me. I could hear the voices of people speaking to me and I continued to see their lips moving, but I did not register what they were saying..

The Grossman home was on Bayshore Drive, with a beautiful view of the back bay that stretched from Atlantic City through Ventnor and Margate, and onto Longport. Michael's parents had lived there for years, long enough to raise four children, who had paired up to become eight and eventually bringing in ten rambunctious little additions. We arrived to find the whole family sitting down to dinner for a Labor Day barbeque.

Sharon was waiting with my clothes. Michael's parents, Marsha and Stanley, welcomed me at the door and asked if I was hungry. I declined, and from the corner of my eye I could see everyone staring at me. The large living room and dining room grew silent. Unbeknownst to me, it was the beginning of what would become commonplace- silence and discomfort.

Michael's mother, Marsha, a thin, elegant woman with a strong mind, and kind heart, led us to the bathroom and handed me a large, dark gray bath sheet. "Here you go, honey. If you need anything else, let me know. There's soap, shampoo and cream rinse in the shower stall."

"Thank you," I replied. Sharon murmured her thanks, too. Then Marsha shut the door behind her.

Sharon's hair was slicked back into a short ponytail, as usual. A slender wisp of a woman with a small frame, she was dressed in clean crisp clothes, as was her custom. She always looked put-together, even if she was just wearing shorts and a T-shirt. She was one of the kindest people I knew, with a very even temperament.

She put down my bag of clothes and I began to slowly undress. Even then, in such a dark moment, I thought, "How can I get naked in front of her? She's skinny, I have cellulite. She's going to think I'm a cow."

I was not a cow. I had a fairly nice body after having two kids, but I was not S.K.I.N.N.Y. I was not toned, I was not camera ready. And then I took off the T-shirt I had been wearing since the beach, and the pink bikini underneath it, and got into a hot shower. It felt amazing. The goose bumps that had been on my arms and legs melted into the heat, and the pounding hot water was the first real feeling of something familiar since the accident.

I stepped out of the shower and Sharon handed me my towel. I felt the cool twists of cotton absorb the water, and I was swathed in a temporary blanket of calm.

After I dressed, Sharon asked, "Do you need me to do anything? The kids are being taken care of. We're taking turns. Christina and Gary are at your house now. And I'm going to go back there. Don't worry about them, they're in good hands."

"Thank you," I said.

"Here's a bag with a change of clothes." She lifted the bag. "We spoke to Brad, and Craig called Rich and Freddy. They're going to meet you at the hospital. We tried to call Michelle and David but there was no answer. I'll keep trying."

And there it was, a machine in motion. Friends getting together to help, and even though we were part of that nucleus, we were not a part of the mechanization.

We walked out of the bathroom, and Mark was waiting to take me to Philly.

3. ATTENTION DEFICIT

When we arrived at Jefferson, I asked to see Alex. The woman at the front desk asked for my insurance card, which I promptly produced. Then she put us in a small waiting room that was closed off from the rest of the ER patients. It was dark outside and the lights were bright, as they are in all hospitals. We walked into the small, rust-colored room, which oddly enough was carpeted, and there were our friends Rich and Fred both of whom lived in Philadelphia..They had beaten us there.

Both got up to hug me. "I'm sorry," they said in unison.

Just then Brad, Alex's best friend from childhood, walked in and hugged me. "How are you doing?" he asked. Then added, "Don't answer that. I know...you suck, this sucks, everything just sucks."

Brad was never one to mince words, and I appreciated his candor. I was surrounded by some of Alex's closest friends, and there was comfort in that.

But it didn't last long. A man with a white coat walked in and introduced himself. I shook his hand. I knew I was supposed to be attentive, but my mental prowess was on hiatus. Gone fishing without a pole. There was that buzzing again...I was fading out. The

18

good news was that Rich and Mark were both doctors and they looked like they were listening attentively.

Fade in. "…and we've put a halo on him to stabilize the neck. A halo is a bit of a contraption. It has four long rods that stabilize the head and neck in place. We had to drill four holes into his skull to set it with substantial-sized screws; two are located in the forehead and the other two are located directly behind, in the rear of the skull. The bottom parts of the steel rods are attached to the bodice, which looks like a solid plastic vest with a sheepskin-like lining. "

Fade out…*Medieval*, that's what I was thinking. *But hey, I'll reserve judgment.* If the visual of his head being balanced on his neck by the solid steel contraption was supposed to make me feel better, it missed the mark.

Fade back in "…he is intubated, and tomorrow when Dr. Vacarro gets here, he will assess the situation. He will need surgery to stabilize his neck. This is done by putting a titanium plate in the back of the neck. Dr. Vacarro will explain it further, because he is the orthopedic surgeon who does this procedure."

I looked around the room. Everyone was nodding except me. I guessed I should, too.

"Any questions so far?"

"Yes," I said. "Where's the closest bathroom?" If I didn't have Inflammatory Bowel Syndrome before, I had it now.

When I returned, the doctor was patiently waiting. Everyone had their eyes on me. I smiled faintly, because this is what I was trained to do as a child.

Brad led with, "You're going to sleep over my apartment tonight, and I will bring you back in the morning."

"OK," I said. The rest of our friends thanked the doctor and said their goodbyes, hugged and kissed me and told me they would

19

see me tomorrow, and then left. I, too, thanked the doctor, and began to walk with Brad towards the exit.

At the apartment, Brad's partner, Lee, greeted us at the door. He gave me hug and said," Let me show you your room."

I quietly followed him upstairs to a room on the second floor, where he put my things down. The room was warm and lit by several incense candles that I found immediately soothing. He opened the doors to a porch filled with pots and planters. On display was his citified garden, sprouting into beautiful flowers, plants, and herbs. He picked some mint and some chamomile, and said, "I'll be right back."

I changed into a nightshirt, and within minutes he was back with a silver tray, a teacup, a small teapot with steaming water, and a small bowl of sugar cubes. With hell raining down, I was still reminded that a cup of chamomile tea, known for its calming ability, could settle one's restless soul.

"Oh my God, that is so nice, thank you. You are so sweet."

"Gail, you don't have to thank me. Just try and relax a little. When you're done with the tea just put the tray outside your door and I'll get it in the morning."

I quietly slipped under the covers and looked out at the moon. It was a beautiful summer night, and even though the fall would creep in towards the end of the month, this was the end of the summer for me. The rest of the season would be spent indoors in a frigid hospital.

I lay there, alternating between staring at the ceiling and looking at the clock. The red neon numbers changed from midnight to one, one to two, two to three. I could no longer bear to be in bed. My eyes would not stay shut. I kept thinking of Alex, intubated, with some God-awful contraption on his head. What if he died? Was I going to be a widow? Would I be raising two babies without their father? Suddenly, I needed to get back to the hospital. How could I relax? He could die!

I knocked on Brad and Lee's bedroom door and Brad answered, dazed.

"Do you think you could take me back to the hospital?" I asked.

"Sure, let me just put on some clothes."

We drove back to the hospital in silence, through the deserted streets of Philadelphia. We parked the car and went up to the Neuro-Intensive Care Unit. It was quiet except for the sounds of the heart monitors rhythmically beeping. We checked in at the nurse's desk and I told them I was Alex's wife.

"Do you know how he is doing?" I asked.

"Why don't you two wait in the waiting room and I will check in with his doctor," the nurse said. "Let me show you where it is."

She walked Brad and me over to the waiting room, which was dark and empty. The lights were off, but we could see the chairs from the fluorescent lighting in the hallway. This would become my new home for the next two weeks. We sat down on the aubergine-colored chairs, and I watched as Brad tried to close his eyes. Every time I tried to close mine, they would pop right open.

Within minutes, a doctor walked in. He introduced himself as the resident on Alex's case, and went on to say, "Alex has had another MRI, so the surgeon will know exactly what he is looking at tomorrow. We can't tell if his spinal cord is severed at this point. Those who have a spinal cord injury with a severed cord never regain any function. The level of injury for your husband is C6. He is paralyzed from the nipples down. But it is still early. There is no way to know how much, if any, movement or sensation he will get below his injury. He has been sedated and is on a morphine drip. Right

21

now, he is not breathing on his own, but after the surgery we hope at some point to remove his intubation tube. There is a risk of him getting pneumonia, and being intubated increases that risk. Do you have any questions?"

"Yes, can I see him?" I asked.

"Let me check with his nurse. Maybe you can take a peek. I'll be right back."

When he returned, he nodded, and I left Brad to follow the doctor back behind the closed and locked doors of the Neuro-Intensive Care Unit. The hallway was brightly lit, with a bland gray linoleum floor.

Alex was in his own room and had more tubes and cords in him than the back of a television, with cables going every which way. The difference was that his tubes were hooked up to lifesaving devices and were mostly transparent, with fluid running in and out of his body. I watched the monitor as it beeped rhythmically. His IV dripped fluids into one arm as a catheter dripped fluid into a bag filling with urine. It looked like his halo was holding his head in place on the top of his body. He had an endotracheal tube going into his mouth and an oxygen mask over his nose. He was a mess.

As he slept in this induced state, I thought about how much I loved him. I kissed him on his cheek and whispered in his ear, and then I turned around and looked at the nurse, who said, "We'll tell you if there is any change."

I turned towards the exit and walked through the hallway, back to Brad in the waiting room. He was asleep, so I stared out the window, waiting for the sun to rise, waiting for the beat of daytime.

4. THE WAITING ROOM

When I woke, I could feel the crick in my neck from sleeping like a crumpled piece of clothing. It was cold in the waiting room and once again I had goose bumps.

It was 7 a.m., and there was a changing of the guard. Nighttime nurses were preparing to leave and the daytime nurses were familiarizing themselves with their patient load. The waiting room, where we had dozed on and off, had taken on its daytime hues of deep purples and blues.

Brad looked at me and asked if I wanted coffee.

"No, thank you." I didn't drink coffee, and I had no appetite whatsoever. There was a payphone right outside the waiting room. "I think I'm going to call home and check on the kids."

When I turned around again, the room had started to fill up. A young man had just been brought in from Altoona, Pennsylvania. He had been in a bad car accident and was wrapped in so many bandages that he looked like a mummy. His parents were divorced, but they were sitting in the waiting room like they were glued together. They were staring out the window, waiting for an update from a doctor or nurse.

As I sat down, Mark Dannenbaum walked in and kissed me hello. He sat down, as well. "Any updates?"

"Not yet," I responded. "His surgery is today. My mother is supposed to come in today. And right now, that's all I know."

Brad stood up and said, "Gail, as long as Mark is here, I'm going to go home and take a shower. I'll be back a little later, if that's OK with you."

"Of course it is. Thank you so much for staying with me."

I felt hollow, like a person inside me was speaking the pleasantries; someone who knew that I was supposed to respond appropriately. But the real me, she was still floating around somewhere.

As the minutes ticked by, I felt them. Each and every one was slow and prolonged. Time itself became painful, a throbbing reminder of how a simple, carefree life could flip within seconds into a dark reservoir of fear and isolation.

Michael Grossman walked in a few minutes later, and he, too, kissed me hello.

"Mrs. Kiejdan?" a nurse asked.

"Yes."

"Your husband is being taken down to surgery soon. The doctor would like to meet with you. Would you like to come back into the NICU?"

"Yes, I would." I stood up and followed her back through the locked glass doors, which she opened with a magnetic keycard. I felt like my lips were turning blue, it was so cold up on the seventh floor. I made my way to Alex's room, which was on the left-hand side of the hallway, with a beautiful view of parking lots and rooftops.

In Alex's room, Dr. Vaccaro introduced himself and said, "I will be performing Mr. Kiejdan's surgery. I am an orthopedic surgeon with special fellowship training in spine surgery."

You look really young, I thought. *Focus, Gail.*

He continued, "A few years ago I was involved in developing a way to stabilize the spine after a fracture, using titanium plates."

When did you start, when you were fifteen? I thought. *Focus.*

He continued, "This procedure, insofar as technique is concerned, allows us to stabilize the spine and enable it to fuse properly. We will open Mr. Kiejdan up both anteriorly and posteriorly at the level of his injury."

"C6," I interjected.

"Correct. The goal is to insert both plates, gain alignment and create stability. At this point we do not know the extent of the damage. If his spinal cord is severed, I'm afraid he will not gain any usage back. But because there is substantial swelling, he may get a level or two. We don't want you to get your hopes elevated that he will walk again because that happens with a very small percentage of patients. Do you have any questions?"

"Yes, how long will the surgery be?"

"It should take a couple of hours. I will be back here when it is finished."

"Thank you, Dr. Vacarro," I said.

"You're welcome," he responded. And with that, the orderly came to take Alex to pre-op.

I went back to my anointed chair and began to wait. Friends began to file into the waiting room, and for some reason I had the sense that it was more like sitting Shiva, the traditional Jewish mourning period following death. I could hear the elevator dinging from a distance. And I could hear our friends talking to each other

25

in the distance... at least, it felt like the distance. In reality, they were sitting right next to me.

I could not engage in conversation, so I just sat there. I stared at the poor people at the end of the room who were here from Altoona. Their son was going into surgery later that day.

I began to close my eyes, and as I did, I felt a familiar presence. I opened them, and there, to my incredible relief, was my mother. I stood and hugged and kissed her.

It had been two years since my father had passed away, and my mother's uncommon strength never ceased to amaze me. She had persevered, grabbed hold of the reins, and set a quiet course as to how she would live her life without him. There she was, solid, strong and energetic. Yet on the inside she was kind, compassionate and smart.

"Mom."

"I'm here, honey. I took the first flight out this morning." She had come straight from the airport.

"Alex is in surgery. They said it would take a couple of hours."

"Have you eaten anything?" she asked.

"No, but I really have no appetite."

She rolled her suitcase into the corner, said hello to all of our friends, and we sat back down to wait. By this time, I had begun to give out the number of the pay phone that was on a wall opposite from the NICU waiting room. That was where I could be reached, because this was where I would stay.

At around 3 p.m. the doctor came to the waiting room. I stood up and walked into the hallway with him.

"Mrs. Kiejdan, as far as the procedure goes, everything went well. I was able to go in through the anterior, which is what I had hoped to be able to do. That is where we placed the plates. Right now, your husband is in post-op. You will be able to see him in an hour or so. The next step for him is to get him off the ventilator, and then we will go from there. Do you have any questions?"

"Yes, when can I see him?"

"Well, after they bring him up from post-op, the nurses in the NICU will let you know."

"Thank you so much," I said.

"You're welcome."

I turned around and my mother was right there. "Honey, I'm going to get a ride to the house and check on the kids. Are you coming home tonight?"

"I don't know yet. I'll call you later, OK?"

"OK, sweetheart. I love you."

"I love you too, Mom."

And with that, she kissed and hugged me goodbye.

Alex was carted back up an hour later, but he was so heavily dosed with medication that I knew he would not wake up until much, much later.

I slowly became a denizen of the NICU waiting room. I had a pillow and blanket for nighttime and I began to eat all of my meals there. Our friends, who were in abundance, brought lunch, dinner, and coffee. Alex had five siblings, all living at the shore. Most came sporadically, although Robert, the brother he was closest to, came religiously with his wife, Fern. His mother Molly came up with his sister Renee, with whom I had been at odds for years.

Molly said "Gail, please, look at Renee, she is suffering so badly. She is in so much pain."

Ice. That's what I felt from Renee, and that's what I gave back.

Molly's friends were there, too: Richard and Betty, Inga, Rosalee and Sidney. "Richard, go look at him," Molly said. "See how I suffer?

How can this be happening?" They had all stopped by to visit a distortion of what was once their friend, their brother and a son, but not many saw him while he was still in the NICU.

Alex stayed drugged as the shock of his catastrophic trauma took hold of all who loved him. Fortunately, he was in intensive care and not in the waiting room where he could see the looks on their faces, or hear the way they spoke of him—as if he was no longer with us.

"He'll get better, you'll see," his mother said to me. "He is a strong boy. We have fight in our blood. We survived the camps."

Day one became day two, which became day three, all at a glacial rate of movement. I had slowly been bringing his friends and family back to say hello to him one at a time. He was still intubated, so he couldn't speak.

On day three, I went back into the NICU with Michael Grossman, who was one of his closest friends. Alex's eyes were open.

Michael asked how he was feeling and joked, "Well, I think this is one way to throw a party."

Alex just looked at us and mumbled something incomprehensible.

We decided to write out the alphabet on a piece of paper and began to point to the letters so Alex could tell us his thoughts. He would blink to communicate when I hit the right letter. I began pointing, and we finally came to an I, then a W and then an A and then an N and then a T and then another T and then an O and then a D and then an I and then an E. He was done. Tears fell out of the corner of his eyes.

Michael said, "Alex you are still heavily medicated. I know you want to die, I get it. I get that this is overwhelming. But give it some time."

Alex tried to shake his head, but all he could do was move his eyes.

"Alex," I said, I love you, you have two beautiful children, and there are at least 15 to 20 people in the waiting room. Your mom is here, Renee and Michael are here, Robert and Fern are here. They all want to see you. Do you want to see anyone? They're here because they love you."

We then wrote down YES and NO so he could choose his answer. I pointed to a YES, no response. I pointed to a NO, he blinked.

He had no desire to see anyone; he just wanted to be dead.

"Well, you have to just see your mother. She's been waiting for a while now."

I walked out to get her. "Molly, come see Alex."

She stood up with her handbag and briskly walked toward me and the NICU doors. I held them open for her.

Alex's nurse was in his room, checking the monitors. Molly looked at her son for the first time since the accident and said, "Oh, mine God. Mine kin." She went to kiss his forehead, and once again tears came out of the side of his eyes. "I love you mine kin. You'll get through dis," she said. "You'll see. We are survivors, you are tough like me. You'll see. You will be OK." She rubbed his arm and kissed his forehead again. There was a small chair by his bedside and she sat down. She started to rock herself ever so slightly. "You don't have to worry about anything. You just get better."

It was not lost on me that she was talking about the family business, which was real estate. Alex worked there in tandem with his brother Ralph, who was also in the waiting room with his wife Susan. The family owned apartment buildings, and quite a bit of land around South Jersey. The whole family worked for the business, some more than others. Alex managed the apartments.

The nurse peeked back into the room and said, "I spoke with the doctor. I think we are going to take him off the ventilator later today. That's good news."

"See Alex, you're already getting better," his mother said. "I'm tired; I've been here a long time. I'm going to go home but I will be back. I love you, mine kin." She kissed him once more, picked up her handbag, and walked towards the exit.

5. OXYGEN

That evening, I went home for the first time in days. My mother, Edith, was in charge. She had taken over caring for the kids and our little dog Pepe. I kissed everyone hello, and then she presented me with a list of people who had been calling.

"Honey," she said, "you don't have to call anyone back right now if you don't want to. I am going to be here. I will help you with the children, and we will figure out a schedule. And, most importantly, we will get through this together."

I looked at her. "Thank you, Mom. I love you so much."

"I know you do, sweetheart. I gave the kids dinner and I made something for us. I know you haven't been eating, but if you're going to maintain any stamina you have to eat."

I nibbled at dinner, and I was happy to bathe the kids. They were my oxygen. My lungs filled with the energy of their little bodies as they giggled and splashed in the tub. I was temporarily me.

Adam and Danielle were still small enough to share the tub. Danielle was playing with her yellow duck and Adam was playing with his tug boat. Danielle saw something moving in the water and began to swat it. When I looked down, I saw that she was swatting Adam's penis.

"Danielle, that's not a toy. It's Adam's penis. If you hit it, it will hurt him."

"Mine."

"No, it's his, honey, please don't do that. Here, play with this." I handed her another plastic duck.

After they were done, I read to each of them and tucked them into bed.

When I was finished with my shower, my mother walked into the bedroom. The phone had been ringing every fifteen minutes, and every time she looked at me to see if I would pick it up, I just shook my head no. I was not capable of speaking. I could talk to her, and the kids, but the rest of my energy had been drained like the pool at the end of the summer. I didn't care who was on the phone. Alex couldn't talk; he was in the NICU. The rest didn't matter.

"What if it's the hospital?" she asked.

I hadn't thought of that.

She picked up the phone. "Hello? No, she can't come to the phone right now. Sure, I'll be happy to take a message, but I can't guarantee when she'll call you back. She's not home very much. OK, I will. No, this is her mother. Yes, thank you. Yes, I will. OK, goodbye."

That's when I knew that, on top of everything else she was doing…she had become the phone police.

I pulled the covers up just as Pepe jumped on the bed. He snuggled next to me and I thought my aching would fade. He sensed that something was wrong and burrowed in further. I knew he wanted me to feel better, but even he couldn't stop the nuclear fallout.

"Good night sweetheart," my mom said. "Get some sleep."

32

"Thanks, Mom," I replied. She turned out the light as she made her way to the back bedroom.

I tried to close my eyes, but they kept popping open. Exhaustive insomnia was my new best friend. I just stared into the shadows waiting for morning to arrive, but I was so happy to be in my cocoon. The kids were the first to rise, followed by me, then Pepe, and then my mom. It was the first day of school. Our friend Siobhan had gotten Adam into the Hebrew Academy's preschool so he had a place to go every morning. They normally didn't accept kids until they were potty trained, but given the circumstances, they made an exception. Adina was coming to stay with Danielle. She was our babysitter, a blonde, statuesque young lady with translucent pale skin, whose demeanor said she was 25, not 17. She carried a sense of calm and intellect, and inner knowledge combined with an unwavering faith in God. She was a Jehovah's Witness and we attributed her strong sense of self to her belief in God. She spent her time in school and at Kingdom Hall, and when she heard Alex was injured she had brought over pamphlets to help us get through it. She knew we were Jewish, but she thought they might help. It was an act of kindness, and all prayers were welcome.

John and Helen Glowacki lived next door. They were devout Christians. Both Helen and John prayed for Alex, me, and the children. It did not matter to me which God you were praying to, prayers were prayers. They were asking for help in the name of a higher power. Again, it was an act of kindness.

I got ready with my mother to go to Philly. I decided to drive Alex's car. He had a white BMW 5 Series with a gray leather interior. It was a five-speed, and under any other circumstances it would have been fun to drive. But for now, it was just a car to get us somewhere.

When we arrived, the waiting room was already filled with a smattering of people in it. The Altoonas were still there—I couldn't remember their names. Altoona, Pennsylvania was several hours away from Philly, making it impossible for them to go home and come back overnight. They had set up a makeshift hotel with blankets and pillows, hospital chairs as beds, and one of the corner tables for toiletries and vending-machine food. That was how I had lived for the first few days and I understood completely.

"Any news on your son?" I asked.

"Well, he has pneumonia. They put him on a new antibiotic. They're hoping that does the trick. We're just praying it does."

"Oh God, I'm sorry." It seemed as if the situation and the conditions of our loved ones called for only one thing: prayer. People around me seemed to have more faith than I did. Or maybe they didn't know what to say or do. After all, there was nothing that anyone could do to change the situation.

I remember at the time that I did not feel a connection to God. I wasn't interested in praying, and as time went on I would find that it was easier to distance myself from God than ever before.

"Mom," I said, "let's go check on Alex." We made our way to the double doors, picked up the phone, and told the nurse who we were. The doors buzzed open and we walked back towards Alex's room.

"Oh my God!" I shouted. "Your tube is out!"

He looked at us, and when he saw my mother he began to cry.

My mother went right over to hug him. "Hi, honey, I'm here. I am so sorry."

Alex tried to speak but his voice was hoarse. "Hi Edie," he managed to say.

She hugged and kissed him and said, "Unfortunately, you've been served a plate of shit and you're going to have to eat it."

My mother was a woman who had a saying for everything, but she did not swear. This one, I had never heard before in my life. I was briefly shocked out of my daze.

"I'm going to be here awhile," she told Alex. "I'll take care of the kids, while Gail takes care of you."

"Thank you," he managed to get out.

"We all love you, and as far as I can tell, you have a waiting room full of friends who love you, and don't forget those two adorable children at home."

The nurse walked in and said to me, "Excuse me, Mrs. Kiejdan, the doctors made their rounds this morning. They told me to tell you they will be back later this afternoon to talk to you. Will you be here?"

"Yes, I'll be here, thank you."

Only two visitors were allowed in the NICU at a time, so I went back out so some of our friends could visit with him. But before I left, the nurse came in and told me that since Alex was stable, they were going to move him into the step-down unit.

My mother got a ride home with Robert's wife, Fern, around two, so she would be there to help the kids get situated.

Late in the afternoon, the neurologist came by and introduced himself. He was young and of Slavic descent. I couldn't remember his name, let alone how to pronounce it.

I knew right then and there that I would have to learn the terms of the medical hierarchy. Because that is how they introduced themselves. Did I know the difference between an intern, a resident, a fellow or an attending physician? No I did not. But I would learn, whether I wanted to or not.

Interns are medical school graduates in their first year of residency. Residents are physicians who are done with their first year of residency, fellows are doctors who graduated residency and went on to specialize, and attendings are physicians who are done with their fellowships and in charge of the residents. But to simplify things…they're all doctors. At this point, that was all I cared about. This was a teaching hospital, after all, and this was where they honed their craft.

As Alex lay there, and I tried to listen, the doctors began to discuss his prognosis in terms of his level of injury. The neurologist began by running a pen-like instrument up and down Alex's foot. No response. Then he took a reflex hammer and tried it on Alex's ankles and knees. No response.

"Alex, can you feel anything?" the doctor asked.

"No," he responded bluntly.

The neurologist and his residents began testing Alex's body. They tried to test it with temperature variations and pin pricks, and when they reached the area just above his nipples, he felt something.

"Well, this coincides with your MRI so far," one of them said. "Alex, right now the scans show that your injury is at level C6."

"What does that mean?" he asked.

"Well, a spinal cord injury has four levels. S, which is your sacral nerves, that's at the base of your spinal column. L , which stands for your lumbar, and it involves your hips and legs. T one to twelve is your thoracic area, and it involves anywhere from your upper trunk down, and C is your cervical area, which is the level of injury that you have, and can involve anywhere from the top of the neck down to C8, which can include hand movement."

We had just been sprayed with bullets and had nowhere to hide.

He continued, "As an example, Christopher Reeve is a C2 and is on a vent. You, fortunately, will not need a vent."

Good news at last, I thought sardonically.

He went on. "Now with a C6 injury, you could at some point transfer, which would be quite helpful in maintaining some independence. We will have to see how much function you get back in your triceps. You are paralyzed in your trunk and legs, and you will not have the use of your hands. You will have the use of some of your diaphragm and you will be able to speak, as you already know, although your lung capacity will be diminished. You might be able to bend your wrists back and forth. You will not have bladder or bowel function. You will be able to move in and out of a wheelchair with assistance, and you may be able to drive a vehicle with adaptive equipment. Now, I know this is a lot to process, so we do have a spinal cord handbook that you both should read—" he said as he looked at me "—to familiarize yourself with the injury. It's pretty substantial. So obviously, no one is asking that you read it now. But at some point you will both find it quite helpful."

That was enough focusing for now. I began to fade out. "Thank you," I said, and Alex just stared at the ceiling. I was grateful he was still on a morphine drip. What human being could process all that? And, what did I need to take to get through this?

I went over and kissed him. He wasn't in his body, and I knew exactly why he'd left.

We were on day four, and as I walked back into Alex's room, a gentleman followed me. He was a tall, slender man with a graying hairline. Just as I was sitting down, he poked his head in the door and introduced himself.

"Hello, Mr. Kiejdan. I am Dr. Ditunno, and I am your physiatrist."

It was the first time I had ever heard the word physiatrist. Since I was raised with a modicum of medical knowledge, I was baffled. I had met the neurologist, the neurosurgeon, the orthopedic surgeon, the residents, the fellows, and the interns. *Is a physiatrist like a psychiatrist?* I wondered. *Because God knows, I could use one of those.*

Not even close. I was about to meet a completely new kind of doctor, at least to me. "What exactly does a physiatrist do?" I asked.

He began with, "Well, we are doctors of physical medicine and rehabilitation." Then he looked at Alex. "It is my job to ascertain what you can accomplish physically, and to help you become as functional as possible. We also help to manage pain care. I understand you are a C6. We don't know yet whether you are a complete or incomplete. If you have a complete injury, that means your spinal cord is severed and there is no chance of you getting any function or feeling back below your level of injury. If you have an incomplete injury, well, that is different. You could possibly get back some sensation and movement below your level of injury. Since all your vitals have been stable, they should be moving you to the step-down unit today. There you will find you have more freedom with visitors. We will also be taking you down to physical therapy."

He tested Alex's reflexes, which didn't exist below his nipples, and said he would be back again tomorrow.

"Well, that was uplifting, wasn't it?" I said after he left.

Alex looked at me and said, "I miss my kids."

"I'm working on it, Alex, but they're not allowed into the NICU. Remember, they're germ carrying agents for the dark side. I promise that when you can see them, I will bring them in."

Once Alex was out of the NICU and in the step-down unit, I could see his temperament changing. He was off the morphine and no longer felt like Picasso. He also kicked out a psychologist.

"Alex, maybe you should talk to one of them," I said.

"What the fuck do they know about being paralyzed?" he asked.

I couldn't argue. They were walking, and he could barely lift his arms or feed himself. He wanted to speak to someone with actual knowledge; someone who actually knew what it was like to be paralyzed. He had no problem talking to strangers, no matter who they were, but he had needs that had to be met, and they were all physical. It was way too early to entertain the thought of therapy, at least for him.

Today, Dr. Ditunno walked in carrying a file and a large cerulean blue notebook. He had begun to discuss the future. Who could think that far in advance? Getting through an hour at a time was where our heads were. He had tested Alex's reflexes, and again he had none. No neurological response in his knees, ankles, or toes.

"There is still time for him to get his reflexes back," Dr. Ditunno said. "But as time goes on those chances will fade. You pretty much have up until a year, but the majority of patients if they are going to get anything back, get it back with in the first six months or so. After that your chances lessen. If you get movement back during the acute period, well then we can be hopeful. Either way, though, you will have to learn to deal with your level of injury in practical terms. When you are ready, you will go to Magee for rehabilitation. There you will be taught how to deal with your injury through physical and occupational therapy. When you are stable, in another few days, we will put you on a different floor. After a week or two you will be moved to Magee. Do you have any questions?"

Of course we didn't have any questions. We didn't have a clue as to what we were in for.

Dr. Ditunno handed me the thick cerulean blue notebook entitled "Spinal Cord Injury Handbook." Of course if you didn't have the use of your hands, calling it a handbook was adding insult to injury.

"You should both read this cover to cover; it will let you know how to handle most situations. It is very informative. And before you get discharged from here, I would like to meet with a group of your friends and family, those whom you would consider to be a support system. You are going to need one. They will come in to be trained on what to expect and how to handle your injury. These are people you should be able to call in a pinch. This is not an injury where you can go it alone."

The next time we would see Dr. Ditunno would be right before Alex was discharged from Magee, about four months later. Magee was the rehab hospital affiliated with Jefferson. The one thing I knew for sure was that when he got out of rehab, I would probably be going in. But until that happened, we had a lot of territory to cover.

Alex's closest family members and friends would be part of the support brigade. I had to choose the people whom I thought would be there for Alex when he came home and who would also be within driving distance, his inner circle of trust. It was an easy decision to make: his brother Robert, Mark Dannenbaum, Michael Grossman, Craig Altman, Jeff Alper, and myself. We were the friends and family members who were going to do the heavy lifting. Dr. Ditunno would enlighten us on how important it was to have a support system with this injury, and he would teach us the ABCs of spinal cord patient care for the home environment.

When I think back, our friends were truly amazing. They visited, brought in food, kept us entertained, and made us feel like we were somehow going to survive this nightmare. Michael Gottlieb drove in from Pittsburg during a horrific rainstorm. Charlie Garfunkel flew up from Savannah and left to be home in time for Shabbat. Stewart

Kessler came in from Florida, Jon came in from Boston. My friends Meryl, Patrice and Ted, Amy and Harry came in from New York, and Lauren came from DC.

Our Philly friends made it their business to stop by the hospital almost daily, which was an amazing feat. I thanked God for Sharon and Craig, Rich and Barbara and Fred and Mindi and Brad and Lee. Then there were the commuters: Michael and Siobahn Grossman, Michelle and David, Christina and Gary and Justin, and Val and Jeff and a host of others. Alex's family came from the shore and my family flew in from Cleveland and Atlanta.

After a few more days, Alex was taken to the dungeon. It was a floor at Jefferson that seemed more like a way station. Compared to where he had been, it was the bowels of the hospital. This was the step-down unit, where they began to focus on what he had to work with before they sent him to Magee.

He hadn't had a shower since the injury, excluding bed baths, and his anal cleanliness was getting the best of him.

"I need to wash my hair, I need a shower," he said. "I take showers three times a day!"

His nurse said politely, "Alex, we don't give showers or baths three times a day. While you are here, you will get a shower every other day."

He was off the morphine, and all he could think about was seeing the kids. "How are they? Do they miss me?"

"They're OK," I said, "and of course they miss you. Adam says every day, 'I want to see Daddy.' Danielle, not so much." Adam was three and Danielle was one-and-a-half, and Adam was more aware that his daddy wasn't home than Danielle. My mother was doing an excellent job managing their schedules, and I had brought pictures

41

of them in to sit on Alex's hospital table, but he was a hands-on father who had just lost the use of his hands and the rest of his body.

It was then that I realized that, in a sense, I was going to be a single mother. The holding, the nurturing, the potty training…it was all going to be me. *Stop thinking about the future, it will do you no good.*

"I miss them so much," he said.

"I know you do."

"Can you bring them in to see me?"

"I'll ask one of the nurses." I walked into the hallway to find a nurse. When I walked back in, there was a nurse waiting for me.

"I'm going to teach you how to help Alex with a quad cough," she said. "The reason you do this is because even though at some point he may get the use of some more of his diaphragm back, his lung function is diminished. Because of this, he will be more prone to pneumonia."

She began to raise Alex's bed. Earlier that day, they had put T.E.D.s on his legs. T.E.D.s are white knee-highs known as anti-embolism stockings. He was sedentary and they didn't want him to get a blood clot. They also put on electronic air compressor sleeves that fitted over the T.E.D.s. The sleeves kept his blood pumping, to increase circulation in his lower extremities.

"So," the nurse told me. "What you need to do to help Alex have a full productive cough is force your hand in on the diaphragm like this," (she placed the bottom of her hand under his ribcage) "and push in and up, so he can cough. Try it," she instructed.

And so I did. None of this seemed real. Was I actually trying to help him cough? Yes. If he couldn't cough, it would be much easier for him to choke on something. Every day I was learning about his losses.

By the time we were through with that, it was time to go to the cafeteria. Alex had so many people visiting, and they weren't all allowed in his room, so we had to meet at the cafeteria. It felt like a party, minus the catering. It also smelled like a cafeteria.

Andrea and Gary and Diane and Randy were there. Diane had brought two boxes of Krispy Kreme donuts from Atlanta. Three were missing.

"Sorry," she said. "I got hungry on the ride from the airport."

Michelle and David, Craig and Sharon, Gary and Christina, Michael and Siobahn, and David Adler were there too. Barb and Rich and Mark and Margie came a little later. Wow. We were so lucky to have such an amazing support system.

The nursing staff and the doctors had started to train me to think in terms of a support system. "He will need a support system." I had begun to hear it over and over. They had put Alex in his first wheelchair to go down to the cafeteria. It was manual and dated. His abdominal area had to be strapped in because he didn't have the use of his trunk, and his legs had to be strapped down, as well as his feet. Since they were lifeless, if his feet came off the pedals, they could be run over. There was a urine bag hanging from the side of his chair. He had his halo holding his head in place and that morning he had decided to shave the mustache that he had since high school. Of course he couldn't use his hands, so a nurse or an aide did it for him.

I actually hadn't seen him without a mustache, ever. I met him with a mustache at American University and every picture I had ever seen him in, he was sporting a mustache. His family members all looked like each other but now that he didn't have a mustache…he looked most like his sister Renee. They were a dark and Semitic looking group with brooding dark moods match. I had experienced those moods since before we got married. But the only mood swings I had room for were Alex's, and of course the kids.

Still, I had hope. Maybe this accident would rally them together to help their brother.

What I was about to learn was that this was the time for many valuable lessons. I was going to get schooled on who was made of what. Nothing brings out truth of character quite like a tragedy. It became easier for me to read the truth, as well as the illusions.

6. THE LEARNING CURVE

Alex was transferred over to Magee on a stretcher. I went with him in the ambulance. Magee was a few blocks from Jefferson, so it was a pretty short ride. After he was situated in his room, a personable young nurse came in and introduced herself as Beth. She said that Alex was her patient, and she would help him get acclimated.

"Alex, at Magee you will be going to physical and occupational therapy every day. You will also learn to use adaptive devices and equipment. This is the place that will help you get back into the world."

Thank God she didn't say back on his feet.

"Right now we are going to fill out some paper work," Beth continued. "Do you have an advanced directive?"

"No," he said.

"Do you have a DNR?" She meant a Do Not Resuscitate, a written order instructing health care providers not to do CPR if his heart or breathing stopped.

"No," he said.

"I will need you to sign here so you can be resuscitated."

"I don't want to be resuscitated."

"Yes you do," I said.

"No I don't," he said.

Beth interjected. "Well, we can address that a little later after you two talk about it. Do you have a living will?"

"No," he said.

"Well, now would be a good time for you two to talk about what your thoughts are on the legal matters that might come up. In situations like this, it makes sense for the uninjured spouse to seek out the advice of an attorney."

He looked at me. "Gail, you're going to need to have power of attorney over me. What else?" he asked Beth.

"Actually, that covers it for now. The training you will receive here should start tomorrow. You will meet your doctor tomorrow as well. Her name is Dr. Bea (an alias). She is a physiatrist. You will also meet with a social worker and a psychologist. Since you are a quadriplegic, you will be measured for a motorized chair while you are here."

STOP!!!!! WAIT!!! Neither one of us had heard that term applied to Alex before.

He looked at me and I looked at him. We were both dumbstruck. Because he had partial use of his arms, we had thought he was a paraplegic.

"Are you hungry?" Beth asked. "I can bring in a tray."

"No, thank you," he said.

"OK, that's it for now. I'll be back. Here's the buzzer if you need anything."

"Goodbye," I said. "It was nice meeting you." And off she went.

"What the fuck!" he said in disbelief.

"I know, I can't believe it. You're a quadriplegic!"

"This sucks more than I thought. I feel sick to my stomach."

Alex looked at me, and I could see that he was shaking... was it a response to finding out he was a quadriplegic? At first it was subtle, but then it became more pronounced.

"Are you cold?" I asked him.

"Yes," he said.

"You're really shaking."

Actually, he was quaking. His entire body was in motion. He began to look like he was convulsing. I buzzed Beth and, as we waited, I started to put his blankets over him.

When she walked in the room I asked, "Do you think he has a fever?"

"No, I took his temperature and blood pressure when he arrived. Actually, this is not uncommon. Alex, do you need some more blankets?" I had already put two blankets over him as he continued to quiver.

"Yes," he responded.

"Alex, because your injury is a high-level injury your body can no longer regulate temperature. So if you are cold, like you are now, it means your body is unable to respond properly. You are going to have to stay out of the extremely cold weather or you will risk going hypothermic. Also, if you overheat, your body's mechanism to cool you off, which is sweating, no longer functions. Since you can't sweat, you will become hyper-thermic. So from this point on you will have to avoid extreme heat and extreme cold. Unfortunately, since the cord is damaged, your body can no longer send the warning signals." Beth looked at me. "I'm going to get a heating pad; that should help you warm up a bit."

It was the warmth of the pad that did the trick.

"Now you can't turn it to high, because if it burns you, you won't feel it."

There was so much to learn. We were swimming in a strange new pool of information and I couldn't help but think that we would be treading water for a very long time. I could feel my head bobbing up and down, gasping for air at the surface, but Alex had had to do that literally to survive the ocean.

I was slowly getting bits and pieces out of him about what happened at the beach. At first he was too drugged to talk, but now as I sat by his bed, he started to unload the details…ever so slowly.

"I was talking to Scott Saks," he told me, "and I was saying, 'This is ridiculous.' We were talking about the guy in Ocean City who had broken his neck the week before. I couldn't catch a good wave. Every time I tried to take a wave in, I would get beaten up. So I decided to come in. On my way in, I found it hard to walk through the current. I was fighting it, then I thought I would use a wave to help me get in. But the wave broke early, and instead of me riding it in, it pushed me down on my head. I heard a snap. Then there was a loud, reverberating sound in my ears like a tuning fork. My whole body was numb, and all I could do was pick my head up. I took a deep breath and put my head back down. And then someone grabbed me and pulled me out of the water."

"Well, there were two people who saved you," I said. "Bud Graves and his son Chris, who is a lifeguard in Longport. The Longport beaches were closed, so that's why Chris was in Margate."

"I wish they hadn't saved me," he responded.

I had no words.

I went home after he had settled down. I sat on the couch as the kids ran around the house. My mother was talking to my brother Gary and his wife, Andrea. Gary handed me a glass of wine while I stared blankly into the room. I knew they were talking about me. I was fading in and out again. I was pretending I was in a warm, cozy room without any window or doors…just a big, cushy, white couch and my dog.

"Gary, do something," my mother begged.

"What do you want me to do? There is nothing any of us can do." He was the logical attorney, and he was right. I looked dispassionately out the window in the living room. I began to know the feeling of isolation in a room of people you knew and loved. I was the elephant.

"Do you like the wine?" Gary asked me.

"It's fine." I replied.

My mother asked, "What are you going to do about the house? It's not accessible."

"I know," I said. "I spoke to Molly; she told me we should get a lot and build a house all on one floor. I don't have the energy for that."

"What other options are there?" she responded.

"Well, I spoke to Robert and he said we could either put an extension on the back and have our bedroom downstairs, which I don't want because then Alex wouldn't be able to put the kids to bed. Or, we could add an elevator by extending the outside of the house. That seems to make the most sense, because then he won't be stuck downstairs all of the time, and he'll be able to check in on the kids. I'm just grateful Robert's an architect."

We were fortunate that Alex's family were builders, so we wouldn't have to do much investigating. Robert was aware of the ADA measurements needed for a wheelchair. And we had the staff at Magee to tell us what we would need to do in regard to the shower.

I realized that I was supposed to muster up the energy to feel grateful. So many patients were unable to come home to a place that would be restructured for their needs. But I didn't have the energy.

"What side are they going to add onto the house?" my Diane asked.

"The left gable if you are facing the house," I responded. "They're just going to add feet onto the end of the house so we can add the elevator, enlarge our closet, and enlarge the shower so he can be rolled in. Plus they have to enlarge all of the doorways so he can roll in to every room."

"When does the construction start?" Andrea asked.

"Really soon, as soon as Robert gets the approvals from the city. I guess in about a week."

"What can we do?" my mom asked.

"Well, I'm going to have to empty out our closet and put all of the clothes downstairs in the back den. But I think that could wait for Thanksgiving."

"What are we ordering for dinner?" Diane asked. She was always thinking about her next meal because she had blood sugar issues; she was hypoglycemic.

"I'm not really hungry," I said. "You guys order whatever you want." I had already dropped six pounds without even trying. Nerves were a beautiful thing. Even though I was not heavy to begin with, the weight just fell like autumn leaves off a tree. The only thing I ate with wild abandon was Jagielky's homemade chocolate, a Margate institution. Their chocolate was my therapy, my best friend, my total consolation, and the best way I could self-soothe. I smiled when someone brought it to the hospital, or dropped it off at the front door. It was my sustenance and my only craving. I was truly grateful for Jagielky's

"I want to go to bed," I said. "Do you mind watching the kids? I think if I go to bed, maybe I won't feel so tired."

"Sure, no problem," my mom said. "We'll feed the kids and give them their baths."

I went up to bed, showered, and climbed under the covers…but again, my eyes were not closing. Wide-eye syndrome had been haunting me every night. It was time for sleeping aids, and I knew just how to get them. My friend Amy who lived in New York, was a psychiatrist and could write a script for Restoril, and then eventually I would sleep.

At home we found a rhythm against the chaotic backdrop. I would drive the hour home from Magee and pick up Adam from preschool. Then we would go home and he would have a snack. Danielle would nap and Adam would watch a little television. My mother would make dinner, and afterwards I would bathe the kids and get them into bed.

Before we took Adam to see Alex, I was worried how he would respond to his new, non-physical father. I had been dropping him off at school in the morning and one day in the car, early on in the injury I said, "Adam, you know Daddy had an accident, and that's why he's not home right now."

"I know, Mommy."

"Well, Daddy is in a wheelchair, because his legs don't move anymore."

"When is he going to get out of the wheelchair?" he asked earnestly.

"He's not, honey. He broke his neck right around here,"—I pointed to the area with my hand—"and that will heal, but he's not going to be able to walk anymore."

Adam burst into tears and I could see that it was more information than his little body could handle. I had to tell him; I couldn't pretend that everything would be normal, because normal

51

was waving goodbye in the rearview mirror. The only normalcy I had came from the kids, and they were completely unaware that they were the reason I got up in the morning and pulled myself out of bed. They made us the family that we were, and I was going to keep it together…for them.

"I don't want him to be in a wheelchair anymore," he cried.

I pulled into the school parking lot, parked the car and turned around to face him. "Adam, Daddy doesn't want to be in a wheelchair either, and I don't want him in it any more than you do," I explained gingerly. "It was an accident that none of us saw coming, but we'll all be OK. It's just going to be different."

"It's not fair," he said through his tears.

"I know, honey, I know." Explaining to a three-year-old that life isn't fair is futile. I got out of the car, unbuckled his car seat, picked him up, and hugged him. I brushed the hair out of his eyes and gently kissed him on the cheeks. "Nothing is going to change the fact that Mommy and Daddy love you. We all have to be strong, OK?"

He frowned with a forced acceptance and, as I put him down, he grabbed my hand so we could walk towards the school.

Inside, Ms. Lolly, a diminutive woman with blonde hair and a preppy J. Crew sensibility, was waiting for him with a huge smile and welcoming arms. "How's my Adam today?"

"Good."

"Great. Let's see what we can play with today. I have a new animal that you might like."

And with that, his mind moved onto something else.

"Bye, pumpkin, I love you," I called.

"Bye, Mommy," he responded with a smile on his face.

Ms. Lolly turned back. "By the way, Gail, as you know, the children have to be potty trained."

"Yes, I know."

"And of course, we made an exception for your circumstances. I just want you to know that we are making progress."

"You are? Because I'm not home most of the day."

"Well, don't worry about it. We all go into the bathroom with him at reading time, and that's usually when it happens."

"Well, if you can make headway there, I'd be forever grateful," I responded. "Thank you so much," I added. Then I thought, *thank God I don't have to potty train him, our private preschool dollars at work…* and then I left for the hospital.

When I got there, Alex was with a woman named Mary Grace. She wasn't really a woman—she seemed more like a young adult, fresh-faced and steady. She would become Alex's Magee wife, and I wouldn't be the slightest bit jealous. I was glad he found a confidante at his new home away from home. She was pretty, with an olive complexion, big brown eyes, and shoulder-length dark brown hair. She had an easy demeanor and was relaxed and friendly. I knew immediately that she understood how being in an institution could be depressing, because she began bringing cappuccino every morning to Alex before they started occupational therapy. To him, it was a taste of the pre-injury life, the 'before-institution' life. A taste of what still waited out there in a world that would be less welcoming.

Mary Grace began to teach Alex about all the adaptive devices that he could use instead of his hands, as well as how to push himself along in a manual wheelchair. She helped to raise his spirits in ways that only a young, beautiful woman could. He was shallow, and that part of him wasn't injured.

He saw me looking at him. "Oh, there's my beautiful wife."

I kissed him hello. "Hi Mary Grace, how are you doing?"

"We are great. Alex just told me he was having trouble breathing through his nose."

"All I want to do is pick my nose," Alex said. "I can't breathe, I can't use my fingers. Look at what Mary Grace made."

She held up a fake finger with a fake nail attached to it.

"Looks like that nail is long enough to make some headway," I said.

"Finally, I'll be able to breathe."

There it was, another thing I took for granted...blowing my nose.

"Alex, tomorrow we are going to practice going to the cafeteria and learning to use utensils. I will bring along some adaptive equipment, so at some point you can begin to feed yourself."

Up until then, Alex had minimal use of his hands. He could barely hold a soda can and lift it to his mouth. We were still hoping he would get some movement back, but so far there was nothing.

When he was done working with Mary Grace, I pushed him back to his room. There in his room, where he would stay until sometime in January, it was just the two of us. We could hear the other patients in the hallway; most of them were in the same boat. They, too, were trying to get used to an alien way of living, too. In some ways, they were students in this teaching hospital, learning to live in a world that had turned from friendly to foreign overnight.

"How are you holding up?" I asked him.

"I really don't want to do this," he responded.

As I kissed him on the lips, his hazel-green eyes twinkled and his black lashes fluttered. I opened my mouth and he opened his. I knew perfectly well that this was the way to get his mind off the present. Kissing was his magic carpet ride. Lost in the sensuality of the mouth, we briefly forgot our surroundings.

Alex's nurse Beth walked in to check on him. "Alex, we have to set up a bowel routine. At the hospital we usually do it at night, but when you go home you might want it to be in the morning. What do you prefer?"

"The morning," he responded immediately. "I like to shower, shit and shave in the morning."

"Because your body is sedentary now, you will need to take daily medications in order to be able to go regularly. That way you won't have to worry about having to go in the daytime when you are out or busy. It becomes part of your morning routine. Would you like to go down to lunch?"

"No thanks, Gail brought me something from home. I'll eat that."

"OK. I'll be back a little later with your medication."

After she left, Alex began to imitate Nurse Ratchet from *One Flew Over the Cuckoo's Nest*: "Medication time, it's medication time."

I smiled and said, "I brought food from Fern today; she made you egg salad and tuna fish. I put it in the patient's refrigerator, let me go get it." Fern, his brother Robert's wife, lived in Margate and had dropped the food off that morning.

At this point Alex could not feed himself. He couldn't hold a fork, he couldn't hold a spoon, and he would never be able to hold a knife again. I fed him from the plastic containers that Fern had sent up, and I brought him a can of soda and put a straw in it. I lifted the soda can so he could have a sip, and I thought about how life can change in a split second.

The phone rang. Alex couldn't answer, so I picked it up myself. "Hello," I said. "Hi," pause…" we're doing okay. He's right here. Hold on a sec I'll give him the phone."

I turned to Alex. "It's your mom."

I held the phone to his ear as they spoke and I realized that he would need a portable phone that he could somehow pick up and keep on the hospital table in front of him. When they had finished speaking with each other, I put the phone down for him.

"It's time for me to go," I told him. "I have to pick Adam up at school today."

"Please don't go," he begged. "I feel like you just got here."

"I know, honey, but I've been here a few hours already, and I'm here almost every day."

"I'm lonely. I miss you. I miss the kids. All I have is their pictures to look at." He stared at the windowsill and then out the window. Then he looked at me, and I realized it was time. He was out of the woods.

"How about if I bring them up this weekend?"

"Oh my God, that would be amazing. I just can't take it anymore," he said with relief on his face. "The nights are the worst. My mind wanders. I just think that you would be better off without me. You're young, you're beautiful, and you're still marketable."

"Marketable?" I responded. "What am I, Special K?"

"You know what I mean. You should have a life."

"You and the kids are my life," I said.

"Think about it," he responded.

"Yeah, I'll think about it when I'm on the couch relaxing. Now, I have to go before I hit rush hour traffic."

"How's my car?" he asked. "Did you drive it up here?"

"I did," I said. "It's fine."

"I'm never going to be able to drive it again. I loved that car."

I didn't know what to say. I knew he loved his car. He loved the way it looked and loved the way it handled. You could see it in the way he drove, and especially in the way he took the curves. There

56

was true joy, and a little bit of the crazies in his driving. Every morning he would shower, get dressed, get in his car, and stick his head out the window to dry his hair. He had been born with that sense of wild abandon, and now it was gone.

"I'll call you later," I said. "OK?"

He looked so defeated. "OK."

We kissed each other goodbye. And I drove home.

7. A NEW HOME

Four to five days out of the week I got a ride up to Magee with Fern. Robert's wife was a colorful blonde from northeast Philadelphia who wore fuchsia lipstick 90 percent of the time. Perpetually tan, and encrusted with diamonds, she initially didn't carry a handbag. She left her wallet in her car, which was her secondary residence. In the beginning of Alex's injury, fuchsia was just the color of her lipstick and her nails. But years down the line it would be splashed everywhere, like a heavy perfume. It began when she bought Bulgari sunglasses with hot pink frames, and a few years down it would make it to her Louis Vuitton handbag. Of course she contrasted it with black, her go-to color.

Fern, too, was a woman of contrasts. I had seen both sides of her, and I could see she had a bite—she was bling with a sting. She was also a dragon who could breathe fire and smoke her enemies. She came across as having no fear, a tough woman who spoke her mind and could have run the women's division of the Jewish Mafia. But there were two sides to Fern. The other side, she kept hidden from public view.

She would pick me up and without a thought say, "What up?" while lowering her voice. It was obvious that she had excellent driving skills, as she manipulated in and out of traffic at an illegal speed. Her brother David raced cars, and her husband, Robert, whom Alex was closest to, was a quiet, gentle giant, whose height topped off at six foot three. He had the family stomach, which gave almost all of them an accentuated girth. Yet between the two of them Fern had the swagger, and she seemed to be the boss.

It was still early in the injury, but Fern would see to it that I didn't have to drive to Philly every day. Her parents still lived in northeast Philly, so after she dropped me off she would go visit them. They were survivors of the Holocaust and, as I learned with Alex's family, not only is there a difference between survivors and non-survivors, there is a difference in their children.

I had been going to Magee almost every day since the middle of September. It was an institution, with institutional food, vinyl floors, pale yellow paint on the walls, bland nursing stations, and places for Physical Therapy and Occupational Therapy. The only way to get a breath of fresh air was on the rooftop, where patients were allowed to start a garden or get some actual sunshine.

It was the middle of fall and Alex's withering mood needed light. So I pushed him in his manual wheelchair to the elevator and then up to the sun, in hopes that it would make him feel better. It was there that we met Tom and Kathy McMeekin. Tom was an Atlantic City fireman who had been in a horrific car accident with three other people, when he and his friends were hit by a lumber truck. Tom was the only survivor. He, too, was a quadriplegic. The question in Tom's case was: who was really the lucky one? The one who survived to be severely disabled? Or the ones who didn't survive? It is not an uncommon question.

Kathy and Tom were two people who set an example of the road we were about to go down. With two teenage boys, and a strong family support system, they managed to maintain an outwardly optimistic attitude. They were friendly and warm, and put us at ease within seconds.

"Do you have kids? Kathy asked.

"Yes, we have two, both in diapers." Alex replied.

"I'm going to bring them up this weekend," I said. "They're missing their daddy an awful lot."

"And he's missing them," Alex said.

"Boys? Girls?" Tom asked.

"One of each. A rich man's family, that's for sure," Alex responded.

"Well, we'll look forward to meeting them," Kathy replied.

As we looked beyond the rooftops I could see the congestion of a busy city. Alex could not look over to see the city streets, but he was happy to absorb the heat of the sun. I was still not consistently aware of the effect the outdoors had on him, and thought the warmth would do him good. But as I would learn, his injury would not allow his body to cool down through the normal process of knowing when it's too hot to get out of the sun. He had no way to know if it was too hot or not. One minute he was freezing, and another minute he was overheating. His body couldn't regulate temperature. And he wasn't in tune with the foreign feeling of having no feeling below his nipples. He was also in a manual wheelchair with a high back, and he couldn't tilt his head back because he was still wearing the halo.

But the sun's warmth has a healing effect beyond any medicine a doctor can give you. We sat there quietly, listening to the street noise below—the honking of cars, the screeching of brakes, the sounds of a city...life continuing without interruption. I looked at Alex sitting uncomfortably in his wheelchair, with a large bag collecting urine from a Foley catheter. The catheter was an indwelling tube that went up through his penis to his bladder, so urine could drain into the bag that was hanging ever-so-gracefully on his chair. Later on, we were warned that it would be a source of infection, and that as a source of infection it could lead to other complications. But we hadn't gotten the lecture on that one yet. Maybe I should have read the handbook.

Nope. Not a shot in hell. The only reading I could focus on was for preschoolers.

After the rooftop visit we made our way to Physical Therapy, or PT, where Alex was to be stretched. Donna, who was Alex's physical therapist, called it range of motion. It was something I needed to learn how to do, because after he went home it had to be done twice a day- in the morning and in the evening. Alex had been working on his triceps. He had minimal muscle movement in them, but since there was something there, it was worth working on. Triceps were the difference between dependence and independence. If you could transfer using your triceps, you could use a transfer board to get your butt into a car, or rotate a steering wheel with an adaptive device. Alex could transfer into a bed with help, and onto a commode chair to go to the bathroom. His arms were still defined from his workouts this summer.

Flashback: Alex running on the boardwalk.

I hadn't even closed my eyes. It was strange, because I never had flashbacks before. Now I was starting to have them on a regular basis, but I didn't dare tell anyone. They came out of nowhere and at any time of day. They were my escape hatch...ready for me to slip away without notice. They were comforting, because they were always of something good.

"Gail!"

61

"Yes," I said, snapping back to attention.

Donna said, "Alex is progressing. Hopefully, in time, he will be able to steady his body enough to transfer."

I looked at the elevated, navy-colored matt. It was the size of a double-bed and was raised off the floor on an oak platform about two-and-a-half feet high. Alex lay back on it, balancing precariously on his elbows, with the rest of his body splayed out in front of him.

"If he can manage to get up on his hands for an extended period of time, you may not need a Hoyer Lift."

"What's a Hoyer Lift?" I asked.

"Well, it's a bit of a contraption. It's kind of like a sling that is big enough to hold a man, and it hooks up to a heavy metal pole. You can manipulate it under Alex's bottom, and help him get into bed." She looked around the room until she saw one one. "I'll be right back."

She went to the other side of Occupational Therapy, or OT, and pulled over an enormous metal pole, with a large sling attached to a metal overhang. It reminded me of the mothers who slung their babies across their bodies, except those slings were as natural-looking as breastfeeding, while this was a mechanical monstrosity. I did not want it in my bedroom with our solid, hand-carved rosewood furniture that we had bought on our honeymoon in Hong Kong. I wanted to live in the past as long as possible, because just a few weeks ago we were living in the world of the walking.

"Well, let's hope we don't have to get one of those," I said. What I wanted to say was…"Seriously? You can't make that thing more esthetically appealing?"

I looked away, trying not to imagine a future with a thing like that. First I looked at Alex's face and then I looked at his bare feet.

"Oh My God," I said, so that everyone in the room looked at me. "Look at his feet, Donna. His toes are moving!" I felt a rush of adrenaline, mixed with relief and joy. "Look! They're doing it again!" His toes were moving and he had no idea.

Alex looked down. Donna ever so gently said, "I know, Gail. Those are spasms. They are very normal. It doesn't mean anything."

I ignored her. "Alex, try and move your feet, or your toes." I looked at his face. "Are you trying?"

"Yes Gail, I am. It's not working."

I don't know who felt worse, him or me.

"I try all the time to make things move...I'm sorry."

"Don't be sorry, it's not your fault."

This guy was the best apologizer in the world. It was probably one of the reasons I married him. He recognized when he was wrong. But right and wrong had no place with an injury like this. Fault had no place either. It was still early in the trauma, but I knew there was no room to look back.

"It's still early, but spasms can become quite severe, especially in quadriplegics. Let's hope Alex doesn't have to contend with that," Donna said.

Out of the corner of my eye I spotted Dr. Bea, Alex's physiatrist at Magee. She was walking through the physical therapy unit. She had the look and demeanor of Popeye's Olive Oyl, except she was highly educated. Her personality was that of a walking flatliner.

"Hello Alex, how are you feeling today?" she said with a soft, monotone voice.

"Great, I woke up with wood so I know my pole is alive."

"Really?" she inquired.

"Alex, come on," I said.

"No, not really. But now I know how to get a rise out of you."

She didn't smile. "I have a therapist coming to see you tomorrow. Mrs. Kiejdan, it might be good for you to be in on the session."

"What time is it at?" I asked.

"It will be right after lunch, around one o'clock."

"I don't want to see another therapist," Alex said. "There's nothing they can do for me. Unless they're in a chair, they don't have a clue as to what this is like. And if I need to complain, I can talk to my wife."

"Alex, it's an opportunity to talk about your fears, and your expectations. It's all a part of the process of getting you back into a place where you feel emotionally secure. In addition, I know you have two small children. Your wife should not have to go through this alone, either."

"Fine. I'll meet with him."

"It's a *her*. Her name is Dr. Vinchenz. She'll meet the two of you in your room tomorrow, so you can get acquainted." Dr. Bea smiled perfunctorily, turned around and walked away.

"With all of her personality she shouldn't be working with spinal cord injuries," Alex said. "She should be on the brain injury floor."

I ignored him. "Look at you!" I said. "Most people only have one therapist, and now you're on your fourth." He ignored me.

The following day at one o'clock exactly a woman with long brown hair and bangs walked into Alex's room. I was sitting in one of those guest chairs that could lean far back enough to become a chaise lounge, and then a bed. I was randomly popping Jagielky's chocolates in my mouth. I popped them like a drug, and my imaginary therapist told me that they would make me whole again.

If one were to ask what got me through all of this, I would say it was Jagielky's. Back then, my favorite was the milk chocolate-covered butter creams and the milk chocolate fluff. But, unbeknownst to me, someday I would evolve and choose an inexplicably delicious new favorite. Since food held no interest, I could literally eat at least a half-pound of chocolate a day.

Dr. Vinchenz introduced herself to us. She was petite, and Alex and I couldn't take our eyes off of her. She had been in a fire and her face had been badly burned, along with other areas of her body. The scars were huge. It looked like second- or third-degree burns had left a painful-looking disfigurement over most of her face and the left side of her body.

Shock therapy! That's what the doctor wanted for us. Simply put, everyone has shit.

"It's nice to meet you," we said in unison. I couldn't help it, I tried not to stare.

I had already been practicing my smiling on the other patients— don't stare too much, don't make them feel uncomfortable. Smile, say hello. They are not invisible, so don't make them feel as if they are. If you pretend you don't see them, you're an asshole. Seriously, how hard is it to smile or say "hello "or "how ya' doing?" I thought.

The big question was, where did that fear come from? Why are we initially so afraid of those who are in wheelchairs or those who have facial disfigurations? I was learning that they are no different than us, except for one enormous exception: their lives were much more difficult. They had hardships we couldn't imagine, and for the most part their injuries made them stronger. Regrettably, I would learn that they were perceived as weaker.

They may be muscularly weaker, but they are mentally stronger. They are survivors.

But I was taking my cues from Alex now. He was leading the questioning. "Dr. Vinchenz, how long have you been a therapist?"

"About five years or so," she answered.

"What got you started?" he asked.

"I wanted to help people. And I found myself uniquely qualified to do so. As you can see, I've had a little experience with learning how to adapt to a life with different circumstances."

"What happened to you?" he asked.

"When I was eighteen years old, I was in a house fire. Now I have a few questions for you Mr. and Mrs. Kiejdan."

"Shoot," Alex said.

She had her pen and paper in hand. And she began to write down the basics. Where are you from? How old are you? Do you have children? What are their names? Who's caring for them? How did your injury occur? She wasn't bad, because they weren't bullet point questions. They were peppered with polite conversation and an understanding of how the injury had affected him so far.

Dr. Vinchenz was on staff at Magee and began to focus on his stay there. "Alex, how have you found the staff here? Is there anything you need that you aren't getting?"

"Yes, I need to go home."

I interjected. "Alex, the house is under construction; you can't come home until the house is ready."

"I have an idea," Dr. Vinchenz said. "Why don't we see if we can make arrangements for you to go home for Thanksgiving Day?"

"That's in a couple of weeks," I said. "My family will be here for Thanksgiving."

He looked out the window. "Okay."

"Let me talk to a few people. We're going to have to get it OK'd by insurance, and we're going to have to get you transportation. I'll put the wheels in motion so you can spend Thanksgiving with your family."

"That'd be great," Alex said.

"This was very productive," Dr. Vinchez said. "If I can do anything else for you to make things easier, please call me. How about if we meet again next week?"

"Do you want me here, too?" I asked.

"Actually, I would prefer it. This is a challenge for the whole family. I'm sure you will have things that you are worried about or need to address, and if I can help either one of you, or give either of you tools to handle certain situations, then this will be beneficial for everyone."

Dr. Vinchenz was the fourth psychiatrist that Alex had seen, but she was the first one that he hadn't kicked out of his room. She didn't patronize him, nor did she ask him how he was feeling. The others did, and after that they were gone.

8. GOING FOR NITRO

Nighttime after dinner for Alex was boring. During the dinner hour, he always had visitors who brought him food: sushi, Thai, a little something from the Redding Terminal—he ate it all with a little help from whoever was there to feed him. Then, around seven or eight o'clock, everyone had to do their bowel movements. That was the schedule. After eight the place smelled like crap, literally. The weekends were even busier. That's when friends made the trek up from the shore.

It was Saturday morning and I had fed the kids and Pepe their breakfasts. Today was a big day-the kids were going to visit Alex at Magee for the first time. I packed a baby bag for Danielle and Adam with a change of clothes, and Mom and I put the kids in their car seats and headed towards Philly. Mom was in the passenger seat, while I drove. My Volvo was the perfect family car and it was known to be as safe as they come. But it wasn't vomit proof.

"Mommy," Adam said from the back.

"Yes, honey?"

"I don't feel good."

"What's wrong, baby?"

"My tummy hurts. I think I'm going to throw up."

"Can you wait until I can pull over, Adam?"

"Mommy, I ...." The sound of a three-and-a-half year-old retching is no different than that of a thirty-year-old man after a night of binge drinking. It's loud, and comes out like a shooting comet, splattering everywhere. I was just pulling over with my flashers on, but it was too late. Masticated Froot Loops were all over the back seat, the floor, and Adam. Danielle made an icky face and pinched her nose with her fingers.

I went to the trunk and pulled out the wipes and a change of clothes. I cleaned him and the car as best I could, and we were on our way. By the time we got to Magee, I was drained.

"Mom, can you take the kids in while I find a towel to clean the rest of this up?"

"Honey, let's all go into together. Danielle hasn't seen Alex since before his accident. I'm sure there are cleaning supplies you can borrow, so we can deal with it later."

I looked at Adam and the pallor of his face was back to normal. "How do you feel, buddy?" I asked.

"Fine. I want to see Daddy."

"We're here, we just have to sign in and ride the elevator."

We walked in the revolving doors that could fit wheelchairs, and the kids just kept going round and round while I signed us in.

"Come on, kids," said my mother. They ran over to the elevator, both trying to push the buttons with Danielle standing on her tippy toes to reach.

"Me, me," Danielle said, and she pushed Adam out of the way.

"Mommy, Danielle won't let me push the button."

"Adam," I said, "you can push it once we're in the elevator."

"You'll take turns," my mother interjected.

From my point of view, Danielle had a little bit of bully in her, but I honestly didn't have time to address it. As we walked off the elevator on the seventh floor, we rounded the corner to the right. Alex's room was the third one on the left.

"This way," I said. The kids had turned the corner with us but then they both took off, running. Hospital corridors bring out the child in everyone!

"Don't you want to see Daddy?" I called after them. I went in and rolled Alex into the hallway. As we came out of his room, Alex said, "Kids…come on back to say hello."

But neither one listened.

I turned to Edith. "Mom, I have to go catch them, I'll be right back."

I grabbed their hands and walked them back to the room. Once we were back, neither child paid any attention to Alex. They weren't interested, and he was hurt.

"Adam, Danielle, kiss Daddy hello," I said.

Adam shook his head and Danielle followed suit.

"Come on," I cajoled. I picked Danielle up and put her on Alex's lap. He kissed her and she squirmed out of his arms to check out the room.

I grabbed Adam's hand and walked him over to Alex. "Say hello."

"Hi Adam, I miss you so much. Don't you miss me?"

Adam looked at him and said nothing. "Mommy, can we go?"

"Adam, say hi to Daddy."

"Hi, Daddy." He glanced at Alex, then looked up at me. "Can we go?" he asked again.

"Not yet. We're going to visit with Daddy and then we will go home."

My mother started pulling the crayons and paper out of the bag.

"Nana, draw an animal," Adam demanded.

"Ask nicely, sweetheart," she said.

"Please."

She smiled. "That's the word I was looking for."

"I'm sorry, I don't know why they're acting like this," I said to Alex. I had built it up so there was some anticipation to see him, and then there was absolutely nothing.

"Danielle hasn't seen me in almost a month," he said. "She's one-and-a-half. That's a huge chunk of time." I could see the sadness of another loss on his face, time with his children.

"I'll bring them up every weekend from now on. They're also not used to you in the halo, or in a wheelchair." I looked him over. "Well, at least your mustache has grown back. You were looking too much like your sister."

He cracked a smile.

"That's better," said my mother.

"Edie, thank you so much for being here for Gail and me and the kids. You know, you're looking good!"

"You haven't been in here long enough for me to look that good. But you are welcome, honey. We'll all get through this one way or another."

Danielle took off down the hallway again and I ran after her.

There was a new nurse on duty. We had learned that they rotate. It made sense—his night nurses rotated, his daytime nurses rotated, and his weekend nurses rotated. We never knew who was going to pop their head in the door. Today's menu was serving one with a side of non-verbal attitude: "I don't have time for you, and you'd better get used to it." Nurse Ratched had competition.

"Why don't we take the kids up to the roof?" I suggested.

"Okay," Alex said. "Adam, Danielle, do you want to see a roof garden?" Adam agreed and Danielle nodded.

"Up," she said, as she reached for me to pick her up.

"Adam, would you like to help Nana push Daddy?"

"No," he answered.

"Let's just head to the elevator," Alex said.

As my mother pushed Alex into the hallway and around the corner towards the elevator, the wheel seemed to get stuck on something.

"Whoa, wait. Something is tugging." We all looked down and saw that Alex's urine bag had been run over by one of his wheels and had ripped in half. The urine had leaked all over the place. The nurse on duty had hung the bag too low and it had become a casualty.

"I can't go up there now. I need to change my bag. Can you buzz the nurse?" He was angry and frustrated.

I buzzed the nurse, whose name was Sissy. When she came in, she had an irritated hustle to her walk. "What do you need?"

"My leg bag split underneath my chair. I'm going to need a new one."

"Alright, let me get you back in bed, and I'll change you over. I'll be right back."

"Clean up aisle five," I said. "Mom, can you take the kids up to the roof garden?"

"Gail, just go with her," Alex said. "I'll come up after she's changed my bag."

"Okay," I said. And the four of us made our way back to the elevator.

Within two days of that incident, Alex had his first urinary tract infection. To an uninjured person a UTI can start with burning, a low-grade fever, or a sense of urgency. But not to a quad. What we

72

would both learn is that because of the lack of feeling below his nipples, Alex would experience something more severe, and it was called autonomic dysreflexia.

I had wheeled him over to OT, and we were talking to Mary Grace. "I have a headache…" Alex started. Then he began to lift his arms towards his head. "OW, OW, OW," he started to scream, "Help me! My head, OW, OW."

Mary Grace ran to the phone. "It's an emergency, page Dr. Bea, get me a nurse."

"Oh my God, oh my God," he was moaning. "My head it feels like it's going to explode. Shit, oh God!"

It took a few very long minutes, but Dr. Bea made her way to Alex, pulled out a blood pressure cuff and placed it round his upper arm. She put a stethoscope on and began to take his pressure. She was listening carefully to the beat of his pulse.

"Okay, your BP is 240 systolic, 136 diastolic." She was on the phone in seconds, asking for another nurse to bring her nitropaste. Alex was turning gray, and his lips were colorless. I was quietly panicking. Dr. Bea put on a pair of gloves as the nurse who rushed over opened a fresh tube of nitropaste. She measured out a half-inch of paste while placing it on a pre-cut piece of rectangular paper the size of a bandage. She slapped it on his forehead as quickly as she could.

"Alex, you're going dysreflexic. The nitropaste that I just put on your forehead will bring down your blood pressure. You should be feeling better shortly."

She took his blood pressure again. He couldn't even lie down; there was nothing for him to do but sit there and wait. Dr. Bea looked at her watch, and then repeated taking his blood pressure.

"200 over 120," she said. "Okay, Alex, you're going in the right direction. Has anyone talked to you about autonomic dysreflexia?" She looked at him and then me. I shook my head, and he said nothing.

"She looked at her watch. "Let's wait a few minutes and take it again." The white paper was still on his forehead. "Since you are still in the acute part of your injury, this is new to you. It is not uncommon for quadriplegics to go dysreflexic."

"What is it?" I asked.

"That's a very good question. Since his body no longer has sensation from his nipples down, there has to be a way for it to communicate when something is wrong. For example, if he has an infection, or bowel problems, or he even hurts himself again and is unaware of it, instead of feeling the pain, the body sends a signal that something is wrong. That signal is very high blood pressure, which is accompanied symptomatically with an excruciatingly painful headache."

She looked at her watch again, and began to take his blood pressure again. "140 over 88. Okay, let's take the nitro off." She took off the nitropaste with her gloves still on, wiped his forehead with a clean piece of gauze, and then asked the nurse to wipe it again with soap and water.

"We don't want you to bottom out either. Alex, how are you feeling?"

"Better, but I still have a headache."

"That should subside soon," she said.

He looked wiped out. "I want to lie down; I really don't feel well"

"Okay, why don't you head back to your room and I will come in and finish explaining to you what you just went through."

I rolled Alex back to his room and buzzed for his nurse. We sat there and waited. He was no longer an emergency, so waiting was what you did. After about twenty minutes, Autumn came in. She was a beast of a woman. She came in with citytude, heavy on her feet, and smelling like onions.

"What do you need, Mr. Alex?"

"Can you please put me in bed? I don't feel very well."

"All righty," she said. As she was transferring Alex over to the hospital bed, Dr. Bea walked in.

"Are you feeling any better now, Alex?"

"Little bit. I'm happy to be getting into bed. I guess I'm wiped out from the headache."

"Let me continue to explain what just happened to you. As I was beginning to say before, autonomic dysreflexia is your body's response to something that is going wrong. It is a serious syndrome and can lead to life-threatening hypertension for the majority of spinal cord patients above level T6, but most assuredly for C level injuries, and that is you. The risks for a stroke, myocardial infraction, which is a heart attack, seizures, and even death are of enormous concern. That's why when you feel sick with a headache, it is truly like an alarm going off. And as you experienced, the first thing that we do is take your blood pressure."

She had come in with a portable blood pressure cuff and began to take his pressure again. It had normalized. "Autumn, can you get a urine sample from Mr. Kiejdan?"

"Yes, Dr. Bea."

"How were his bowels last night?"

"Let me get his chart, I think they were productive."

"Alex, we are going to check you for a UTI, urinary tract infection, then we will go from there."

I interjected. "Dr. Bea, Alex's bag was hanging low on his chair, I guess it really wasn't placed properly and he ran it over and the bag broke open. Do you think he got his infection from that?"

"It's a possibility; we'll see when the test comes back. Until then we will have to watch your pressures, Alex."

He said little. He was drained and wanted to rest.

"Honey, why don't you nap," I said. "The social worker asked me to stop by today, after noon, so why don't I do that while you are resting." I put my hands on his cheeks, kissed him on the lips and left the room.

I walked down the hallway towards the physical therapy unit. On the right-hand side, right before the physical and occupational therapy unit, there was a small cubby of an office with a woman sitting behind a desk facing the doorway. Her name was Mrs. Elaine Schilly.

I poked my head in. "Hello, I'm Gail Kiejdan. I think we had an appointment."

"Oh yes, please come in and have a seat." She stood and shook my hand. "How are you doing?"

"I'm good, how are you?"

"Well I'm just fine, thank you." She looked at me with a smile that telegraphed, yes I understand how you really are. And I looked back with a smile that said, "no, you don't really know."

I sat down in front of her desk piled high with papers, which I imagined as a stack of nightmares. This is where she decided what her patients needed from the insurance companies, and in return, what the insurance companies would allow us to have. She pulled our file from the top of the stack and started to read it, "I just want to see something here," she said without looking up.

Elaine had a short blunt haircut just below her ears. Her stout body went perfectly with her disheveled graying hair, and the octagon, wire-rimmed glasses that sat on the bridge of her nose. She pushed her hair behind her ears and continued. "I understand that you have been coming almost every day to see your husband."

"Yes, I have."

"Might I advise that you come only three to four times a week? I have been here quite a long time. I know you drive up from the shore, and from past experience, there can be a heavy toll on the patients' caregivers, which is what you have become. You need to pace yourself to get through not only your husband's stay here, but when he returns home. May I ask who is taking care of your children?"

"My mother came to help me take care of them."

"Thank God for mothers," she said.

Not all of them, I thought. Alex's mom was not exactly pitching in. She was planning when she could go to Florida, and I think she was going to leave before Thanksgiving.

"Yes, I am very lucky." I had noticed that I didn't have the energy to engage in a conversation that wasn't perfunctory.

"Also, I have checked with your insurance, and they will pay for you to have a hospital bed in your home."

"Why will he need a hospital bed at home?" I asked.

"Unfortunately, Alex will no longer be able to sleep in a regular bed. He is going to have skin issues and skin breakdown and he will need to sleep on a water mattress, which really is best for the skin."

This, I was not comprehending. What was she talking about…we weren't ever going to sleep in the same bed again?

"I'm going to make an appointment for you two to meet a bed specialist. The sooner we get the paperwork done on that, the better.

As you will learn, insurance approvals take a while." She looked up at me. "They also okayed a Hoyer Lift."

NO! I DON'T WANT A HOYER LIFT IN MY HOUSE!!!!!

"You must have good insurance," she said.

"We do," I responded. "It's not really something you should skimp on."

It wasn't the first time or the last that I would hear that remark.

"I think that's it for now," Elaine said. "It was nice meeting you." She stuck out her hand for me to shake, and then repeated, "Gail, you really need to slow down the pace and only come three or four times a week."

"All right," I said as I shook her hand. "Thank you."

Why did I continue to thank people for bad news? Thank you for telling me I'm never going to sleep with my husband again, thank you for the fucking Hoyer Lift, thank you for seeing me in a dimly lit office that depressed the shit out of me.

Enough. I went back to Alex's room and popped a Jagielky's chocolate in my mouth. It was a milk chocolate-covered marshmallow, and when it melted in my mouth, I melted a little with it. I felt a little better. I knew it wouldn't last but hey, whatever works.

I called Fern to come pick me up. She had gone over to her father's store in northeast Philadelphia.

Alex was sleeping. I nudged him a little on the arm. "Honey, I'm going to go home now." He didn't seem to care and that was OK with me. I needed a break. "I'll talk to you later tonight."

I kissed him goodbye and made sure that the portable phone that we had purchased was near his bed. He could no longer answer a desk phone because he couldn't hold the handset, and that was all they had in rehab. At this point he couldn't even push the buttons. But with the speaker button. and an adaptive device that had a pencil attached, he would eventually be able to push a button. If someone was in the room with him, they would answer the phone for him. Fortunately, he had a lot of visitors.

By the time I got into the car with Fern I was exhausted.

"Bad day?"

"Yup."

She looked me in the eye with a flash of pity. "Do you want to go shoe shopping?"

"No thanks. I'm tired."

"What happened?"

I shook my head in disbelief. "It's just overwhelming," I said.

"I know, it sucks, it's just beyond," she replied.

"It really is," I replied. "Let's just go home."

I thought about the shoes. I knew shoes made me happy. Sometimes I didn't even wear them. Maybe I was a shoe collector, like other people collected art, or mementos from traveling. I loved putting my shoes in a line-up. I was their judge and jury. Yes, you may come out of the closet. No, you are never coming out of the closet. You, yes you will be worn and worked to death, because I own you. You will be worn because I need to look professional! I was master of my shoe domain, and that was my kingdom, and that was all I was master of.

I thought about my professional life. Sharon Pearce, who was my boss at Bally's Casino, had called a week ago to see how I was faring, and I hadn't returned her phone call. Sharon was one of the kindest human beings I had ever encountered. Honest and straight forward. She was also a worker bee who had ascended by pure diligence and hard work into an executive position in charge of advertising and public relations. I had known her since she hired me for the opening of the Taj Mahal Casino in 1990.

When I moved to the Atlantic City area from New York I had a difficult time finding a job as a copywriter. I started out commuting to Philadelphia, freelancing for one agency or another. Then there was an opportunity to freelance closer to home. And so I began a long and fruitful relationship with a woman who would become an integral part of my survival. She had heard that Alex was in an accident...we lived in Tiny-Town after all, and what did my mom always say? "Good news travels fast, and bad news travels faster." It couldn't have been more accurate. When I got home, I called Sharon back.

"Oh God, Gail. I am so sorry. Is there anything I can do?"

"Actually, not right now."

"How are you? How are the kids?"

"Well, fortunately the kids are doing okay. Adam has had a hard time, but I hope with time he will come around. Danielle is one-and-a-half so she seems to only care about my whereabouts right now. And I...I am not in therapy yet, so I guess I'm OK."

"Who's taking care of them?"

"My mom is here. And she is amazing. I really don't know what I would do without her. She makes sure the kids are on their schedule so I can go to the hospital. She's even doing the laundry."

"Well, at least you are lucky in that regard, Gail. Don't worry about work, and I don't want you to worry about getting paid. I will make sure that for now, I can work something out."

"Thank you, Sharon. But I honestly don't know when I'll be back. I really have no clue how long Alex will be in rehab, and I go to the hospital every day."

"Well just don't worry about it. Your job will be here whenever you get back."

Godsend. That's what I thought. A gift amongst the rubble.

"Thank you, Sharon. You have no idea how much I appreciate it."

"Don't thank me, Gail. But please call me if you need anything. I can watch the kids, I can clean your house."

"You don't even clean your own house," I said.

"I know, but I'll clean yours. Just call me if you need anything at all."

"I will, I promise, I'll talk to you soon."

9. THE BRAIN INITIATIVE

It was a Saturday afternoon, and I remember it so well because we had found a routine in the midst our chaos. Chaos by its very nature is unpredictable and messy. We were living the messy life to the fullest extent of the term, except for the kids, who we somehow managed to keep on a schedule. Fern had made egg salad and tuna fish salad to send up to Alex. She was dropping it off so I could visit him with my mother. The front door was open and the screen was still in place. I heard the scream and then froze.

"Gail!" My mother screamed. "Gail!" she screamed again.

I was halfway up our circular staircase and something told me to look for Pepe. What if he'd been hit by a car! I couldn't take it. I felt like I couldn't move, but I had already pushed myself through this far. So I came down the steps and with trepidation opened the screen door in search of a body.

It was not the dog that I saw lying there, it was my mother.

"Jesus! What happened! Oh my God, how did you fall?"

She looked up at me. "I had just gotten the mail and I was walking back to the house, and I guess I was looking down at the mail and I tripped on the pathway light," she said.

I tried to pick her up, and she said. "No, no, no, I think something is wrong with my wrist, use the other arm." So I pulled her up by the right arm and guided her up the stairs into the house.

"Let me call Alex and tell him we're not coming," I said. "Then I'll take you to the hospital."

I heard two car doors slam, and Robert and Fern walked into the house. "What happened?" asked Robert.

"She tripped and fell," I said. "I can't go see Alex, I have to take her to the hospital."

"I'm OK, Gail," my mother said. "It can wait until tomorrow."

"Are you crazy? It cannot wait," I said.

Fern interjected, "Why doesn't Robert take you to Philly, and I'll take Edith to the hospital? We were just going to dinner anyway."

My mother looked at her gratefully. "That sounds like a good idea. Gail, I'll be OK, you go see Alex."

"You're not going to miss anything, Gail," Fern said. "We're just going to sit in another waiting room."

"Yeah, the emergency room at Seaside Hospital, that's a picnic," Robert added.

"All right," I said. "Adina will be here in a few minutes to look after the kids, and Robert and I will go up to Philly."

My mother said, "Let me get my purse Fern, and we'll go."

"I'll carry it," Fern said. "I don't trust you."

"I don't blame you," my mother said. She kissed me goodbye and they were on their way.

As soon as Adina came, the kids ran to the front door. She always had an adventure planned for them. Then Robert and I headed up to Magee. The minute I got into the car, I fell asleep.

I was a baby. Pure and simple. I could not handle another "all men on deck" situation. I was barely getting through with Alex in

83

rehab, and caring for two small children. Adding my mother to the cauldron seemed to be creating some kind of dangerous brew that was going make me boil over. But instead of boiling over, I reverted to infancy and checked out the only way I could. I slept the whole way.

When we got up to Alex's room, Alex's friend Michael Gottlieb was there, standing beside Alex's bed. He was not one who sat and relaxed, but on top of it, he had just driven almost five hours from Pittsburgh, which is where he resided.

I kissed everyone hello, and Robert said hello as well.

"You are not going to believe this," I said.

"Where's your mom?" Alex asked.

"She fell. Fern is taking her to the hospital, and Robert brought me up here."

"Is she alright?" he asked.

"I don't think so," Robert said. "I hope it's a sprain or something."

"How was your drive in, Michael?" I asked.

"Not bad. I'm staying overnight, I just wanted to see how Alex is doing. He looks pretty good, all things considered."

"Oh, do you like his new hardware?" I said, referring to the magnificent-looking halo.

"I don't think he'll be able to sneak through a metal detector or anything, but it does add a little badass look."

"Are you hungry?" I asked. "We have takeout menus from around town."

"Or, we could walk to the Redding Terminal and pick something up," Michael said.

"Or, I have egg salad and tuna salad from Fern," Robert said.

"I'm in the mood for Thai," Alex said.

"There's a great Thai restaurant right down the street from the terminal," Michael said. "I don't know if it's still there, though."

We were still ruminating about our food when Alex's phone rang. I picked it up and it was Fern.

"What's the verdict?" I asked. "Shit." Pause. "Double shit. No. I don't want to do it down there. Michael Gottlieb is here, I'll ask him. Okay. We'll figure it out. Thanks. Bye."

I looked around the room. "Her wrist is displaced, she has a distal radius fracture, and they said she needs surgery."

Michael was an ENT who had gone to medical school at Temple University. He knew the orthopedic surgeons in the area, and he knew who was good and who wasn't. "Let me make some phone calls," he said. "If I remember correctly, there's a guy, I think he trained at Hahnemann, his name is Greg Israelite, he's good."

"Rich is at Hahnemann," I said.

I called our friend Rich Zamarin. Michael had somehow reached Dr. Israelite, who said he would call scheduling and try to fit my mother in first thing on Monday morning. Rich concurred that he was an excellent surgeon. So, we were set. I called my mother and told her she was having surgery on Monday morning at Hahnemann.

"I don't think anyone has set a surgery date faster than what we just did," I said after I hung up.

"It pays to know people." Alex said. "See, I have really smart friends. I don't know why they're friends with me, but they do come in handy."

"What's for dinner?" asked Robert.

"Thai," I said feeling better now that we had a plan.

"Do you know how long you're going to have to be in here?" asked Michael.

"They haven't told me yet. I guess I have a lot to learn. First I have to be put on a bowel program so when I go home I won't have to worry about getting on the pot in the middle of the day. I'll just get it over with in the morning. On the bright side, it will still be shit, shower, and shave like everyone else."

"He also has a lot of rehab ahead of him," I said. "He has to learn how to transfer, and feed himself, and all kinds of things that we all take for granted."

Michael was sensitive, and the magnitude of the changes were not lost on him. His eyes grew misty. I imagined that he was remembering how bad they'd been together not too long ago. The partying, the girls, the late, fucked-up nights—those were now just memories.

"Hey Robert, how is the house coming?" Alex asked.

"Well, we're just waiting on the approvals from the city."

"What's the problem?"

"In a word, Marie. She is just sitting on it, for no good reason."

"That old bag should retire," Alex said.

Robert continued, "There's nothing we can do until we get the approvals. Unfortunately, you give people in a small town a little bit of power and they think they have complete control over you."

"Well she does!" I exclaimed. "How can he come home if we can't get the construction started? I know what I can do, call a lawyer or the ADA." I looked at Michael and said, "He needs to come home, and God knows how long it's going to take to put in an elevator, not to mention change all the doorways, and build an accessible bathroom."

"I don't want to feel any more stuck in here than I already do," Alex said.

"You feel stuck? Let's make a poster," Robert retorted. He walked out of the room to the nursing desk, grabbed a magic marker, tape and some paper, and returned with a smug smile on his face. He began to tape all the pieces of paper together into one giant rectangular and then he started writing. We all looked at it and started to laugh. He hung it up on the window so that anyone driving on the Vine Street Expressway could glance up and see the words:

HELP ME...I'M A PRISONER AND THEY WON'T LET ME OUT.

Gary and Christina walked in with their son, Justin. They had been visiting regularly, just like Michael and Siobhan, Mark and Margie , Michelle and David, Craig and Sharon, Rich and Barb, Freddie and Mindi, and Valerie and Jeff. They were all our small miracles. When Alex was busy with his friends, he didn't need me to be there. I was feeling even more emotional exhaustion after my mother's fall and I wanted to get home to her. When I finished my Pad Thai and Gai Med Ma Moung, I asked Robert if we could leave.

"I won't be here tomorrow," I said to Alex. "I'm going to have to take care of my mom. Will you be okay?"

"Sure."

"I'll definitely be back on Monday. Her surgery is in the morning." I kissed everyone goodbye. "Michael, thank you for making that call. You saved me from another breakdown. Of course, I haven't gotten through the first one yet."

"Anything for you guys," he said.

Monday morning came very quickly. Fern picked us up around 6 a.m. so we could get there in time to fill out the forms and do pre-testing. Her surgery wasn't scheduled until 11 a.m., and that would happen only if the doctor was running on time.

Fern dropped us off and, after I got my mother situated, we waited behind curtain number two. They took her insurance card, her history, a list of the medications she was on, and made her sign a waiver. Here I was, checking out my fourth hospital within eight weeks.

"If you want to go see Alex now, I'll be fine," my mother said with a smile. "Don't worry, I'm in good hands."

"I know you are," I said. Fortunately, Hahnemann and Magee were in walking distance of each other.

Fern popped her head behind the curtain. "Ladies, how are we doing?"

"Will you stay with my mom while I check in on Alex?"

"No problem, do what ya gotta do."

"I'll be back, Mom, before you are out of surgery." I smiled at Fern. "Thank you, Fern, for doing this."

I kissed them both goodbye and scooted over to see Alex. He had just come back up from breakfast, and by then it was 9 a.m.

"I'm not staying long. My mom has surgery at eleven, and I want to go back and make sure everything went alright."

"You look a little frazzled. Why don't you sit down for a minute?"

I tried, but I was like a jack-in-the-box without a lid. I pushed myself to sit and just kept popping up. "I have shpilkes."

"I'm usually the one with those," Alex said.

I felt that while I was at Magee, I should have been at Hahnemann, and when I was at Hahnemann I should have been at Magee.

Discomfort was my only option. Once again, I was counting minutes and hours. I looked at my watch and popped one of the last Jagielky's from the box. You don't need food when you have chocolate. I felt the chocolate's immediate impact; I started to relax and enjoy the calming effects it had on me. It was the same effect I could get from a Valium, or a shot of tequila, or buying a pair of really expensive shoes.

"Okay, I have to go back."

"It's only eleven," Alex said.

"Yes, and she's in surgery now. Sorry, gotta go. I'll be back."

So, I walked back over to Hahnemann and found Fern in the waiting room.

"She just went in. The doctor said from the X-ray that she's going to need pins."

"Shit."

"How's Aloosh?" That was Alex's Polish name.

"He's okay. Obviously, I didn't stay long."

At about twelve-thirty, the doctor came out and started talking to Fern.

I stood up. "Excuse me, I'm Mrs. Desberg's daughter."

"Oh, I'm so sorry. It's just that I saw your mother talking to—"

"My sister-in-law," I interjected.

"Anyway, everything went as expected. She should be out of recovery in about an hour. I have to say you have some very insistent friends—first I hear from Gottlieb, and I haven't heard from him in a while, and then I heard from Rich. How do you know them?"

"They're both really good friends."

"Honestly, between the two of them, I felt I had no choice but to get your mother in first thing this morning."

"I'm sorry, but we have a lot going on."

"I know, Rich told me. How is your husband doing?"

"He's doing okay. He's in rehab now, and I'll be going in when he gets out."

He smiled. It was a kind smile and I truly appreciated it. "Now, regarding your mother, I have an office at the Shore. I would like to see her in a week and see how things are going. I'm thinking as of now that the pin will be in for up to six weeks. When I see you in my office we can discuss physical therapy, and so forth."

"Thank you so much for fitting her in. I really appreciate it."

"Yes, thank you," Fern said.

"You're both very welcome."

I sat there, with that buzz in my head. It was becoming way too familiar.

"Do you want to go back and see Alex?" Fern asked. "I'll wait here until your mom gets out of recovery."

"He wanted a falafel. I guess I could find a street vendor. I'll be back soon."

"Take your time. We're not going anywhere."

"Okay, thanks."

By the time I got back from Magee, my mother was dressed and ready to go.

"Hi, Mom! How are you feeling?"

She smiled. "Good as new."

"Not really," I pointed out. "Your arms in a sling, and you have two pins in it."

My mother was the eternal Pollyanna. She never had anything but a smile on her face and an optimistic outlook. She also never complained, nor would she ever say anything unkind about anyone. Obviously, I didn't inherit those genes. But, she was also tough—tough as nails, as my dad used to say. She was born in Karlsruhe, Germany, and immigrated to the United States when she was eight years old. The writing was on the wall, war was coming, and Jews all over Europe were in trouble. She was fortunate that she and her parents were sponsored by distant cousins to come to America. The first thing she did upon arrival was intensify her studies, so she could learn English. She spent her childhood with her head in the books, and since she and her parents ended up in Cleveland, Ohio, eventually she worked her way to college, attending Case Western Reserve. She would graduate Magna Cum Laude and would become a chemist and eventually work for Union Carbide.

But before all that, she would focus on assimilating and losing her accent. My mother was proud to be an American, and grateful that this country had opened its arms when no one else would. She cried when we went to Washington D.C., and said that I would never understand how fortunate we are to be in such a great country.

But I was beginning to. I knew that we had access to a fine health care system. That so far, the nurses and doctors that we had encountered were topnotch. And here was proof: she'd broken her wrist on Saturday, and by Monday afternoon she was out of surgery and ready to go home. I was grateful that she was okay.

By the time we got home, my mother was ready for bed. I walked her up the steps, helped her put on her nightclothes and helped her into bed. Pepe knew intuitively that something was wrong. He jumped on the bed and snuggled in beside her. She fell asleep within minutes.

I went back downstairs. "Thank you, Fern."

"No worries, I'm just glad she's okay. I'll talk to you later."

The kids were outside playing, my mother was upstairs sleeping, and I curled up on the living room couch to take a nap. Except it turned out to be an internal freak-out. I began to think for the first time in two months. Up until that very minute, I hadn't had a second to myself. *I cannot do this. I cannot continue to function like this.*

Was I really functioning? Everyone was still alive, but the overwhelming magnitude of the situation was beginning to hit me for the first time. I did not want to be there anymore. I did not want to be anywhere anymore. I couldn't sleep and I didn't like what I was thinking. I sat up and walked into the family room.

I picked up the phone, which I rarely did anymore, and I called my sister to tell her that my mother's surgery had gone fine. "She fine, you know Mom. She's a trooper."

"Is she still going to stay there?" Diane asked.

"What do you mean?"

"Well, don't you think you should send her home? How can you take care of everyone? How can you take care of Alex, Mom, and the kids?"

"I'm not sure, but maybe that's why I want to roll up into a ball and lie on the couch," I responded.

The doorbell rang, "Diane, someone is here. I'll call you later."

I opened the front door and there stood Molly and Bogie. Bogie was Molly's companion/housekeeper. She cleaned, she cooked, she was Molly's companion. She was from Poland and didn't speak any English. Molly spoke Polish, German, Yiddish, and English. Bogie was carrying a basket filled with food. I had an instant flash of Little Red Riding Hood. There was a container of matzah ball soup, a plate of broiled chicken, a small container of compote, some rolls, and another small container of heavily overcooked green beans.

"Wow, come in. That was so nice of you." It was truly unexpected.

Molly walked in first, even though Bogie was doing all the heavy lifting. "How's your mother?" she asked.

"She's tired. She's upstairs resting."

"Don't vorry, Gail. She vill be okay," Molly said. "I vill help."

"Thank you for making the food. It smells delicious."

"Bogie, put the food in the refrigerator," Molly said to Bogie. Bogie did as she was told.

Molly truly liked my mother. She always said, "She's a lady."

"We will bring dinner again tomorrow night," she said when Bogie came back from the kitchen.

"Thank you, Molly. Thank you, Bogie."

"Prosze," Bogie said. I kissed them both, and they left.

A few hours later, I went upstairs to check on my mother. Her eyes were just beginning to open.

"Mom?"

"Em hmm," she responded.

"How are you feeling?"

"Just a little groggy. Oh, it's late," she said as she looked at her watch.

"Molly made you dinner. She brought it over with Bogie but you were still sleeping."

"That was so nice of her. See, no one is all bad."

Molly and I had had a rocky history. It wasn't always bad, but after Alex and I had kids it seemed to exacerbate.

"I know, Mom. Listen, I was thinking, wouldn't you be better off going home and recuperating there? I think all of this is just too much. It's too much for anyone."

She looked at me with a kind smile. "It's absolutely out of the question."

"Mom, no offense, but there's not much you can do. You have a broken wrist, for God's sake! And if you went home, I wouldn't have to worry about you."

"Gail, I will be fine. I can assure you, I will not be a bother. Besides, you need the emotional support."

I knew then that I wouldn't get her out of the house without a bulldozer. When she made up her mind, she dug in and let the world work around her.

So for the next few weeks we all made do, and I called the doctor and made an appointment for myself. I needed Prozac, or Zoloft or Wellbutrin—something to take the edge off and allow me to function. So I made an appointment with my GP and we decided on Zoloft.

It was towards the end of October, and I realized that I hadn't gone clothes shopping for this kids. I had simply forgotten. But I really didn't have the time, either. We were all on a schedule. I was lucky that my friends had continued to drop food off at the house. I didn't have the time nor the inclination to cook, and I had no desire to run into anyone at the grocery store. And I was grateful that it was something a group of people did out of their own volition. There were some friends who asked me what I needed, and instinctively I told them, "I'm fine, I'm managing." Really, what I needed was a private jet and a vacation in the Maldives, but that just wasn't on the agenda.

The other thing I needed was someone to do my thinking for me. I did have a few friends who were on the brain initiative. They were the intuitive ones. They didn't ask questions. They just dropped things off, loaded the refrigerator, and left. They didn't need to speak to me; they knew I was limited.

Fern had been going to northeast Philly, where she was born and raised. She had come back with piles of clothing for the kids, enough to get them through fall and into winter. Mindi had offered to fill in their wardrobes by buying their winter coats.

As the seasons changed, so did I. My hair had started to turn prematurely gray. I needed to get it colored, so I wouldn't look as old as I felt. I decided the best approach to how I was feeling was camouflage. Michelle's mom had told Michelle to always wear lipstick. If I wore lipstick too, maybe no one would notice that I was dead.

My clothes had started to hang on me, which was astonishing given the amount of chocolate I was consuming. It was Alex's injury diet, and he had done what Weight Watchers, Pritikin, and Nutrisystem couldn't. This diet allowed me to mindlessly vacuum pounds of chocolate at a time into my mouth, and still lose weight. Not that I had ever been fat or overweight, but at five foot seven and 127 pounds, immense amounts of chocolate could make a difference. That was perk number one. Perk number two was that Miss Lolly was potty training Adam.

Christina was dropping salads off. Lisa Brezel was dropping off bagels, and Siobhan was helping to shuttle the kids to and from their activities. Sharon and Craig, and Rich and Barb were ordering from their favorite restaurants and bringing dinners in to Alex, as opposed to the inedible dinners he was eating in the dining room. Jeff and Valerie were doing the same. Michael Grossman went up to give Alex his shot of optimism, as did David and Michelle. Alex didn't consider himself lucky, but with the flow of friends and family that came and went, he was.

Once in a while someone would say, "You're lucky, it could have been worse." These people, and I will not name them, were stupid. You do not tell someone who will never walk again, hold his children again, shower by himself again, get dressed by himself again, and go to bed without help again, that he is lucky. Someday, in the very distant future, Alex might feel lucky, but it would be intermittent.

I watched as he tried to entertain those who visited. It was interesting to see him act one way with the visitors and another when he was alone with me.

One Saturday afternoon, Aunt Helen and Uncle John paid a visit. They weren't blood relatives, but they were high on our list of family. Aunt Helen and Uncle John lived next door and had been so supportive and close to us that they were family. They were devout Catholics and we appreciated their strong belief in God. Since the day of Alex's injury, Helen had been praying for him.

"You know you have a lot of praying to do with him, and it's not just for the injury," I had said.

"Oh, I know. He's fresh, that one. I have some Holy Water that I want to put on his forehead. It was brought over from an actual holy place in France called Lourdes."

"Helen, we'll take whatever we can get," I said.

As I was sitting on Alex's bed one Saturday, I saw Aunt Helen and Uncle John coming down the hall.

"Alex, here comes Aunt Helen and Uncle John."

As they walked in the room, he began to convulse. His eyes rolled back in his head and he started to drool.

"Oh my God," Helen said. "Buzz for a nurse! Jack, do something!"

John ran to the nurse's call button to push it.

"Alex, stop it!" I said. "You are scaring them!"

With that, he straightened his head and started to laugh. "Gotcha!"

"That is not funny!" Helen said. "I ought to smack you, broken neck or not."

"I'm sorry," Alex said. "I just get bored in here."

"I thought I was going to have a heart attack," said John. "You really scared me."

"It looked pretty real, didn't it?" Alex responded.

"Yes, it did. I need to sit down," said John.

"You know, we came all this way to put Holy Water on your forehead, and say a prayer, and I brought a relic that a friend of mine keeps in a safe. But I don't think you deserve it. It was blessed by the Holy Father and everything." Helen sounded irritated.

"Really, I'm sorry. I'll be good," he said.

"You don't know how to be good." She looked at me and said, "I don't know how you put up with him. It's a good thing we love you. Jack, give me my handbag, it has the relic and the Holy Water in it." Jack and John were one and the same; she called him Jack, and mostly everyone else called him John.

He handed Helen her bag and she pulled out a little frosted glass bottle that had a brass top with a cork underneath. She said the blessing and sprinkled it on Alex's forehead.

"It burns!" he screamed. "Did you guys see the exorcist ?

"Not funny. This may help. You don't know," she retorted.

"Helen, I appreciate all the help I can get. I have a friend who is a deacon in a church, and he had the whole congregation praying for me."

"Hey, stranger things have happened," she said. "I don't know about you, but I believe in miracles."

"I don't," he said. "But thank you anyway."

"You know, we're going to try and get Alex out for Thanksgiving," I said.

"Really? Are your sister and brother coming too?" she asked.

"They are. We're working on getting it approved by insurance. He's only allowed to leave for eight hours and it's an hour drive down and an hour drive back. They have an accessible van that they are going to use."

"Are you excited to come home?" John asked.

"Very," Alex said. "I haven't been home in two-and-a-half months; it'll be weird. But I can't wait to see the kids, and Pepe. My mother is leaving for Florida right after Thanksgiving, so I guess she'll come visit."

"Well we won't bother you at Thanksgiving, we'll see you afterwards," said Helen.

10. GIVING THANKS

It had felt like an eternity. I was on pins and needles waiting for the van to pull in the driveway. Alex was still in a manual wheelchair and I had been taught at Magee how to get him up the front steps of the house. Fortunately, the driver who brought him down was also trained and did the work for me.

We had ordered Thanksgiving dinner in from Casel's market in Margate. My mother set the dining room table with a hand-embroidered white linen tablecloth and napkins, our fine china, the silver we got for our wedding, and our Baccarat crystal, and she did this all with her arm in a sling.

It was gray and cloudy outside and it mirrored what I was feeling inside. None of us knew what to expect when he came home, so when the driver pulled in I screamed to the kids "Daddy's home!" and began to feel an emotion unrelated to fear and trepidation for the first time in two-and-a-half months. I was excited and relieved, and all of a sudden very aware that for months I had been feeling a jumble of things that started at numbness and skyrocketed to internal hysteria.

Pepe was barking like a pit bull. He had no idea he was a Chihuahua. I had to scoop him up in my arms so the driver could bring Alex into the house.

"Can you sign this pink slip, Ma'am?" he asked after he brought Alex inside.

I put Pepe on Alex's lap and the two of them were like long-lost lovers. Alex burst into tears. Pepe began by intuitively licking Alex's neck, and then his cheeks, and then his mouth. He licked the tears away, and there was a dawning of relief and relaxation on Alex's face. They were so happy together as Pepe stood on his hind legs, reaching the crevices of Alex's face that he hadn't been able to get to for so long.

Everyone in the family surrounded Alex, hugging him and kissing him. He was home.

"Welcome home," I said, kissing him on the mouth. Pepe stood up on his hind legs and began to lick Alex's throat again. How the hell did that dog know his neck was broken?

"Adam, Danielle, come say hi to Daddy." The kids had been running around the house with their cousins from my side of the family, building a pillow-fort in the living room, and playing hide and seek. All the kids were in the same age range and when they came over to Alex, it was not with excitement. It was with trepidation. Gary and Andrea's daughter, Sara just stared, as did her brother, David, and Brandon (Diane and Randy's son).

"Hi, Daddy," Adam said. Danielle was not talkative yet. She was a climber and decided he was her Everest. So she put her feet on his feet, which were strapped onto the pedals of his chair, and began to climb the mountain.

"Not yet, sweetheart," I said. "Maybe after dinner."

Gary asked, "Alex do you want something to drink?"

"I would love a can of real Diet Pepsi. They only have Shasta at Magee."

"We've got that in the garage fridge," I replied. "I have straws in the drawer, hold on a minute."

"All they have at Magee is the cheap stuff, it tastes like fake soda." I hadn't seen him handle a soda can, and since he would never be able to use his fingers to pull the tabs again, I opened it for him and put it in front of him. He grasped the can with his knuckles and lifted it to his mouth. It was the first time in two-and-a-half months that I had seen him do anything for himself at all. He had gone from not even being able to breathe on his own, to being able to sit in a wheelchair, and now he could handle a soda can. That was progress to be thankful for.

My mother interjected, "Why don't we eat this lovely dinner while it's still warm?"

Randy, Diane's husband, pushed Alex's chair to the dining room table, but the side arms barely fit under.

"I guess we need to do something about the table," I said. "I'll put it on the list."

I cut his food, which was something else I would have to get used to, then I cut Adam's food, and then Danielle's. It was not lost on me that I was cutting everyone's food, and by the time I got to mine it was cold.

"At Magee they made this adaptive device so I could use a fork. It's in my knapsack, could someone get it for me please?" Alex asked. "I'm also on a medication schedule, my pills are in the backpack, too. Please pull them out, away from the kids."

Andrea went to his knapsack. As a radiologist, Gary's wife was always quick to get up and respond. These doctor's credentials put her first in line for nursing duties.

"Thanks, Andrea," Alex said.

"I guess you've been demoted," I said to her.

"It's no problem, I'm happy to help."

My mother said, "I think this is as good of a time as any to raise our glasses. I would like to make a toast to you, Alex. You have endured so much these past months, and you continue to persevere under such very difficult circumstances. You are a tough cookie, so here's to a fruitful continuation of your road to recovery."

"I have a toast too," he responded. He tried to grip his soda can and the soda spilled all over the white linen tablecloth. At this moment, I didn't give a shit about a stupid spill that would have irritated or even infuriated others. It didn't matter anymore.

Alex looked at me. "I'm so sorry, Gail. God, I hate this. I'm so clumsy now."

"Don't worry about it, it's just a tablecloth. I'll bleach it and you'll never know what happened." I grabbed paper towels and began to sop up the spill.

"What were you saying, Alex?" my mother asked.

"I just wanted to thank you all for being here. That's it."

"No problem," Diane said. "Can we eat now? I'm starving."

The phone had been ringing all through dinner, and for the first time in months I got up to answer it.

"Yes, hi. Yeah, we're great. No we're just finishing up. That's no problem, we're here. See you soon."

I turned to Alex. "That was your mom. She's coming over with Bogie."

The phone rang again, "Yes, we're here, no problem. Well, the van driver said he was going to pick him up at seven. Okay, bye."

Within minutes, the doorbell began to ring and the Pitbull /Chihuahua began to bark.

"Someone please pick up the dog," I screamed. No one inside the house was afraid of him, but he instilled fits of terror in strangers. I opened the door and Molly walked in with Bogie. Following them were Robert and Fern, and then Ralph and Michael.

Alex was truly happy to see them. "Mine kin, mine kin, it's so good to see you at home."

"Did you have a nice dinner?" Molly asked.

"Well it sure beats the cafeteria food at Magee."

"Hello, Alex, how are you?" Ralph said as Michael walked in behind him. Ralph had a voice that could drain godliness from a nun. His tone was flat, nasal, and indifferent. He very well may have cared, but he emitted no emotion.

"How ya doing, Alex?" asked Michael.

"I'm good, happy to be home with my family."

It was amusing to me that he looked so uncomfortable in the chair, and everyone around him seemed so much more uncomfortable than he was. No one seemed to know what to say, or what to ask. And it wasn't like he was a stranger! These were family members who hadn't spent much time with him at the hospital. Maybe they had gone to see him once or twice, but their discomfort was palpable. It would become a prevailing theme in our lives, the discomfort of others.

Most of them left as quickly as they came.

"We just stopped to say hello."

"When are you getting out?"

"As soon as the warden approves my bail," he responded.

"I guess when they feel he's ready to re-enter the earth's atmosphere," I interjected.

"Happy Thanksgiving," they said as they left two by two.

I shut the front door behind them and heard a beeping from the driveway. I looked out of the windows and realized our time at home was up.

"Your driver is here, Alex."

"Tell Nate I'll be out in a minute."

I hadn't realized until then how worried I'd been while he was home. Would his wheelchair fit in through the back hallway? Would he make it up the ramp we had built in the back of the house? The elevator shaft was done, but the elevator hadn't been installed yet. He hadn't wanted to ruin the look of the entryway in front, so we had built a ramp in the back that he could access through the side walkway. Once the elevator was installed he would be able to get out of his van, which we didn't have yet, and roll into the garage, where there would be an access door to the elevator, which wasn't built yet. It would take him from the garage to the first floor, and up to the second floor into a newly-built landing that wasn't there yet either.

As we all said our goodbyes, I thought of how quickly the day had gone. "I will see you tomorrow," I said. I looked into his bright green eyes, with their long black lashes, and kissed him goodbye.

Gary and Randy put his coat on him, which was no easy task. They had to lean him forward and hold him there, since he did not have the use of his trunk muscles. Then they had to lift his arms one at a time and feed them into his coat sleeves, then they had to zip him up. He said his goodbyes to the kids, the rest of the family and Pepe.

And after he left I closed the door.

"Clean up time," my mother politely instructed. As we began to clear the table, the house grew quiet, but only in my head. I am sure that everyone heard the screams of the kids and the clattering of the plates and the dog's barks, but I faded into oblivion, my favorite space.

I felt alone in my pain. It wasn't the sharp, throttling pain that I could take an aspirin for, it was an emotional pain that came with an aching and longing that would not disappear. I ached and longed for a husband I would never have again. As those bright green eyes were shuttled off to Philly, I felt the shadow of despair take over my body, my head, and my heart. Lost in one world, with a foot in the other for Adam and Danielle.

"Gail." My mother said my name again.

"Yes?"

"Where did you go?"

"I was on a plane, on my way to Paris. Sorry I couldn't bring you."

"That's okay, we'll go together next time. Would you mind helping me put the leftovers away?"

"No problem, I'll get the Tupperware."

It was Thursday night, and a repeat of *Friends* was on, and I found great comfort in watching a program that would take me somewhere else. I knew that traveling like this was the only way for me to go anywhere, so I put myself in someone else's living room.

11. THE QUEEN

As December approached, Molly began to ready herself to go to Florida. She had Bogie pack up the car with her things, which would be shipped by truck to North Miami near her apartment in Aventura.

"I am sorry," she said to me on the phone. "The only reason I am leaving is because there is noting I can do here. You have your mother helping you. Believe me, if I could give him my spine I would... I feel sorry for you, I do."

What could I say? Saying what I really felt would do no good. "Have a safe trip, Molly. Enjoy the sunshine."

"Vhat, are you crazy? I can't enjoy myself. Do you think I'm going to have fun when I go? I'm going to be suffering just like you. I do what I can. Please call me."

"I will, I'll let you know how he is doing. I'll talk to you soon."

"Thank you," she said.

Okay, bye." I never knew what to say to her. I knew deep down that she was waiting for me to leave him. I felt her anger towards me in her intonation. She hadn't come out and said it, but I heard it loud and clear. When she had been over the other day she'd referred to me as "The Queen," which pissed me off more than anything,

"Vhat does the queen think?" she had said.

106

"What are you talking about?" I asked.

"Vell, you're the queen, aren't you?"

I literally was in shock. I could not speak, and all I could do was wonder where the hell that had come from. All I could think was, *What have I done? I'm barely keeping it together for two little kids, plus I have a disabled husband! I am going to and from Philly every other day!* What the fuck did I do to deserve that sour, condescending tone of "You're the queen aren't you?" I was exhausted, drained, and on the verge of insanity, but I didn't even have time for a breakdown because I was trying to be a good mother and wife, while my husband was in rehab and I ran around like a mouse in a maze! *It's your son I'm taking care of!* I screamed inside my head. But I said nothing. I was so fucking polite, I hated myself.

Then two days later, when I thought I couldn't take any more, I had to. We had finished dinner and I was helping my mother with the trash. Pepe was sniffing around the side of the trashcan. He perched his legs on its top, leaned in, and grabbed the bone from a chicken breast. Little dogs are notoriously fast, and as I turned around I caught sight of him as he ran with it. I gave chase while he squeezed behind the couch and chewed and swallowed the bones. There was no putting my fingers in his mouth and pulling them out because they had been downed within seconds.

"Shit!" I screamed. "What do I do?"

"Call the vet!" my mother implored. I ran to the phone and dialed the number. An answering machine said they were closed, but to dial another number for emergencies.

I dialed the other number and left a message. "Hi, my name is Gail Kiejdan. My dog Pepe just swallowed chicken bones and I don't know what to do. He is a Chihuahua, about twelve pounds. Please call me back when you get this message. My number is 555-0823. Thank you."

Within half an hour, Pepe threw up on the living room couch. It looked like bile, blood and a few ragged pieces of chicken bone. He gagged again, but nothing came up.

Gary Lowenstein, who was an electrical engineer, had been in the back room looking at the elevator installation. He was meticulous about everything he did. He was Mr. Clean with hair. He must have heard the commotion as he walked from the back hallway into the kitchen.

"What's going on out here?" he said.

I told him.

"Maybe you should call the University of Pennsylvania's Veterinary School," he said.

"That sounds good, and they're in Philly. Two patients, one city."

As I went to pick up the phone, it rang. It was our vet, offering to meet me at her clinic.

I grabbed Pepe and jumped in my Volvo. I put a towel down on the leather seat on the front passenger side of the car and put Pepe on top of it.

Dr. Miller was a stern professional, whom one could call humorless. She didn't smile much, but I had great faith in her abilities as a veterinarian. You could see how much she loved animals by the way she handled them.

She picked Pepe up and brought him into the examining room. "Let's see what's going on here, Pepe."

He was shaking, the way only a Chihuahua can. She pulled her stethoscope out of a drawer and began to listen to his heartbeat, then his lungs. Then she began to squeeze his glands, and felt underneath where I assumed his stomach was. "You say he threw up twice?"

"Yes, the first time had blood and the second just looked like bile."

"Did you see any bone?"

"Yes. The first time had a few pieces. They looked a little shredded."

"Okay, this is our game plan. I'm going to call the Garden State Veterinary Hospital in Tinton Falls. I will let you know when they get back to me. You will probably have to take him up there first thing in the morning. Unfortunately, a chicken bone can kill a dog, if it tears the lining of his stomach, and it sounds like it has fragmented a bit. But if anyone can help him, it's the Garden State Veterinary Hospital. They'll probably take X-rays and he may need surgery. Please call me and let me know what they tell you."

"What about U of P?" I inquired.

She nodded. "You could use them, they are excellent too, but it is a teaching hospital so I would go with Garden State right now."

"Okay, thank you so much."

I left the hospital shaken. Pepe and I got back in the car and drove home in the dark. He sat on my lap and I felt his warm body comfort me, as it had so many times. If you would have asked how I had gotten through these past few months, where I got the most relief from the stress, I would have told you that it was from my little, blonde, twelve-pound, big-mouthed, yippy dog.

The next morning, Pepe and I traveled to Tinton Falls. It was easily an hour-and-a-half drive. When we arrived, he jumped out of the front seat onto the pavement like nothing was wrong. It made me feel 100 percent better. We walked into a large, open waiting room. I checked in at the front desk and we both sat down while I filled out the forms.

After about 15 minutes a young woman, who must have been a veterinarian's assistant, came around from the back and said, " Mrs. Kiejdan?"

"Yes?" I responded.

"You and Pepe can come with me."

We followed her dutifully down the corridor into a bright blue examining room, where she weighed Pepe on a digital scale. "The doctor will be here in a moment."

She left, and about five minutes later another woman walked in. She introduced herself to me as the veterinarian and gave Pepe a kiss. "Well, how are you feeling today, Mr. Pepe?" she asked. And then began to ask the same questions as Dr. Miller. She, too, felt Pepe's abdomen, listened to his chest, and then put her stethoscope down. "Well, quite honestly, there is nothing that I can tell from this examination. If you don't mind leaving him here, I would like to run some tests and take some X-rays. I should know what we can do, or not do, for him by the morning."

"Okay," I said.

"Has he vomited at all today?"

"No, he hasn't."

"Well that is good. "How old is he?"

"He's almost fourteen."

"Hmm," she muttered. "Here is my card." She handed it to me. "Go home and I will call you as soon as we know something."

"Thank you," I said. I looked at Pepe, knowing I was leaving him there. He looked at me and I could feel him imploring me to take him with me. The guilt was unbearable. What little emotion I had left to feel seemed to take over my body. I knew I was doing the right thing; he was in the best possible place to be taken care of. I just felt like I was betraying him by leaving him there. I looked him in the eyes, I kissed him and held him in my arms and said, "Mommy loves you. I just want you to get better. I will be back to get you really, really, soon. I promise."

And with that, the veterinarian took him from me and left the room.

I drove home on the Garden State Parkway. It was a cold, bright blue sunny day. The emotions that I had experienced had subsided. I was back to being numb. By the time I got home, I was exhausted—was that a feeling? I believe it was, but it wasn't a feeling of emotion. Those were on hiatus, probably on sabbatical in some exotic locale.

My mother was waiting expectantly in the kitchen. "How did it go?"

"I don't really know. They're going to call me tomorrow after they perform some tests."

"Were they optimistic?" she asked.

"No. But they weren't pessimistic either."

"Maybe, it's not as bad as it seems," she said. My mother was in full-blown Pollyanna mode again. I don't know how or why, but she always, always, looked on the bright side of things. And for that I was eternally grateful.

The next morning, I decided I couldn't go up to Magee. It was too much. I called Alex, updated him on what was going on with Pepe, and told him I needed to stay close to home. As the day wore on I felt myself thinking of Pepe constantly.

By 2 p.m. the phone rang.

"Hello," I answered.

"Hi, Gail? This is Dr. Oliver from the Garden State Veterinary Hospital."

"Hi. How are you? How is Pepe doing?"

"He's doing well. We ran some tests and took some X-rays and what we found is that the bone is just sitting in his stomach. That means it's probably not going to go anywhere. If he were a younger dog we would operate and remove it. But because he is fourteen, we decided he could live with it in his stomach. It really shouldn't hurt anything. I think he's going to be OK."

"Oh thank God! Thank you so much! I'm so grateful!"

"You're welcome. You can probably pick him up tomorrow."

"Thank you so much, Dr. Oliver." I hung up the phone, I hugged my mother, and I was a new woman. Then I called Alex and gave him the good news.

Relief is a strange thing. You don't really know how tightly you're wound until you begin to feel the release of stress. I knew I was a breath holder since I was a child, but this was different. I wasn't trying to get dizzy and make myself unconscious. This was the opposite—I was gasping for air all of the time. I just didn't know it.

By nighttime, I felt completely relaxed. I went to bed knowing I'd get to pick up Pepe in the morning and bring him home. I had taken a Restoril to help me sleep, like I had taken almost every night since Alex's accident. I liked it. I had tried other sleeping medications, but this left me without side effects, and didn't make me feel groggy in the morning.

At 2 a.m. I awoke, startled and frightened. The phone was ringing and I knew that it could only be bad news. I picked it up, not knowing who was on the other end. Once again, all thoughts were frozen.

"Hello?" I said.

112

"Is this Mrs. Kiejdan?"

"Yes." In my heart, I knew it was Alex.

She continued. "This is Karen Granicy, I'm from the Garden State Veterinary Hospital. I'm so sorry to tell you this, but Pepe passed away this evening."

"Oh no! Why?"

"I don't really know. We thought he was fine and I know you were supposed to pick him up tomorrow, but he just didn't make it. I am really so sorry. You can call back in the morning and we can make arrangements for you to pick up his body. I really am sorry."

"Thank you," I said. And I hung up the phone. With that, I began to wail, deep uncontrollable sobs, like screams. The tears were cascading down like they were coming from a fountain. I gasped and let out another sob. The kids were sleeping and God knows, I didn't want to wake them and explain, but the pipe had burst.

I looked up for a second and saw that my mother was standing in the shadows of the doorway.

"What happened?" she asked quietly.

"Pepe died," I sobbed.

She came into the room and I knew she'd been afraid it was Alex. "I'm so sorry, sweetheart." She grabbed a tissue and handed it to me as she sat on the bed and held me, while months' worth of strain poured out of my eyes.

"I thought he was going to be fine," I cried.

"Did they tell you what happened?" she asked.

"They didn't know. I'm supposed to pick up his body. I don't want to pick up his body."

"Don't worry, honey. You won't have to drive an hour-and-a-half to pick him up. I will handle it."

And I knew she would, because I couldn't handle one more thing. Was this the last push before I fell off the cliff? I absolutely thought it was.

The next day I went to see Alex to deliver the devastating news. Robert drove as I cried the whole way up. He didn't have a dog, so I knew he couldn't understand my near-hysteria. Plus, what can you say to someone who is inconsolable? Nothing.

At the same time, my mother got on the phone to coerce someone from Garden State into cremating Pepe and illegally shipping his ashes to us. She did not take no for an answer. She had a card up her sleeve, and she used it. It was the quad card.

12. THE HALO

We were entering holiday season, and the kids were incredibly excited for Hanukah. Was it Aunt Fern's latkes, or the dradle game, or the lighting of the menorah? No. It was the notion of eight nights of presents. I needed to buy eight nights' worth of gifts for both of them, and the only store I had been to in the past few months was the grocery store, where I slowly plodded through the aisles not giving a crap-and-a-half about what I was going to buy to feed us. But somewhere in my cavernous brain I recognized that it was also a good time to thank every one of our friends who had been so helpful with the countless things I didn't have the time or energy to do while Alex was in the hospital. Kindness was not in short supply. Friends dropped off bagels, some filled my refrigerator, and others filled the freezer. There were the ones who helped me with carpooling, and the ones who took the kids for play dates, picking up and delivering. I suppose if ever there was a time to ask for favors, this was it. But I didn't. The greatest kindnesses were from those who did without asking. I had no idea what I needed, but some friends seemed to know anyway.

On the other end of the spectrum there were also those who could no longer say hello. I would be lying by omission if I didn't admit my thoughts. *You're scared? You're uncomfortable? How the hell do you think I feel?* My new station in life, "quad wife," had changed others. Some just didn't know what to do or say, so they remained quiet or murmured amongst themselves. What do you say to the newly-minted quad wife? Was it personal? Hardly. But time would teach me what angels walked among us, and how to look past the thin veneer of the exterior and into the heart.

As the New Year approached I continued to wish for Alex to walk again, and every day I looked for signs of movement. I also continued to have visual flashes of him walking. I told no one. I didn't have time for therapy, and if my mind was forcing hallucinations on me, I was happy for the split-second delusion.

Up until his injury, New Year's had always been a celebration. We had fresh lobsters flown in from the Trenton Lobster Pound in Maine and had a small party every year where we boiled the crustaceans in sea salt and seaweed in large pots in the garage. I would make a large salad or homemade coleslaw and baked potatoes, and someone would bring the appetizers and desserts.

It was not to be this year, nor any other year. Sometimes when a door closes you don't even hear it; you don't see it happen, but there is something within you that tells you that the large, open window with a wonderful world of possibilities is disappearing, too. There were all those possibilities, and then they were gone. This New Year's Eve, I would drive to the hospital with my mom and the kids during the day and come home to go out to an early dinner with my mother. No celebration, no magical kiss, no wishes for a Happy New Year, just a vacuous feeling and a small sense of optimism and hope for Alex. Next year will be better. The magic of hope was that it stirred the imagination, and offered a rope through an obstacle course that even Special Ops would find challenging.

It was New Year's Day and we went back to Magee late in the afternoon. Our friends Valerie and Jeff Alper had brought Alex a surprise. They had continued with the tradition of boiling lobsters at their home, and Valerie had made her amazing Caesar salad with her own dressing, and had laden the top of the salad with fresh lobster. At Magee, she had gone up to the indoor area of the rooftop and set an elaborate table with a tablecloth, candles, plates, bowls and silverware that she brought from home, and topped it off with champagne glasses filled to the brim with ice-cold bubbly. It was simply an extraordinary kindness.

I rolled Alex up to the rooftop and you could see his expression change dramatically. Within seconds he went from a retreated state of depression, to surprise, and then to joy. It was beyond thoughtful; it was cathartic.

"How's my favorite quad?" Valerie asked. The kids went off and running as we sat down to a type of dinner we hadn't seen in months: warm, loving and inclusive.

"Better now. Wow, you are amazing. This is amazing. I can't believe you did all of this," responded Alex.

"Valerie, this is amazing," my mother said.

"Well, Happy New Year, everyone," said Jeff.

"We brought champagne," Valerie interjected.

"I don't know, he's on a lot of medication," I said.

"Drugs and alcohol? Well, maybe you'll get an even better buzz for the New Year" she said.

"What the hell" said Alex. "I'm already in a hospital, so if there's a problem let them deal with it."

"So, when are you coming home?" Valerie asked.

"Soon, we hope. The goal is to get him home sometime in January," I said.

Valerie responded, "That is soon. So, within the next two or three weeks? We should have a party!"

"I don't think he'll be ready for that right away. He'll need to get situated a little bit first. He hasn't been in the outside world for a while."

Valerie and Jeff lived two doors down. Valerie also had a history with Alex, since they had both grown up as Holocaust survivors' children. Their parents were not only the best of friends, they were survivors from the Vilnius ghetto. They had all made their way to Mays Landing, New Jersey, after the war was over and separately they began their new lives as chicken farmers.

Valerie loved to party and was known to throw some of the best. Thanks to Valerie and Jeff, we were sitting down to a New Year's dinner that was our own private respite, a retreat from the feeling of a long, drawn-out hospital stay. She had tied helium-filled balloons to the back of the seats and had brought an endurable enthusiasm, erasing the hospital setting we had grown accustomed to.

"Here's to china, crystal, silver, and lobster. How bourgeoisie!" I said. I felt the hope, coming from such a small place. And thought, *light creeps in even when it's dark*. That evening she brought both.

A few days into January, the doctor decided it was time for Alex to get his halo taken off. He was understandably nervous. I drove up to Magee to meet him. And together we rode in the back of an ambulance over to the Rothman Institute a few blocks away, so Alex could have his halo removed. Neither one of us had any idea of what was entailed. They pulled into the parking lot and the drivers came around back to unload the package. How do you get used to an ambulance? This must have been the third or fourth time we had ridden in one since September.

The Rothman Institute's waiting room was crowded with all kinds of injured patients waiting to be seen. There were enough crutches, walkers, canes, wheelchairs, and hardware to set off several alarms. When they called "Mr. Kiejdan," I wheeled Alex back around the bend.

We were led down the hallway to a patient room by Randall, the same gentleman who had come to Magee weekly to tighten the vice.

"Hello Alex, how are you today? I bet you can't wait to get this contraption off!"

"No, I can't. I also can't wait to wear regular clothes."

"That is one of the challenges with the halo. Some patients wear their vests on the outside with their clothing underneath, and others wear the vest underneath their clothing. I guess it's a personal choice," Randall said.

"I wear the halo underneath my clothes, it's easier to get dressed and undressed without taking it off and on."

"That makes a whole lotta sense, Alex. OK, you two, I'm going to get Alex up on this table and then we'll be in business."

Randall took the wooden transfer board out and transferred Alex to the table. Then he removed Alex's shirt so we could see the Sherpa-lined vest underneath, and all the metal rods that were holding his head in place. He put a pillow on the table and leaned Alex's head back onto the pillow. Actually, his head looked suspended in mid-air, with the rods resting on the pillow. Then Randall turned around and pulled out an electric rotary tool that would unscrew the screws in Alex's head. I learned later that it was like a Dremel.

"Do you want me to hold your hand?" I asked

"OK," he said under his breath.

Randall said, "Alex, why don't you close your eyes. It won't take more than a minute."

Alex did as he was told, but I daringly kept mine open. It sounded like we were in a dentist's office. As Randall inserted the Dremel to the screws in Alex's head, and began to unscrew the bolts, I saw what I could only describe as a blood geyser coming out of the first hole on his forehead, and then the second hole. A gusher, that's all I could think of—two gushers, bubbling up and then subsiding.

Randall quickly cleaned up the bloody stream with gauze and a bandage. He turned Alex on one side and then the other, unscrewing the bolts with precision. When that was finished he put a brace around Alex's neck, and removed the bodice of the halo.

"This is yours to keep, Alex," he said regarding the halo and the vest. "How do you feel?"

"It hurt more than I thought it would, but I feel a little bit of freedom."

Everyone does," Randall responded. "Let's get you transferred back to the chair, and you can be on your way."

"That's it?" Alex asked.

"That's it."

"This feels weird."

"You'll get used to it. Give it a little bit of time, now your head is really screwed on tight."

"Thank you, Randall," I said. It was at a time like this that one recognized the progress that Alex had made. He was nearing the end of his stay, with a frighteningly new world to navigate.

At home, when we were finished with the last touches of construction, and the painter had finished putting up the new wallpaper in our bathroom and painting the hallway, I felt our house was ready enough for Alex to come home. Besides, his time was up.

They were done teaching us how to access the world in a chair, and the insurance coverage for his hospitalization was coming to an end.

There was one last touch that, unbeknownst to me, Danielle felt was necessary to add. With her almost-two-year-old wisdom, she took a permanent black magic marker and streaked it down the walls of the upstairs hallway. Then she went into her room and did the same on her beautiful wooden whitewashed-oak furniture.

When I walked upstairs and saw what she had done, I exploded. "God damn it, Danielle! What the hell were you thinking?"

What the hell was I thinking? She wasn't even two, the world was still her canvas!

Edith interjected immediately, picking Danielle up with her good arm and managing with her bad one, saying, "Gail, the painters will be back tomorrow. They will fix this. It's fixable."

Where and when had I lost perspective? It was fixable, and it was just stuff. I had stopped caring about stuff. One of the largest lessons in life had been shoved down my throat, and I still lost it. I started to cry. But these weren't the sobs that had prevailed when Pepe died; these were stress tears.

"You're right, Mom. I'm sorry, Danielle." I lifted her from my mother's arms. "You shouldn't be holding her, she is too heavy." I kissed Danielle and said, "I love you, Pumpkin," and put her down, and off she ran.

13. RE-ENTERING THE EARTH'S ATMOSPHERE

After months of Alex being away from home, and months of us wading through the dirt and debris of construction on the house, it was time for Alex to return. The elevator was finished, the doorways had been widened, the paint was dry, again…and the ramp to the backyard was complete.

Our friends Paul and Laurie Provost owned Loving Hands, a nursing agency that provided nurses for in-home care. Laurie, who was a registered nurse and had started Loving Hands, began to interview nurses and then send them to Alex to interview. Initially he had asked for an all-male nursing staff, and together they found several male nurses who were willing to commute to the shore and had spinal cord injury experience.

Before he came home I had to learn to transfer him, with a wooden board, in and out of a car. I also had to learn how to get him up a curb and steps while he was in a manual wheelchair. I was taught that once he was in his electric wheelchair, there would be no way for him to get up steps or a curb; he would be dependent on curb cuts, elevators and modifications. And I had to spend a night at Magee, where they taught me how to do his bowel program and change his catheter. All these things I needed to know in case a nurse didn't show up. As I trained, it became clearer to me that his life would be filled with obstacles; the things that he would never do again just kept adding up.

The phone rang about three weeks before Alex was scheduled to leave rehab. I was upstairs in our bedroom and my mother picked it up downstairs on the first ring. Edith was the phone police, and she was still on active duty. I had only picked up the phone a couple of times since Alex was injured because I didn't think I would be able to carry on a conversation that didn't involve his care.

My mother shouted that it was Laurie. I picked up the phone.

"Hi Gail," Laurie said cheerfully. "I just wanted to let you know that I'm working on Alex's home care. I spoke to the social worker at Magee to see what he'll need once he gets home. I have a question for you. Do you have a caseworker at Blue Cross?"

"I don't think so. What do I need a caseworker for?"

"Oh God, Gail, you need a caseworker to make sure you get everything you need when Alex comes home from the hospital."

"You know, they're not paying our bills," I said. "We've been getting these enormous bills from the hospitals, and they aren't paying them."

"Gail, that's why you need a caseworker. I'll get on it. And I will call you back when I have more info."

"Thank you." And I hung up the phone. The never-ending feeling of being overwhelmed seemed to fill me with a powerful new surge of dread, to be followed by another bout of numbness. I was self-anesthetizing without the use of actual medication. I was in a walking coma. The bills were coming in, and my mother was organizing them in folders.

Within a few days Laurie called back. "They are assigning you a caseworker," she said. "Once I have her name you will have someone to communicate with about your billing. She will also be able to take care of a new bed, the manual wheelchair, the power wheelchair, the commode chair, the Hoyer Lift and the transfer boards. In addition she will have a list of the soft supplies, as well as the medications he will need. You will need to get that list together before he leaves the hospital. What kind of catheter does he have?"

"A 26 French."

"Well, he will also need extra catheters. You'll need to get gauze, sterile gloves, tapes and a range of other things that you probably aren't quite aware of yet."

I listened, and didn't bother to write it down. I was in over my head, and I knew it. If I agreed to everything and pretended to listen intently to what people were saying, they wouldn't know that I was in my own little private, pretend room. A place with no noise, that was quiet and serene. Just a nice big, comfy couch, covered in a soft velvet. It was cozy and warm, and it was closed off to the world, and it was much nicer than the closet I was standing in now. I heard my name…"Gail."

"Yes," I responded. Laurie was still talking.

"I sent a male nurse named Warren Cunningham to meet Alex. He is a great nurse, and has spinal cord experience. I will be hiring more nurses. Alex will meet and interview every one of them. He asked for all males, so he wouldn't have to worry about a female doing all the heavy lifting. I told him females usually do most of the heavy lifting—as a matter of fact, I'm a prime example. But initially, this is what he wants. He may change his mind. But for now he will have all males. So he is deciding who will be in your home. Actually,

I don't think he wants anyone too good-looking either. Do you have a room where they can put their things?"

"Yes, we have the back room. It's the kid's playroom, but we can change it up a bit. It's under construction right now because we are adding an elevator onto that side of the house."

"Do you have a couch back there? A place for someone to sit?"

"We have a futon."

"That's perfect," she said. "That can be the room where the nurses stay. That way they are out of the way and won't interfere with your daily living."

"It sounds like a plan," I responded.

And there it was, a plan. I laughed at the mere thought of a plan. What the hell was that? Something that had become a meaningless word, not worth a damn thing. Nothing that had happened had been in the plan. This accident had come thrashing like a giant out of the sea, and all we did in response was to pick up the wreckage. It seemed that for many years to come, I would be part and parcel to the cleanup crew.

Laurie, on the other hand, was meticulous about the details. She was a bossy blond who took no prisoners, and truly was enthused by the work she did. This fast-talking North Jersey woman was married to one of Alex's best friends from college, Paul. They had dated since high school. Paul, on the other hand, was more laid back. He was an accountant by trade who had joined in to help his wife's nursing agency. With her knowledge of the medical field and his financial background, the agency began to thrive. Laurie knew the system, and knew how to work it. And pragmatically speaking, she was on our side. She had asked the woman on the phone, a woman who would become our case manager, if she would sign a letter of intent in reference to our case, which would validate that they agreed that Alex would need twenty-four-hour nursing.

So began the process of creating a file, and a way to finally begin to pay the bills. They were in the hundreds of thousands at this point, with no end in sight. I thanked God, and my father. I thanked God for health insurance, and I thanked my father for making sure that we got the very best. He was a urologist, and knew first-hand the ins and outs of insurance. Back when he was still practicing medicine he would say, "You'll see. This country is headed for socialized medicine." He also used to say, "You don't mess around with health insurance. Get the best. You just never know."

When we got married, we didn't know any better. But he did. So we had listened to the wise words that would eventually save us on so many levels. Our insurance policy did not have a cap, and it allowed for twenty-four-hour nursing.

As I hid in my closet staring at the shoes, I knew there were some important decisions to make. The modifications we needed to the house were almost complete. The doorways had been widened. The addition with the elevator was almost finished. The ramp had been added to the back porch. The shower was being modified and enlarged to create a roll-in shower. And the sills in all the bathrooms had been changed into accessible sills. Robert had designed the changes so they were seamless. All I had to do was pick out paint colors and tile. Although while I was at it, I decided to add some new wallpaper. Then I spoke with Alex, whose life in rehab had become a safety zone.

"I think I'm going to redo the closets."

"Jesus, Gail, how much money are you spending?"

"Alex, you need to be able to have access to your clothes. You aren't going to be able to open the drawers in your armoire." Alex

126

could no longer use his hands to open drawers. Everything had to have open access so he could somehow manage to pull it out. Later I would learn that he wouldn't even be able to pull out his sweaters or underwear; his hand function would never return. I'd just add the closet to the list, the really important one that I needed to make.

Silence. This was just another reminder of one of the things he wouldn't be able to do. Barriers were everywhere. But they were not going to be in the house.

I was trying to put myself in his position, something I learned you can never do. I tried to sit in my chair for more than 10 minutes. But thinking about staying there for the rest of my life only made me want to get up. It was impossible to force myself to stay put for too long. Imagining not being able to get up, trying so many times and failing. It was too painful to think about. But the worse situation was actually having to live that way.

There was only one way to make myself feel better; maybe it would be my salvation. I began to embrace diversion therapy. In time I would have many diversions to get me through, but this particular one would have me redecorating. Power over my domain, wink - wink.

I would start by investigating the ancient art of Feng Shui. It developed thousands of years ago, and I would try to ride out the swells of chaos with a positive influence and energy that had managed to attain an Eastern following from one dynasty to another. I could change the *chi* in my house. By changing the colors, I would be able to bring joy and health into the home. Greens stood for health, yellow for happiness and joy. I thought optimistically of Alex no longer being in the hospital, of us being together as a family, of no longer traveling back and forth to Philadelphia, which had put me in a state of zombie-like exhaustion. Things were changing. My mother's arm was healed and she no longer needed to go to rehab. My husband was coming out of rehab…and I wanted to go in.

"Gail," my mom said to me as I was cleaning up after the kids.

"Yeah, Mom?"

"I want you to know that when Alex comes home I will be leaving."

I stopped what I was doing and looked up in shock. I never thought about her leaving. I knew she wasn't staying here forever, but I never thought that she would leave me.

"I know what you're thinking, honey. But you can manage this. You have broad shoulders. I laid the groundwork for your insurance, the kids are on a schedule, you have food in the freezer from all of your friends, the house is finished with the construction. It's time for you and Alex to get things back in line as a family. You really don't need me anymore."

I wanted to scream, "Mommy, don't go, please! I'll be good, I promise!" It actually almost came out of my mouth. But instead I said, "Mom, you have been amazing. We are so lucky that you were here as long as you were. I know it's time for you to get back to your friends in Florida. You probably could use a vacation, with all this crap you had to deal with."

"I love you Gail, and I did what was necessary, and at some point you will probably need a vacation too. So when everything is situated, you'll come to Boca for a little respite."

I walked over and hugged her. "I love you, Mom."

And she hugged back. "I love you too, sweetheart."

And there it was, my unwanted independence. She had left Beachwood in September, and hadn't been back. We were now in the middle of January, and she had to go home to pack her car for Florida, and re-ignite the pilot of her real life. Her organizational skills were impeccable. She spoke three languages fluently: French, German, and English. She was an accomplished chemist, who had had three children and had stopped working to devote her time to raising us. We were all so lucky to have her, and no one knew that more than I did. I was going to miss her strength, and her level-headed decision-making. She was a tough cookie with a "nice mom" exterior. And most importantly, she could handle Alex's family with grace and decorum.

The day before Alex came home, I went up to Magee to pack all of his things. We had sent gifts to the nursing staff and the doctors, and the people in physical and occupational therapy. I had said my goodbyes to those who were around. I was not sorry for him to be leaving, and I had assumed that it was the same for him.

I was wrong. He had grown accustomed to this life and the safety that it had provided. He was comfortable here, because almost everyone was in the same position. They were all handicapped and they all understood that the outside was a place where you were, without question, going to hit the wall. Your wall could be as simple as a curb without a curb cut, steps, buses that weren't accessible, cars that you would never be able to drive again, or a piece of meat that you would never be able to cut. They had been given tools to help them meet these walls, but not all adaptive devices could prepare them for the barriers they were about to face.

14. HOME AGAIN

When the van pulled in the driveway, I didn't know what to do first. I was so excited, the kids were running around and my mom was in the kitchen. I decided to put my coat on and go outside to greet Alex. "Hello! Welcome home!" I said as I came out of the front of the house.

The driver was rolling him down the ramp of the van. I thanked him as I took over pushing the wheelchair.

"Last time you were here we were just starting construction on the house, now it's done. How was the ride home?"

He was very quiet. I saw an area of wetness at the side of his eyes. "Uneventful."

"Your new nurse is here. He's upstairs putting your medical supplies in the closet in our bathroom." Before it was a supply closet it had been a shower, but with the addition to the house we now had room for a closet, which was good because I had no idea how many medical supplies we were going to need.

"That's good," he responded with a flat, lifeless tone.

"Do you want to see the kids?"

"Yeah."

"Let me take you to the elevator."

So away we rolled. I pushed a button and explained, "There are three levels: the garage is one, the main floor is two, and the second floor is three."

"Got it."

I pushed two, so he could see the remodeled interior of the ground floor first. I rolled him into what used to be the children's playroom, and was now the nurse's room. Then I pushed him into the kitchen, where the kids and my mother greeted him.

"Hi honey, welcome home!" My mom smiled at him.

"Hi Edie."

"We're so glad you're back where you belong. The kids have missed you."

"Hi!" he said to Adam and Danielle as they came running in.

"Hi, Daddy," Adam responded.

Danielle, who wasn't much of a talker, began to crawl up his legs and into his lap. She kissed him and hugged him and then sat down.

"Well, that's a nice greeting," he said to her. "I missed you guys, so, so much." He looked at my mother. "So I hear you're leaving us, Edie."

"It's time, Alex I've been here long enough. You kids have to get your lives back on track and that doesn't include me."

"I really appreciate you being here. Gail couldn't have done it without you, and I couldn't have gotten this far without her. We both really appreciate what you've done."

"Well, I love you both, and I'm glad I could help."

With that we heard very light footsteps on the stairs. It was the nurse, Warren, and as we would learn, he was stealth.

"Welcome home, Alex," he said.

"Thank you, Warren."

"I was just upstairs getting your bed and your closet situated. I'll be in the back room until you need me. Let me just check your leg bag to see if it needs emptying."

At that point, Alex's leg bag was hanging on his chair; this was one of the many things that were going to change. Camouflage was going to play a major role in our lives. We were going to hide things, so they appeared as normal as possible to the outside world.

In the back room, the walls were beige, with a red futon against the back wall. The nurse's room was plain. I had put most of the kids' toys away in a newly-built closet that was part of the addition. Warren would hide back there, and with the purchase of a telephone with an intercom beeping system, Alex would be able to call for him by hitting his hand on a button.

"It really is quiet here without Pepe," Alex said.

"I know," I responded. Normally, Pepe would have barked up a storm and not let Warren move. But our little protector was gone.

"How are the kids doing without him?" he asked.

"Well, Danielle is fine, and when I told Adam, I was a little nervous and upset, I guess. I started to cry and he said to me, in all his wisdom, 'Don't worry, Mom. We can get another dog.' And that was that. So, I guess it's just me who is adjusting."

"Looks like everyone has a lot of adjusting to do," he said.

"Yeah, I know," I said.

"Gail," my mom said, "my plane leaves at 11:30 out of Philly, tomorrow. Shouldn't we call someone to take me?"

"Mom, I'll take you. We'll bring the kids; that way I won't have to worry about a sitter."

"That sounds good to me. I'll go upstairs and pack after dinner."

"What's for dinner?" Alex asked.

"Cafeteria food. I know how much you liked it so we brought some home to make you feel comfortable."

"Funny…I used to like cafeteria food…"

"Until you had to eat it every day," I interjected.

My mother was a gourmet cook, and when we were growing up she liked to experiment with her culinary skills. So when it came to eating, we were familiar with a wide array of dishes. While my dad was alive they had a supper club once a month, where we were exposed to an even greater array of epicurean experiments. Needless to say, I could have eaten very well while Alex was in the hospital. But instead, my stomach acids had simmered on low and I was left without an appetite.

"Tonight, we're having Portobello mushrooms with a balsamic reduction, sautéed spinach, and marinated chicken breasts," my mother said.

"Oh my God, that sounds amazing, Edie," Alex said.

"Should I ask Warren to join us?"

"I don't know what the protocol is for nurses eating with us, Mom."

"Well, Gail, while I'm here we will include him. Then you two can do what you like."

"But if he starts eating with us now, will he think he's always supposed to eat with us?"

"That's a good point." Fortunately, the door on the nurse's room/playroom was closed at the time, so Warren wasn't privy to this conversation. "I'm going to set a place for him, and you two can figure this out after I leave."

"That works," Alex said.

After dinner, Warren offered to do the dishes.

"Oh, thank you, Warren, that's so sweet," my mother said.

After dinner, I told Alex I had to bathe the kids and get them ready for bed. He met us upstairs. He hadn't been in our bedroom in four and a half months. He looked towards one end, where our hand-carved Oriental rosewood headboard and mattress sat imperially on the Berber carpeting. On the other end of the rectangular room sat his hospital waterbed. In a metal hospital bedframe, it had hand controls so he could raise and lower it. He could also raise and lower the head and the foot of the bed. But since he didn't have the use of his hands, someone would have to do all that for him.

"Where do I sleep?" he asked.

"I know at the hospital they said that you would never be able to sleep with me in this bed," I said as I sat down on it. "But Warren said that he could probably order you some gel pads for your bottom so you don't get bed sores, and then you would be able to sleep with me." I stood up and leaned over and kissed him.

And then I saw it. Something I hadn't seen since before his injury: the smile in his eyes. He still had it. I could see the flicker of light, the mischievous sparkle that I found so amusing and enticing.

"I want to get in bed with you, now," he said.

"Now?"

"Yeah, lock the door."

"What about the kids?

" Screw 'em."

"Look, I want to, but let me get the kids in bed first."

He looked disappointed, but I was emotionally drained and couldn't think of anything like that for one minute. By that time I was on Zoloft, and my sexual drive was in neutral. Plus, my mother was there, plus Warren was there, plus I thought "it" was broken!

"I want you so badly," he said.

"We will have our time, I promise."

"Promise?"

"I promise."

It was good to know that he still wanted me that way. I just wondered how it was going to work.

The next day, the kids and I drove my mom up to the airport for what one would think would be a tearful goodbye.

It was not. It was an emotional tsunami filled with mild hysteria, and months of internal angst releasing through my tear ducts and running down my nose. My face was red within minutes, I should have been embarrassed, but I didn't give a crap.

"You will be fine, Gail," my mother said, hugging me. She and I were standing outside the car while the kids waited in the back seat. "I raised you well, you are a strong young woman, and I know you can handle this."

"How do you know, if I don't know?" I sobbed.

"I just do," she said matter-of-factly. "Some things mothers just know."

"I love you, Mom," I said as I hugged her.

"I love you too, sweetie."

She opened the back door of the car and kissed the kids goodbye. "You be good for your mommy."

"We will, Nana." Adam said.

"Bye, bye," Danielle said.

She kissed them both and shut the door.

"One last hug," I said. "Call me when you get home."

She looked at me and smiled. "That's not the only thing you got from me." And she was on her way.

When I returned home with the kids, I found Alex in the garage with Warren. I pulled into the right side of the garage. There was debris strewn about from the mess that was left over from the construction, and it left Alex very little room to maneuver. But, given the fact that he was still in a manual wheelchair, mostly everyone around him had to help him push the chair. At Magee he'd begun physical therapy to help him learn how to navigate the manual chair until his new one arrived, and the therapy would continue at home.

I could see that being home was more difficult than he had imagined. Now that he was here, his world was filled with barriers. The camaraderie that he'd developed with the other injured patients was gone. We were walkers, and his world had become a strange new land filled with obstacles.

I unloaded the kids and kissed him hello. "Hi, Warren. What are you two up to?"

"We're trying to figure out how to straighten out this mess."

"Alex, why don't you call Jeff? He said he would come over and clean it up with a few of his friends."

"I don't want to bother him."

"He already offered. Do you want me to call him?"

"Okay." He was quiet and withdrawn.

I looked over at Warren, whom I barely knew, and hoped that he would say something positive.

"Alex, you have a lot to get used to, and it is cold in here. Why don't we go back in the house," he suggested.

But Alex was looking at his bikes, hanging from the ceiling. One was a burgundy-colored hybrid mountain bike that he used to maneuver through the woods when he rode through New Hope, and outside of Philadelphia. He had also taken it on rides to Cape May, Batsto and New Gretna. The second bike was the newer one. It was a Trek 5500 Carbon Fiber road bike. The components were Shimano Durace; Alex had prided himself on his knowledge of the integral parts of all of his bikes. His third and most prized bike, which was the oldest of the three, was black as well. It was a Crescent bike, manufactured in Sweden.

He loved it because of its Racer, Reynolds 531 double-butted tubing. The components on the bike were Campagnolo, with front and rear derailleurs. It was a ten-speed of course, and had been top of the line in 1970. It was heading into antique territory, but the hand-painted lugs and high-pressure sew-up tires that had to be glued to the rim, had made it a racer's dream bike back in the day. And if you got a flat it had to be sewn back up by hand. The inner tube and tire were composed of one piece and he carried a complete tire on the back of his bike. He had ridden in group-rides for 100 miles through the Wharton State Forrest, and I could see the sadness of what would never be again etched on his face.

The kids had scuttled into the house and I began to follow them, "Come inside Alex, we'll get the garage clean later."

"I'm going to sell the bikes, and my car," he said when we got into the house.

"Okay. I guess it doesn't really make sense to keep them."

"I could get good money for the bikes. I'll keep the hybrid for you, and I'll sell the other two. I paid $5500 for the Trek, I bet I could get five grand for it."

"Are you going to put an ad in *The Press?*"

"Yeah, I'll do that tomorrow." He paused, then added, "I want to go back to work."

I thought about it. "Well, there's no reason you shouldn't."

"I know for a fact that the office isn't accessible, at least not from the front."

"Well, call Ralph and ask him if they can make it accessible. It shouldn't be too hard. They're in the building business."

"I will. As a matter of fact, I'm going to call him right now."

I handed Alex the phone. He had an adaptive device so he could push the buttons. He put it on speakerphone, because he couldn't hold the phone up to his ear. From that point on, the majority of his phone calls would be on speakerphone.

I admired the way he wanted to jump right back into work. I didn't know if I could have done the same thing.

"Hi Ralph, is there a way for me to get into the building in the front?"

"No, Alex. If you want to come to the office, just call before you come. We'll have to unlock the back door for you."

"Well, Ralph, I'm coming now."

Ralph had been running the office since the accident. He and Alex had always butted heads. Not only didn't they see eye to eye on how to run the business, they didn't really see eye to eye on anything.

Ralph was the second-oldest son in a family where the daughters were not included in the business. It was old school from the get-go, with a Holocaust survivor's mentality that permeated throughout the business. Alex's father, Pinchus, had made sure that everyone had an equal share in the firm, but not an equal say. After his chicken-egg business ended from a widespread disease that killed all of the chickens, he had to start over. He began by building a home for one of his neighbors. One home led to another, and the income enabled him to buy land, which eventually enabled him to build apartment complexes and strip malls. He invested in land, and he was a shrewd negotiator. Meanwhile, Molly had six children to care for, which meant many mouths to feed, and Pinchus was never home. He was always working to make sure that his family would not go hungry like he and Molly had during the war.

Michael, who was their first child, was born in Germany, and was the one who oversaw the construction workers. Edie, the second child, didn't get involved in the business until all of her children were grown. Ralph who came after Edie, managed the office and the apartments with Alex, who was second youngest. Robert came after Ralph and was the architect and a builder. And Renee, the youngest, worked at the shop where they built kitchens for the apartments.

And now Ralph, who didn't want to share any of the decision-making with Alex, had just had the office to himself for four months. He must have relished the authority, realizing that when Alex went back to work, he would face a rude awakening.

Alex handed me back the phone. "Warren, will you take me to the office?"

"Sure, let me go get my coat."

"Are you sure you're ready for this, Alex?" I asked.

"Why wouldn't I be? What am I going to do at home?"

Warren came back with his coat. "Alex, would you mind if I had a cigarette first?"

"Go right ahead."

Warren was a committed smoker. As we would soon learn, he would get up really early in the morning, around 6:30, use his French press to make coffee, which was strong and black, and go outside to have a cigarette. I did not allow smoking in the house, and that wasn't going to change for anyone.

After Warren finished his cigarette, he transferred Alex into the car, threw the manual chair in the trunk and drove to the office, which was about five minutes away from our house on Tilton Road.

He came home not too long after visiting…in an implacable rage.

"He is a motherfucker!" Alex said as Warren rolled him into the kitchen.

"Who?" I asked.

"Ralph. Do you know what he did? He took all of my files out of my office. And when I asked him why he did that, do you know what he said?" I shook my head, stunned into silence and afraid to talk.

"I went in to start my responsibilities, and I wanted to do some preventative maintenance on some buildings. I brought it up to him that we needed to have a lot of repairs done, and do you know what that asshole said? He said 'No.' And I said 'Yes! I run these properties, I ran them before and I'm going to run them now.' He then said, 'You're not running them anymore.' It was a pure power thing for him. Then he said, 'You have nothing to say here anymore.' And everyone else listened to him because I hadn't been there in so many months. Then I got so angry with him I said, 'Drop dead.' You know what he said to me?"

I shook my head no.

"He said 'You're going to die before me anyway.' Then I said to him, 'You know Ralph, I'd rather be in this wheelchair, than be you.'"

That night Molly called. She was, and would be, a staunch Ralph supporter to the bitter end. There were reasons behind this and they all had to do with the fact that he took care of her. For Molly it was never about loving your children equally, it was about taking care of the people who took care of you. In that way she was dramatically different from Alex's father, Pinchus.

Ever since Pinky had died, Ralph had taken care of Molly. Not emotionally, but he paid the bills, and made sure Molly had what she needed financially. Even though he wasn't the oldest, he was entrusted to take care of the business finances. He wasn't a shining star, but he was honest and he knew how to count his pennies. The two girls, Edie and Renee, took care of Molly in other ways, but Ralph could do no wrong.

"Vy did you talk to Ralph like that?" were her first words.

"Mom, he took away all my work. He took my files out of my office, and he said that there is nothing there for me to do."

"Alex, he's your brother, you're all wrong. He just wants to make life easier for you."

"No, he just wants control, Mom."

"He's not like that, mine kin, he's a good boy. He just wants to take care of you."

There was no use trying to make his case. She was, and always would be, without question, 100 percent on Ralph's side.

This was another level of devastation Alex was not prepared for. He wanted to work. He wanted to feel useful; he needed to feel a sense of empowerment. And together, his mother and Ralph literally stole his dignity and drive. He was fighting for his life, to regain a semblance of normalcy, but the powers that be didn't see it that way, because they couldn't see beyond their own motivations.

"Don't vorry Alex, you will still get a check," she said.

"I know, Mom. I know how the will is written. But don't you get it? I want to work!"

"Vy are you aggravating me, Alex? I'm not a well woman."

"Never mind, Mom. I'll talk to you later." And he hung up the phone without saying goodbye.

"She doesn't give a shit about me," he said to me.

"Alex, I have no words. It sucks. It really does. I can't imagine what she is thinking."

"I'll tell you what she is thinking. She's thinking about Ralph."

It took me a while, but eventually I understood that she wasn't just thinking about Ralph. The cruelty of taking Alex's job away was truly lost on them. But the side effects were something we were going to be dealing with for a very long time.

15. BUYING TIME

The next day, our friend Christina dropped off a delicious non-traditional lasagna she called 'lasagna wheels'- miniature lasagna noodles rolled with a ricotta mixture and topped with mozzarella and a pesto sauce. She also brought a salad, fresh rolls, and butter.

When she dropped off the dish, I was sitting in the cold garage, smoking a cigarette.

She stared at me. "What are you doing? Why are you smoking that thing?"

"I need a vice. I can't drink or do drugs, because between Alex and the kids I really have to be as sober as a judge."

"I thought chocolate was your vice," she countered.

"Oh God no, that's my therapy."

"Well, if it's a temporary feeling, how therapeutic could it be?"

"Retail therapy is temporary, but it's still therapy. And you know all about that, don't you?"

"Oh I do," she said.

"Thank you so much for the lasagna wheels. They look yummy."

"It's different. Let me know how it tastes."

I took the dish from her, stored it in the garage refrigerator, and sat back down on our red velvet antique couch. We didn't really have a place to put it in inside the house. Besides, I began to want an escape from what was going on in the house and the garage took me out of the fray.

Christina sat next to me, bringing her southern California sunshine in the midst of what was turning into a gloomy winter. She stood about five-foot-two. She was an interior designer who also painted abstracts, beautiful scenic landscapes and, on rare occasions, portraits. Her greatest attribute was her disposition. She was always friendly, and said hello to everyone. Sometimes I thought the northeast was not friendly enough for her.

I was lucky to have a small group of very compassionate and thoughtful women friends like Christina, who continued to keep me afloat. I probably wouldn't have made it through without our friends. And as I would learn in the not-too-distant future, some would carry us on their wings, and others would put on their invisible cloaks and disappear.

"How are you holding up?" she asked me.

"I'm okay."

"How is Alex?"

"Well, he tried to go back to work yesterday."

"Good for him," she said.

"Not so good. Ralph told him there wasn't a place for him anymore."

"What an asshole!"

"I know. Pinky would turn over in his grave," I said.

"What is he going to do?" she asked

"I don't really know."

I inhaled the cigarette. It really was disgusting, but for whatever reason, it made me feel better. I then stubbed it out on the garage floor with my foot. I never really finished them. It was just something that seemed to help me relieve stress.

"So how are you doing without your mom?" she asked.

"We're okay. I guess we have a lot of things to get used to."

"She's an amazing woman," Christina continued. "I don't know many moms who would have done what she did."

"I know, I'm very lucky."

"I told her I didn't know how you were going to get through this…you know what she said?"

I shook my head no.

"She said that you were going to be all right. She wasn't worried."

I thought about the worrying aspect. I don't think I had done a lot of worrying, because it just took up too much time. So did going to see a therapist. How many times had people pulled me aside and said, "Are you talking to someone? Because maybe you should. It would help you get through things. You know, figure things out."

That was truly funny. Who the hell had time to talk to a therapist?

Therapy and worrying both took time and energy I did not have. Or, maybe I was just numb.

"Do you know what my mom said to me, Christina?"

"What?"

"Worrying is like a rocking chair, it wastes time and it doesn't get you anywhere."

"I like that," she responded.

"So do I. It's going to be my new motto."

Edith always had a saying for everything. I could never figure out where she got them, but she would always come out with something short, simple and appropriate. I grew quiet, thinking about how much I missed my mother and her unwavering strength.

"Where did you go?" Christina asked.

"I was in Paris."

"What did you buy?"

"Nothing, just doing some window shopping. You want to come inside?"

"Okay, I'll go in and say hello to Alex. How's his mood?"

"Up and down, he's on an emotional trampoline."

As we walked in the house, Alex put a big grin on his face. He was always so happy to see Christina.

She kissed him hello. "You happy to be home?"

"Of course. I'm getting adjusted. But I'm happy to be with my beautiful wife and my kids. Thanks for all of the support and the cooking you've done."

"It's no problem Alex, I hope it's worth eating."

"What, are you kidding? I love your food. How's my little buddy Justin?"

Justin was Gary and Christina's son. Before we had children, Alex would take Justin to the playground once in a while. He loved him from the get-go. At this time, Justin must have been only eight, but he was the most talkative and inquisitive little boy. He had straight blonde hair with a wiry little body, and Alex found him amusing as hell.

"He's okay. He's had some joint problems; his knees have been hurting him a lot, so we've been taking him to a few specialists."

"Sounds like you've had your hands full," Alex responded.

"Yup, everyone's got something. Of course what you have to deal with pretty much tips the scales."

After Christina left, we decided to take a field trip to Sam's Warehouse. I put the kids in the backseat of Alex's car, Warren transferred Alex into the front with a transfer board, and I climbed in between the kids. Part of my education before they had let Alex go home was to learn to transfer him as well.

Word did not find any entries for your table of contents. At Sam's Wholesale Warehouse, Danielle made it her business to push Warren out of the way. He had been pushing Alex in his wheelchair and Danielle decided that she wanted to do the job. She was just about two years old and we were sensing her dominating personality.

While we shopped, I kept my eye on Adam. He had his own little world, and from an early age he was a wanderer. When he was one-and-a-half, Alex had lost him on the beach. They were sitting with a group of friends, Alex's head was turned in conversation, and when he turned around to check on Adam, he was gone. Panic stricken, Alex began to run, but he wasn't sure which direction Adam had gone in. Someone wisely told him to go with the wind. Kids do not go against the wind.

Laurie Provost had set up interviews with other nurses for Alex to meet while he was at Magee. So, when Warren left after a four-day period, a new nurse came on duty.

Warren had set things in motion for Alex's transition. He had put him on a morning bowel program, he had set up his new quad closet filled with medications, bandages, towels, sterile gauze pads, catheters, and chucks.

We were trying to learn how to have a nurse in the home, but nothing prepares you for the loss of privacy and the continuous intrusions. Our home was theirwork place. Some nurses would understand that they were working in a home environment, and others would think "Hey, this is where I work," with the focus being on *I*. The revolving door of personalities was something I would never get used to. I wasn't in control of who was coming and going in my house. I wasn't in control of anything. Control was an illusion, and I had learned that sooner or later that illusion gets shattered.

The next nurse to walk through our doors was a man named Tim, and then there would be another Tim.

Then there was Eric, who on his first night spilled urine all over our bedroom carpeting. Eric was tall, imposing and clumsy, and he had a full head of hair with nothing underneath. He broke several things in the kitchen and couldn't remember how to get from point A to point B without detailed instructions.

On his second night at work, he had a brand new laptop. Our niece Rachael was watching the children.

"Look," he said to Rachael, "Keep those kids out of the back room. I have a new computer and I don't want them touching it."

Rachael, never one to back down from a displaced attitude, said, "Listen, this is their house, not yours. So if you don't want something to happen to your goddamn computer, I suggest you put it where the kids can't reach it. Asshole!"

And when I came home, I was informed by Rachael about what an asshole the nurse was.

"Thank you for doing that." I said.

"No problem, Gail. He needs to learn a few things." And she was the one to school him. I was glad it wasn't me she was schooling.

After Rachael told us what happened, we informed Laurie that he could no longer work in our home.

A few days later the doorbell rang. It was Mike D. He had graying hair, and what I perceived to be beady blue eyes. He looked very untrustworthy, but I invited him in so Alex could interview him. Over time, I would learn that he was honest and dependable. The beady blue eyes would become bright blue as I discovered not to judge a person immediately. And for a man without children, he knew how to handle them. He ended up engaging ours with the pretense of his hand becoming a giant claw. "The claw! The claw! Look out! Here comes the claw!" They were thrilled.

As the months went on, I realized I had more on my plate than I could handle. I was just beginning to recognize that I, too, was in shock, and that state was thawing into a reality that I couldn't grasp. The emotional needs of two small children and the emotional needs of a quadriplegic in essence had forced my needs to the sidelines. I was the main caregiver in the house, with the help of some trained nurses. I thought we could muddle through. As I erased myself from the equation, it became all about getting through the day.

It was then that I felt I had grown. When Alex was first injured, I was getting through the hours one at a time. Now I was taking it one day at a time. But talking on the phone was still a perk that I had no time for.

Alex started to shop for a van. He needed to buy a regular van and then have them send it to a conversion company, where they would convert it into a handicap-accessible van with a ramp that he could roll up and into. The van would also have chairs that switched in and out so his nurse or I could remove the driver's seat, so Alex could pull in his wheelchair and lock down in place and drive. In addition, they would put a three-pronged rubber pin in the steering wheel called a tri-pin that would allow him to pull the steering wheel in the direction he was going. Or if need be, we could pull out the passenger seat so I or a nurse could drive and he could pull in on the passenger side. This van would also enable him to use his electric wheelchair when he got it. They would both take months to get, but when he got them, he would have a renewed sense of independence.

His spasms, which had begun at Magee, seemed to have been getting worse. He had to be continuously strapped down. It wasn't that long ago that I had discovered him in the hallway at Magee, where he had slithered out of his chair. In addition he had sat on his sacrum too long and thus began a war with his first skin breakdown.

Skin breakdowns were no joke. They were rated between levels I and IV, with the unstageable ulcer being the worst. We learned that they could be life-threatening if left unattended. Several patients at Magee had ended up having flap surgery, where the doctor cuts out the necrotic tissue in order for the skin to heal. Then the patient would spend at least six to eight weeks lying on his stomach in bed or on a stretcher, waiting for it to heal properly.

Alex's first skin breakdown, a pressure ulcer, had progressed to level II. It meant that the damage was so deep that you could not detect how far it had gone without imaging or surgery. He would eventually end up just lying on his sides, one then the other, so the pressure ulcer could heal. Stage IV was no picnic either: by then the damage had already gone past the skin, past the muscle tissue and into the bone. Fear the bedsore! It was a dangerous side effect of being in a wheelchair, and it was on our radar as something to look out for. So, every night before bed, Alex had his skin checked, especially his sacrum and ischium.

His spasms continued to increase. Alex's brother Ralph and sister Edie kept thinking they were from nerves or stress. They were not. They were part of the injury.

One night, as Alex lay in bed, tears slipped down the side of his face. He could not turn himself; he had to be turned at night by his nurse. All he could do was stare up at the ceiling. His legs were positioned so he wouldn't get skin breakdown. He had a pillow underneath his coccyx bone, one in between his knees, and one at his ankles. These were all hot spots, where the bone was close enough to the skin to break through. He had spent weeks going from side to side in the hospital and he wasn't going to go through that again. After the kids were in bed, I slipped under the covers beside him. He could no longer sleep under the covers with me. He had to have his own comforter, which enabled him to be moved more readily by the nurses.

"I don't think I can do this," he said.

I knew exactly what he was talking about.

"I love you Gail, but this is too much for me."

"Alex, please just give it some time. You just got home, you're still getting adjusted. Please give it time. You may feel differently down the road. But you won't know unless you try."

"I know exactly how I feel now. And I know I'm not going to get much of anything back. This is it for me. You don't deserve this. The kids need a father who can function. They need someone who can throw a ball, and someone to play with. I can't do shit. I can't even wipe my own ass. I really don't want to live like this. I really just want to die."

And there it was. Something he had said a hundred other ways.

"Honestly Alex, I don't blame you. I think I would feel the same way. But you have two children who are depending on you."

"Danielle won't know the difference, she won't even remember me. And even though Adam's older, he won't either. You can get on with your life. You're marketable. You're pretty and you will find someone else to love."

"I don't want someone else to love. And, what do I tell the kids? Yeah, you're right, Danielle won't remember. But Adam will. And when he goes to your funeral, he'll look down at your casket and not understand, and ask me, 'Why isn't Daddy here anymore?' And in his innocence he'll ask, 'Didn't he love me?' So you see, Alex, you would be leaving a terribly sad little boy behind."

I knew one thing, that man was served guilt on a platter for breakfast, lunch, and dinner growing up. And it had worked on him. But I had never used it, not once in our relationship. I wasn't raised on it either, but I had seen how effective it could be, and this was not the time to be proud.

"Alex, why don't you give it two years. Try life this way for just a couple of years, and if you don't want to be here in two years, then you can do what you want."

He was quiet. He was thinking.

"Okay," he said in a whisper.

I knew I had just bought some time.

16. LEARNING TO BREATHE

Spring was coming and Alex had gotten his new van. It was a Chrysler Town and Country in a metallic forest green. He hadn't gotten his electric wheelchair yet, but that was coming. I was hoping that between the adaptive van and an electric wheelchair he would feel more freedom. Right now, he had to be strapped down with belts that hooked around his manual chair. First I would strap the kids in their car seats, and then I would strap Alex down. Then I would get into the driver's seat, and we would go to an activity. Sometimes a nurse drove and sometimes not. Either way, our family had grown to include an extra passenger.

It initially began with basketball on Sundays at the JCC. It was a family outing and it was difficult to manage.

Adam hated basketball from the moment he realized he couldn't dribble. He couldn't seem to hang on to the ball. But we told him to keep trying; nothing is easy the first time around. And try he did.

"My fingers don't work," he said.

"Well, just keep trying. Maybe it's a matter of practice," Alex responded.

You could see the coach getting frustrated with Adam. Maybe he wasn't coordinated, but it pissed me off that the coach didn't have the patience for a kid his age.

When we got home he went straight to his animals. There he found comfort and solace. He could control their behavior. After all, they were made of resin. He had been fascinated with animals since he was one and half years old. He identified them, separated them by their classifications and their species, and eventually the continents they roamed on. He could tell a Ring-Tailed Lemur from a Japanese Macaque, and he was only four.

When the electric wheelchair finally arrived, I felt an enormous sense of relief. Part of the drawback of being in a manual wheelchair is that you constantly have to do weight shifts in order to avoid skin breakdown. *Life-changing*, that's all I could think. *This will make life easier.* Alex had been measured for the chair at Magee so it would fit him properly. It was a very expensive and much-needed mode of transportation. No different than a new car, other than the fact that it was a lifesaving device. Manufactured by Permobile, the wheelchair was a top of the line road ragin' machine and it was going to be adjusted to fit in his van with a lock-down system, so he could drive. That, along with handicap controls on the steering wheel, would give him the ability to steer and maneuver his new van. Independence day was here!

Along with the nurses, I had been giving Alex weight shifts every couple of hours. In addition, at dinnertime I had to cook, serve, and cut food for four. Then I had to clean up the kitchen. I started to hate cooking. It brought me no satisfaction. I was an exhausted, overworked robot. Adam was getting pickier by the day and Danielle, well, she ate but at this point it wasn't anything more than mac and cheese, pizza, and McDonald's. Not the healthiest of choices, but the easiest for the non-compliant.

As I cleared the table I saw a little flicker of light bouncing off that new $20,000 wheelchair, which was, thankfully, covered by insurance. It had been delivered that day and Warren had taken Alex into the garage to make sure everything was as specified. Alex had stopped trying to push his manual chair on his own weeks ago, due to the fact that it was damaging his rotator cuff on the right side. He needed to use his rotator cuffs to transfer in and out of the chair, and in and out of bed, and in and out of the commode chair.

I heard the elevator door open behind me and turned around to see him with a huge smile on his face.

"Alex, look at you. You can whip around the house, or up and down the street without anyone pushing you."

"Yeah, and I can do weight shifts on my own. Warren and I are going to go out for a test drive."

"Go for it," I said.

The chair itself was not that quiet. It was a noise we were going to have to get used to, not just when he was tooling around, but when he tilted back, raised or lowered the seat, and raised or lowered his feet. Even though he was on his butt all day, the chair would lean all the way back to take the pressure off his sacral and coccyx area.

"Daddy, I want a ride!'" Adam exclaimed.

"Me too! Me too!" screamed Danielle.

"Let me put on your coats and you can go outside with Daddy and each get a ride," I said. "Is that okay with you, Alex?"

"Sure, welcome to Disney! Except these rides are free!"

"I don't think Blue Cross would agree with that one," I said.

Michael Grossman had been calling me on a daily basis. As one of Alex's closest friends, he knew how unstable the situation was.

He was calling Alex every day as well, but he would call me and ask "What can I do? Is there anything I can do to help?"

He had been through the shock of it all with us. For me, I don't think it had worn off. I actually didn't know how long it was going to take. But Michael was so incredibly genuine in his concern, I could sense his loss, too.

There was a world out there that we didn't know how to navigate, and there were still people close to us who were willing to engage us on our terms. Michael was one of those, and initially there were many others.

But this injury grows old pretty fast to those who aren't forced to deal with it. This was not something that I would realize early on.

Michael Grossman used to say," You'll see Gail, in five years he'll be walking."

"I hope you're right, Michael. I really hope you're right." Everyone dangled their own carrots for their own reason.

As we watched television, we got glimpses of Christopher Reeve and his struggles, which were accompanied by his optimism about finding a cure. I had begun to wrap my own head around the need to find a cure. *Because who the hell can live like this?*

I looked at Christopher Reeve and his wife Dana, and I knew that they had it so much worse. He was on a vent; his head had actually had to be placed back on his body. He was the worst-case scenario, a C1-C2, and when the doctors spoke of him you could see that they were sad for a man they did not know. He was completely and utterly dependent on other people. With the electric wheelchair and the adapted van, Alex would have some independence.

As the first summer after the accident approached, I welcomed the warm weather. It was a time to plant flowers, the kids were not on much of a schedule, and we had opened the pool in the backyard. I looked at the pristine blue water as Alex sat under an umbrella.

"It pisses me off to hire a pool company," Alex said. "I used to be able to clean it myself. Do you want to clean it, Gail?"

"Hell no! You don't think I have enough to do around here?"

"I was just putting it out there," he said. "You know you're going to have to do all of the barbequing."

"I know," I responded. I guess I didn't sound enthused enough.

"Don't you think I want to do it?"

"I know you want to do it, Alex."

"It makes me sick watching you run around after the kids. I see how hard you work."

"Then why did you just ask me if I wanted to clean the pool?"

"Because I'm an asshole."

"Well, it's like I've always said, a woman gets two, the one she's born with and the one she marries." I sat down on one of the chaise lounges next to the pool.

"Seriously, I feel guilty watching you do all this work."

"I know, but there isn't exactly anything I can do to make you feel better."

"I remember last summer, when you went up to visit Meryl," he ruminated," I had Adam and Danielle to myself, and I had no problem taking care of them. I met Michael and Siobhan at Smitty's Clam Bar, I had them in the pool. I was a hands-on dad."

"You can still be a hands-on dad."

"No I can't. I can't run after them; I won't be able to teach Adam or Danielle how to ride a bike. I can't pick them up."

I stopped him before he continued the litany of things he couldn't do. "But they can crawl in your lap and lie on you. You can wheel them around in your chair. You can read to them."

157

"How? I can't even turn a page with these things." He lifted his hands up to show me.

"Well, maybe the kids can turn the pages, while you read to them."

"You have an answer for everything, don't you?"

"Yeah, I take after my mother. I'm trying to be positive." It was time to change the subject. "Are you drinking enough fluids?"

I was learning that not only was Alex's body dead weight to him, it had also taken on alien reactions, bringing to life parts that he had no control over. In addition to the spasms, he could no longer tolerate extreme temperatures. Too much heat made his body go dysreflexic—his blood pressure would shoot up to a dangerous level. It could lead to seizures, stroke, and even death. If his body got too cold he wouldn't feel it until he was inside. And we would learn that it would take him hours and hours to warm up. He no longer could sweat below the level of his injury..

This was his first day out in the sun and he had no idea of the reaction the heat was going to have on his body. His body began to heat up and couldn't cool itself down. Since he couldn't sweat below the level of his injury, which is the body's natural control system for cooling, he began to go dysreflexic.

"My forehead is sweating and I'm getting a really bad headache," he said now. "My blood pressure must be going up. I think I'd better go inside."

Warren was in the back room reading Camus. I walked towards the new double glass doors that led right into the family room. We had them installed to make the backyard more accessible.

"Warren?" I yelled. "Alex doesn't feel well."

Warren came out of the back room, took one look at Alex, and opened the backpack that was hanging on the back of his wheelchair.

He pulled out a blood pressure cuff, wrapped the arm piece around Alex's forearm and began to pump up the pressure. Meanwhile, he put a stethoscope on and began to listen to the thumping sounds of Alex's blood. It had shot up to 240 systolic (the top number) and 105 diastolic (the bottom number). Warren ran to get cold wet towels to put on Alex's head, and gave him an ice-cold beverage to drink. He took his pressure again; it was still high. Then he brought out the big guns...nitropaste. He carefully put on gloves to protect it from seeping into his system, then he put a half-inch of nitropaste on a small pre-cut piece of paper that had measured increments of a half of an inch, an inch, an inch and a half and two inches. Then he gently placed it on Alex's forehead.

In minutes, he took Alex's pressure again. It had begun to come down. As soon as the pressure started to drop, Warren quickly removed the nitropaste with his gloved hands and a dry paper towel. Then he wiped Alex's forehead again with a wet soapy paper towel. He put everything in a plastic bag and threw it in the trash.

It was a precarious situation: if blood pressure goes too high you can stroke out. But if it drops too low, you just pass out and die. If you hadn't gotten all of the nitropaste off, it would have continued to seep into Alex's system and lower his blood pressure.

The blood pressure issue would be a dark and dangerous shadow that would follow Alex throughout his life. I couldn't imagine how my blood pressure was reacting to his blood pressure. At this juncture, I seemed to be experiencing emotional plummets with intermittently induced bouts of oxygen from the kids.

Days later, Alex disappeared. I called Jeff and Valerie, our neighbors two doors down.

"I can't find Alex," I said to Val. "Is he down there?"

"No, I haven't seen him," she said.

Where could he have gone in his electric wheelchair?

"Hey Jeff, have you seen Alex?" I heard her shout.

"Nope. Does she need me to help her look for him?" I heard him say from a distance.

"That would be great," I said to Val. "I'm going out on my bike, I'll see if I can find him that way."

"Jeff is going to look in his car. He'll call you if he finds him."

I hopped on the one bicycle that was left in the garage, a crimson hybrid. I felt my heart racing and an internal mechanism of foreboding going off in my head. Where the hell could he be?

I went through Fischer Greens and Fischer Woods: nothing. The day was beautiful. But a beautiful day can easily be erased under precarious circumstances. I went up and down Oak Avenue: more of nothing.

I went back home to call Val and Jeff.

"Hi, did you find him?" Val asked.

"No, did Jeff?"

"He's not back yet, I'll call you when he gets home."

"Thanks," I said.

Twenty long minutes went by. I had asked Alex's nurse on duty, Tim, to help me look. He got on the bike and I waited. In a few more minutes, I was going to call the police. I knew he was not in his right mind. *He's not adjusting, it's just too overwhelming*, I thought. Really, where could he have gone?

Then I walked out front and I saw him riding down the street. I felt my heart slow. I went inside and called Val. "He's coming down the street right now."

"Where was he?"

"I have no clue."

"Jeff is just pulling in the driveway, I can hear his car."

"Tell him thank you for me, please. I'll call you guys later."

"OK Gail, love you."

"Love you too."

I walked back towards the garage, opened its door and walked down the stairs.

Alex was staring at his Sears Craftsman tool chest. It was a red six-drawer homeowner tool center with a bulk storage panel door. Most of his tools were in there…tools that he had collected, and some that my father had given to him. There were hand tools, socket wrenches, a miter saw, a drill press, ratchets, hammers, screwdrivers, wrenches, and pliers. It was a smorgasbord for those who liked to work with their hands and fix things. The drawers were filled to capacity with staple guns, cutters, and snips.

"Hi. Sorry to interrupt your train of thought, but where were you?" I asked.

He looked at me, with his bright, hazel-green eyes, "I went to Route 9."

Route 9 was a major street in our town, two blocks from where we lived.

"What were you doing on Route 9?" I asked.

"I saw a bus coming and I was going to drive my chair right in front of it. I was so close. I really wanted to do it, but then I thought about the kids, and I didn't."

"Just the kids?"

"Yeah, you would be better off. You would get over it. It really would be better for you. You could remarry, everyone would be better off."

"You are so wrong." I said. "Weren't you listening to me the other night?" *Here it comes*, I thought. "Look, I know nothing about this is easy. It's all new. It's still God-awful, maybe it will always be

161

awful. But please, give it some time. You think we'll be better off? I promise you, if you kill yourself we will be damaged for the rest of our lives. I know you're not thinking clearly, but you will ruin us."

He was quiet. I knew it was guilt I was shoveling, but it was the only ammo I had.

"I have to go pick the kids up at camp. I'll be back and we will figure out dinner."

I got in my car, backed out of the driveway, and felt nothing. Numbness was an interesting thing. I was beginning to think it was my very own protective shield. I was also beginning to think it was permanent. Why would anyone want to feel all this? I didn't know if I would ever feel again, and I was grateful.

The next day, Alex insisted that I take the kids to the beach.

"Why do I have to take them? We have a pool in the backyard."

"Because they live near the beach. They need to know what it's like to have sand in their shoes," he responded. "The sooner you get back in the sand, the better you will all be. Besides, it's social down there."

I thought about it, and since I didn't want them to feel traumatized, like I was, I agreed. Except, I had never really loved the beach. I grew up near the woods. There was an enormous park system in Cleveland, and when I was in high school I had explored the streams and rivers with friends. We had climbed on the muddy shale shelves that stuck out over Chagrin Falls, and explored our way through the parks in Chagrin Valley. It was magical, and I had to remember that wherever the kids were now, they would take those memories with them. For them, it was the Jersey Shore.

So I packed up a hundred things to bring to the beach: my chair, their chairs, towels, lotion, buckets and shovels, snacks, drinks, sunglasses and diapers. I settled them into their car seats, and as I drove towards Margate, I could only think that I'd forgotten one thing: a Valium. In my head, I kept hearing *I don't want to go to the beach, I do not want to do this, I don't even like the beach.*

But I kept driving. I knew I had to find a parking space, and I couldn't drop the kids off by themselves at the bulkhead, like the husbands did with their wives and kids. I had to find a space, park, and carry all of our stuff, balancing it with the hands of two small children.

By the time we got to the bulkhead, I was drained. I looked at the expansive seas that calmed most of the souls who were lying there, and knew intuitively that that would never be me. I looked for Gary and Christina and spotted a giant circle where everyone sat. I cajoled the kids to follow me, put a smile on my face, and walked over to say hello.

"Good for you, Gail," Wilma Dannenbaum, Mark's mother, said. "Really, good for you. I'm so happy to see you here with the kids."

"Thanks," I responded. "We're happy to be here."

"How's Alex doing?"

"He's hanging in there." Barely, I thought.

"What's he doing today?"

"I think he's going to go to Sam's. Buying in bulk seems to make him happy."

As I unloaded my things onto the sand and got the kids situated, all I could think of was that I felt like a braying mule. I sat in a circle of friends and felt miles away. The distance that the injury created was something I couldn't explain. I was forever changed, and I felt as if someone had branded me on the forehead with a giant QW (Quad Wife). Even though we were physically at the beach, it was painful. Mentally, I was in war-torn Bosnia. And as far as I was concerned, they were all in Paris, sipping a fine Louis Latour burgundy.

I sat down to build castles in the sand, and as I surveyed the beach, I saw hundreds of happy bakers, glistening under the sun's rays: surfers catching their breaks, the walkers and talkers. There was a young couple holding hands and walking down the beach. It almost brought me to tears. This simple display of affection was something I would never again be able to do with Alex. Would we even grow old together? I doubted it. Would he make it through the kids' formative years? I was not optimistic.

I realized then that I wasn't breathing fully. I really didn't think that Alex had a long time to live. So much had gone wrong so early. Maybe he would see the kids grow up through grade school. I no longer knew what the future looked like, so I stopped picturing it.

I looked at my watch. I decided then and there I didn't have to stay for more than two hours. Then I would bribe the kids with ice cream and we would head home.

I had become an exceptional faker. I smiled and laughed as a front for those whose eyes wandered in my direction. I knew that I, too, was being watched. I wanted to be ordinary…not the strong wife who stood by her husband's side after he was damaged.

Then I thought, he may be damaged on the outside, but I am damaged on levels that no one can possibly imagine.

I made it through the next hour and then asked, "Who wants ice cream?"

"We do, Mommy!" Adam answered.

"Well, why don't I pack up our bags and we can go to Dairy Queen on the way home."

"You're leaving already?" Christina asked.

"Yep. I got them here, and I stayed for an hour-and-a-half. Pretty damn good, if you ask me." I was truly proud of myself for making it back to the beach. Check it off the list of accomplishments.

Mark Dannenbaum said, "Gail, why don't you go pull up the car and I'll walk the kids up to the bulkhead."

I smiled at him in relief. "Oh, that would be great Mark. I really appreciate it. Kids, you wait here with Mark, I'm going to get the car, and he will walk you up to Rumson, so you don't have to walk all the way back to Ventnor Avenue. Okay?"

"Are we still getting ice cream?" Danielle asked.

"Yes we are! I promise."

It was not lost on me that I would be the permanent schlepper, while all the other husbands dropped their wives and children at the beach, and then parked the car. I was a single mother in many respects, and I just had to get used to it.

17. THE PUMP

As the end of the summer approached, we were coming up on the one-year anniversary of Alex's accident. September 2nd was the dark day that we dreaded.

As we broached it, it became clear that surviving the first year had been a step-by-step process; we were constantly transitioning from one first to another. The first months home, the first birthdays, the first summer with Alex in a chair, and the first anniversary of the accident.

I tried to look for joy, and found that any buoyancy came from the kids. The simplicity of their smiles were, and continued to be, my life preserver.

"I think we should have a party on the second. You know, like a Labor Day party?" I said to Alex.

"Why? What exactly are we celebrating?"

"Labor Day, and maybe if you were among friends, you wouldn't feel the before and after so much."

"Whatever you want to do is fine with me."

"I think I'm just going to make hamburgers and hot dogs, grill some corn on the cob, and make a salad. You want anything special?"

"No."

"OK then, I'll invite the usual suspects."

Flashback. I was in the kitchen marinating chicken in Soy Vay. Alex had just come back from a run, Pepe was alive, Danielle wasn't talking, and Adam was playing with his toy animals, herding them in groups by species. There wasn't a nurse in the back room waiting to take blood pressure, empty a urine bag, or trying to stabilize the now out-of-control spasms, which brought up the blood pressure to stroke levels. Flash forward.

"You going to the beach?" Alex asked.

"Nope," I answered. "I don't want to go to the beach today."

"Well, me either." Alex responded, knowing full well that he couldn't get on the beach even if he wanted to.

And from then on, we skipped the beach on Labor Day. For years to come, we would have friends over THAT day and a BBQ would help us mask the flashbacks that were like perennial aftershocks. And I would ask everyone to bring something, so I didn't really have to cook.

As the shorebirds flocked to another area of the country, we continued to struggle with the changes going on. Fall took hold, the kids went back to school, and I was exhausted. We had all survived the summer and the first year. Friends were making plans to go on vacation but for us, making plans was a thing of the past. We had gone out to dinner with a nurse in tow during the summer while Alex's body was getting used to its new state.

There were so many things that we were learning with the injury, the first being that it had a life of its own. "It" was now in control of his body. No one tells you this. They teach you how to deal with the spasms and the blood pressure, and how to deal with being in a wheelchair, but they don't tell you that everything comes with side effects. Infections, which were part of having an indwelling catheter, led to blood pressure issues and spasms. Muscles contorted without warning. Sometimes while Alex was being ranged in the morning, he would spasm, which in turn sent his blood pressure up. Once he unintentionally kicked his nurse Tim in the face. It was then that we decided to get a baclofen pump. It was an internal medical device that administered baclofen, a muscle relaxer and anti-spastic agent, every several hours. It would have to be surgically implanted in Alex's lower abdomen, with an intrathecal catheter that would funnel medication directly into the spinal column's thecal sac. The medications also had their own side effects, and would make Alex very sleepy.

He got the pump put in and it seemed to help. It ran on a battery that would last five years.

Because Alex needed to be turned at night by his nurses, and because we shared a room, I did not have a break from anyone. He also had bladder infections, not uncommon with an indwelling catheter. The only way we knew an infection had begun was through extra spasms, or through blood pressure issues. His body would tell us, but since he couldn't feel pain, the signals were different.

At one point early on, he started to get neurogenic pain, which left him burning… burning as if he were in a five alarm fire. The pain went from his butt and legs down to his feet, and there was nothing he could do except take a Neurontin and endure the pain. Sometimes he felt like someone was cutting his feet with shards of glass. It was one of the great cruelties of the injury. Alex had unrelenting, chronic, pain. He usually wanted to be left alone to deal with the agony.

His moods were all over the place. There were days he just shut down, and there was one continual narrative: he wanted to die, he should have died, and could still die. I knew he could still die. He was in a constant state of de-stabilization. And I was in a constant state of thinking about being a widow with two small children.

Lingering in my mind was a nagging question: could all of this have been prevented? Would a simple five dollar sign have made a difference? That's two questions. Here's a third. Could it make a difference to someone else?

I began to investigate. And, I wrote a letter and sent it in to Governor Christine Todd Whitman, Senator Gormley, and our Atlantic County Safety Director, Michael Schurman. It read as follows:

Dear Senator Gormley,

On September 2, 1996, my husband was swimming with a group of friends. It was the last weekend of the summer, and a windy and rough Labor Day. Hurricane Edouard had blown by the coast and was heading up north and out to sea. The surf was treacherous, and the beaches were open.

My husband entered the waters to body surf as he had done so often in the past. After judging the undertow to be too strong and the waters too unpredictable, he ventured his way back in. He caught a last wave, hoping it would bring him to shore. The current sucked him under and a wave came crashing down on him with neck breaking speed, smashing his head into the sand. He is now permanently paralyzed. He is a quadriplegic who can no longer function with the rest of the world. He can no longer hold his four year-old son or two-and-a-half year-old daughter. He wakes in the morning, opens his eyes, only to wait until someone gets him out of bed. His independent life is now encumbered with tubes and the constant assistance of others. He yearns for a permanent end to a life filled with medical complications.

169

What makes this story even more tragic is that he was not alone on that fateful weekend. Two days prior, a man in Ocean City broke his neck in the ocean. According to Jefferson Hospital, there were five other incidents of spinal cord injuries that weekend, due to the dangerous water conditions. There was an expose done on CBS's 48 HOURS, in which a young man from Cape Cod also received a spinal cord injury from the rough ocean, the very same day as my husband. All this information leads me to one conclusion: The people who frequent our beaches need more information so they can properly judge the ocean's conditions. There isn't a local, state, or national approach to this devastating safety problem.

It is time to begin a safety information system to warn bathers when the water is treacherous. And I hope that with your help, something this important can be achieved. It can be a three-pronged system that does the following:

Introduces flags or signs on the beach to represent the conditions of the water. This can be executed by the lifeguards. Hawaii and Australia have two different yet successful systems in place. Samples of them are enclosed.

Create a scientific standard to judge when the water is too rough for swimmers. The speed of the waves could accurately be taken by radar guns. It is the velocity of the breaking waves that poses the most danger. Currents can also create a tremendous hazard for drowning as well. A constant feed of weather information communicated properly could alleviate some of the danger.

Coordinate information statewide. Plus, institute a system for sharing information from municipality to municipality. The conditions in Ventnor are no different than the conditions in Margate or Longport. (On the particular weekend of my husband's accident, the beaches in Longport were closed; they were not closed in Margate.)

Senator Gormley, the people who frequent our beaches and spend money on beach badges, deserve a program that can keep them safe. As with anything else, there are no guarantees. But if a program like this saves one life, or prevents one family from going through the daily torture that our family is going through, then it is worth it.

I look forward to your reply.

Sincerely,

Gail Desberg Kiejdan

c.c.: Governor Christine Todd Whitman

c.c. Michael Shurman

I received two responses. One was from Michael Shurman, who said the mayor of Brigantine (a town half an hour up the coast) was going to put up the warning signs designed by Ryan LaMonaca, an art director that I had worked with. And the other response was from Representative Frank Lobiondo, through my old boss, Sharon Pearce. She had spoken with her government connections through Bally's Casino and Resort and told me that the towns do not want to be liable for any lawsuits. A sign would make them liable.

Eventually, I decided that there was time enough in my day to go see a therapist. I found a psychologist not too far from our home. She had a very relaxed demeanor and warm smile. Initially, I had no desire to talk about myself and my feelings. I talked about the behaviors of the people around me and, I guess, how it inadvertently affected me. I brought in problems that needed to be solved - lack of privacy with the nurses around 24/7 weighed heavily on my mind. Alex's moods were at the top of the list, as well. I told her that he was already on Wellbutrin and Effexor. She recommended that he should see a therapist, and well, I laughed.

"What's so funny?" she asked.

"I really don't think he thinks he needs one."

"Why? He's been through so much."

"Why?" I responded. "Because he feels that no one can really understand what it is like to be in a wheelchair."

"But Gail, we are trained to give you tools to work with as well as to gain an understanding for people who are not exactly in our position. For example, there are many techniques that we have learned about that might help you or Alex get through what you need to get through."

"Look," I said, "I'll bring it up to him, but I know what the answer is going to be."

"That's all you can do, is make the suggestion," she said.

She would eventually teach me to make space for myself. Something I hadn't done. "Turn a room into a place that belongs to just you. No nurses, just you. Decorate it for yourself, sleep there if you like, just give yourself a place where no one is welcome, but you."

It was the best advice I had been given to date. I had melted into the horizon like a puddle in the desert, and I imagined that I didn't have a wisp of vapor to remind myself that I was still there, other than to facilitate everyone else's activities.

I took the back bedroom and painted it a beautiful pale lilac. I bought a sateen lilac-colored duvet with matching pillow shams and a pattern of pale, vanilla-colored flowers that looked like sprays of lily of the valley, with dark green stems and leaves. I bought a new pillow-top mattress and I reminded myself over and over to not feel guilty. It was a physical separation, but with the nurses in and out during the night I needed to sleep. I needed it, and the kids needed me to sleep, and Alex needed me to sleep. NO guilt, no guilt, no guilt. My new mantra.

Within days after seeing the therapist for the first time, the phone rang. It was Gary.

"Hi Gary, how are things going?"

"Well," he said. I recognized the tone. "Mom fell."

"Is she alright?"

"She is, but she broke several ribs."

"Shit," I said. "Did she trip on something?"

"She said she was distracted, and she wasn't watching where she was going, and she tripped on a sidewalk crack. Don't worry, Gail. She's OK. She's home now. Andrea dropped some food off, so did some of Mom's friends."

"Can she be in the apartment by herself?" I asked.

"She's stubborn. So the answer to that is that she thinks she can handle it. She said not to worry."

"Yeah, I know, worrying is like a rocking chair. It wastes time and it doesn't get you anywhere. Did you call Diane?"

"I did. She thinks mom needs to watch where she's going."

"That's Diane for you. Alright, well thanks for calling me. I'll call her."

"Okay, Gail, I'll talk to you later."

"Love you."

"Love you, too."

I called my mom and got the same response: "Gail, don't worry about me. You have your hands full. I am fine. My ribs are taped. I have pain medication. I'm going to stay in bed and follow doctor's orders. And when I'm feeling a little better, I'm going to pack up my suitcase and my car and go to Florida."

173

"Mom, how are you going to do that with broken ribs?"

"I'm not going to do it by myself. I have friends, and Gary and Andrea. I will manage."

I missed my mother. She had a kind of stamina that I could not even imagine having. She was self-sufficient. She never complained, and she was truly the eternal optimist. I was lucky to have such an incredible role model.

I made up my mind that I would see her as often as I could. Besides, I hadn't had any time to myself since Alex was injured. The therapist wanted me to start carving out "me" time. Ha! Sometimes I thought she was the one who needed therapy. I guess I would make it my business to fly to Cleveland and see her.

"Mom, maybe Fern will watch the kids and I will come visit you."

"That would be wonderful, sweetheart."

Three times a week, Alex had physical therapy. So far, it had been covered by insurance. He looked forward to it because the physical therapist was cute, and without question he was shallow. He didn't pretend to be anything but. Whenever Dale came it lifted his spirits. She was a pretty, blonde Texan who didn't take any of what he had to dish out. She tossed it out as the garbage it was. Petite in size, she was teaching him how to manipulate his new manual chair up and down, and whenever she came over she brought a giant bag of Doritos and a Coke.

One day I was in the garage with Dale and Alex. Danielle had followed me in.

Dale was munching Doritos. She told me that Blue Cross/ Blue Shield called and asked her how busy I was.

"Why do they want to know how busy I am?" I asked.

"They wanted to know if he really needed 24-hour nursing," she responded.

"What did you say?" I asked. I looked down at Danielle, who walked over to Dale. She loved when Dale came over, too.

"Can she have a Dorito?" Dale asked.

"Sure, why not."

Dale smiled and handed her one. It was then and there that Danielle began her affinity for Doritos.

"Anyway, I said that she has two small children, and that she has her hands full."

"Thank you Dale. I appreciate it."

I couldn't have imagined for one minute taking care of two kids on my own, but I was. And now someone out there was thinking of adding a quadriplegic to my list. NO problem there! Two kids under the age of four, and full-time caregiver. Glad we're paying the big bucks for the Medallion Policy at Blue Cross Blue Shield.

"I'm going back in to fix dinner," I said now. "Come on, Danielle, help mommy make dinner."

"Can I stay hewe?" She asked with an unformed r.

"If it's okay with Daddy." I said.

"It's fine, she can just follow us up and down the street," Alex said.

Danielle had started to follow Alex and Dale as Alex worked on maneuvering his manual wheelchair. It was not easy, but he needed to rebuild the muscles above the level of injury. Sometimes he and Dale worked in our bedroom, helping him to transfer from the commode chair to the bed or his electric chair to the bed. He had been working on getting his triceps back. That would make life so much easier; it was the difference between driving and not driving, and getting yourself in and out of bed with the aid of a transfer board, or leaning on a nurse and having him or her transfer you. As long as they kept the Hoyer Lift out of the house, I was happy. How little it took.

I realized then that Alex wasn't the only one who needed a workout. I had stopped what I was doing workout-wise for almost a year. Fortunately for me, Michelle realized this too. She sent over a friend of hers named Lisa Gottlieb. She was teaching at the JCC in Margate, where Michelle discovered that she made home visits as a personal trainer. She then gave several sessions to me as a gift.

It was a huge gift. It put me back in exercise mode, and twice a week I could count on someone making sure I lifted more than the kids. The beauty of that gift was that for several years it forced me into a routine and a time period that was designated just for me. And, I didn't have to leave the house.

I didn't feel housebound at the time, but in hindsight, I was. I wasn't comfortable leaving Alex for anything except the kids' events: birthday parties, basketball, soccer, swimming—the activities that I had been told I needed to sign them up for by my friend Lisa.

She said, "Sign Adam up for this, Benny is taking it. Sign Danielle up for that, Elyssa is taking it. It's two times a week at 2:00, call the JCC and get them in the class. Cindy Hess teaches it. She's great."

So when it came to getting the kids involved, Lisa led the way, and I followed. It was as if my brain had been split into a hundred thousand atoms scattered throughout the universe. And my focus was between retrieving the atoms and getting my kids to school. I knew I had to get them dressed in the morning, feed them, make their lunches, and send them to school. I put a smile on my face, some lipstick and greeted the world that way, but inside I was a lost puppy.

By the time Adam switched over to Seaview Elementary School, I had a brain I could tap. It wasn't mine, but it was still telling me what I needed to do.

Then, one bright sunny morning, when I was working out with Lisa, Michelle called and told me to turn on the television. When I did, the Today Show was on, later than usual. They had continued their broadcast into regular programming. There was a screen shot of the World Trade Center, with plumes of smoke coming out of one side. Even Katie Couric was briefly stunned into disbelief.

Lisa left. I ran upstairs and turned on the bedroom television for Alex to watch. JoAnn, Alex's nurse, was getting Alex dressed on the hospital bed. And we all just stared. Matt Lauer had interrupted his guest at the time to get a screen shot of the first tower. As they were trying to figure out what happened live on air, a second plane hit the second tower.

I knew then and there that the world would never be the same. "We are under attack," I said.

"Holy shit!" Alex exclaimed. Katie Couric was trying to gather information on air, and a few minutes later she went to Jim Miklaszewski at the Pentagon. The Pentagon had been hit. It was a Tuesday morning, and the bright blue skies turned bleak and ugly. I knew that beautiful majestic skies could also change color in a blink of an eye. The ashes that rained down that day sent a wave of disbelief through an entire country. The imaginary bubble had been broken, and we were now a country who had been pulled into a tidal wave of loss.

What I noticed then was that bright blue skies do not fade. You just fail to notice them. You fail to see their magnificent color and impeccable hues. You stop looking for a bright blue sky. You look ahead, not up, and not towards the sun. Just straight ahead. The schools did not let out early, but the world seemed hushed, similar to after a snowfall, except this time it was ashes that were floating down. And the rest of the country could feel the incendiary remnants.

I was supposed to visit my mother that weekend, but there was a massive and unprecedented airline shutdown. Everyone was cancelling flights. Planes had been grounded and who knew when they would be up and running again.

I called her. "Mom, the planes have been grounded I can't come. How does next weekend sound?"

"That sounds good," she responded. "I'm a little disappointed, but I guess it will just have to do."

"Let me call the airlines, I really don't think I will be penalized for a national crisis."

"I was so looking forward to seeing you Gail. I love you honey."

"I love you, too, Mom."

"How is Alex feeling?"

"He's good."

"And the kids?"

"They're good. I've been teaching Adam how to ride a bike without training wheels. You know he's seven, and I think it's time. He's had no interest whatsoever."

"Well maybe he's a late bloomer," she said.

"Well, today he's finally starting to do it, and Danielle is so impatient, she keeps screaming that it's her turn. But I don't want him to feel bad that his little sister could do it before him, so I've negotiated with her. I said, "Once he learns how to do it, it will be your turn." And she said, 'tomorrow can be my turn.' And I said, 'no, once he's finished, then you can learn.' And wouldn't you know it, the minute he put the bike down and said he was done for the day she picked it up and tried to ride it. No means absolutely nothing to her!"

"Gail, that's a good thing," my mother said. "She's going to be a strong young lady."

"I think it skipped a generation."

"Gail, you're stronger than you think."

18. KISS KISS, STAB STAB

I was still fighting a lack of energy. The constant feeling of being drained was from having two little kids and a husband whose only focus was his health issues, and our insurance. At that point he wasn't physically or mentally available.

It was a good time for me to start drinking coffee. Up until then I was the only person I knew who didn't drink coffee, but my lack of energy, and everyone else's needs, required a strong drug, and caffeine was it.

"God damn it!" Alex said one day, looking at the mail.

"What?" I implored. "What's wrong?"

"These assholes are making me sick!"

"Who?"

"The insurance company. Every time I open a new bill I want to throw up."

"You can't throw up, your diaphragm is paralyzed."

"Funny," he responded.

Alex began to have a Pavlovian response every time he received an insurance bill in the mail. Because every time he received a bill, he wasn't sure how much the price was going to go up.

They began to raise our insurance once a year. It started out in increments of ten thousand. We had started by paying $12,000 before his injury, for the best insurance money could buy, as instructed by my father. The insurance we had did not have a cap, which was fortuitous. That was 1995.

Within the next couple of years they had raised our insurance to $22,000, then $32,000, and it kept increasing incrementally until we were way out of the range of affordability. But we were stuck, because now Alex had a pre-existing condition and wouldn't be able to get insurance anywhere else.

We had to take into the fact that he was receiving 24-hour nursing, which was very expensive. After the first year or so, they stopped his physical therapy and he was on his own. And since he wasn't working out he began to smoke cigarettes, much to everyone's dismay.

"What else can I do that's bad for me?" he said. "I may as well have a vice."

I had learned not to argue. At least when it came to his injury. It became my unwritten rule. I listened. No one could possibly imagine what it was like. Even watching him every day, there was so much that I just didn't understand, because essentially I could sit up in bed when I wanted. I could throw my feet over the side of the bed, lean forward and stand up with balance. I could wipe my own backside, I could shower on my own, and I didn't need an enema to make myself defecate every morning. I could also pick out my own clothes and dress myself. I was not a prisoner in my own body, and I still had freedoms that I couldn't imagine losing. So if he wanted a cigarette—hell, if he wanted anything that would make him feel better even if just for a few minutes—then he should have it.

"Want me to light that for you?" I asked.

"Yeah, thanks."

Alex often sat in the garage and stared out onto the street. It was an ordinary street in a nice suburban neighborhood, quiet, with manicured lawns, and a cul-de-sac at the end. So there wasn't much traffic. We continued the conversation we'd started in the kitchen.

"What do you want to do about the insurance?" I asked.

"I'm going to have to ask my mom for help. We can't afford it any more. There are things that aren't covered, and I have to pay for certain medical essentials out of pocket. We pay for chucks, gloves, sterile gauze, non-sterile gauze, the Fleets enemas, and I have to lay money out of pocket and get reimbursed, that's about $15,000 a year. Oh, and diapers, and a blood pressure cuff," he added. "I think that's about it."

"Do you think she'll help us?" I asked.

"I don't know. But I have to ask."

By that time, Alex's mom had built a house on our street. She had told everyone, "It's so dat I could be near my son. He needs me."

In truth, it was so she could be near her daughter Renee. Renee lived on the cul-de-sac, and Molly built a house right next door to hers. She was thinking, and we all knew this, that Renee would take care of her if she needed taking care of. She gave her home in Margate to her favorite son, Ralph. "Ralph is a good boy, he takes care of his mama." Ralph was keeper of the keys and the checkbook. And to Ralph, that was being keeper of the kingdom.

We were approaching the end of spring, and Alex's mother would be home in the beginning of May.

Alex waited until Molly came home to ask in person. She had had a ramp built in the garage of her new home. Bogie opened the door and Molly greeted Alex with her new dog Chichi, who was a

Chihuahua. Alex and Chichi took to each other like metal to a magnet. Chichi didn't like everyone, but he immediately jumped on Alex's lap to lie down. It was love.

I wasn't there with Alex, but he told me all about their conversation when he came home.

"Welcome home, Mom," Alex said. "How was Florida?"

She came over and kissed him on his forehead. "It vas nice. How are you feeling mine kin? Can I get you something to eat? Do you want a cup of tea?"

Molly always had a refrigerator filled to the brim with food, even though it was just her and Bogie. The trauma of having no food during the war was never far from her mind. She remembered going hungry for weeks on end while she was hiding underground from the Nazis.

"No thanks," he responded.

"Vhat do you tink of my new friend?" she asked, referring to ChiChi.

"He looks like a big brown rat," Alex said.

"Vhat? You tink he's ugly?"

"No Mom. He's cute, I was just kidding."

"How's your vife?"

"She's good."

"The kids?"

"They're getting big. Wait till you see them."

"Bring them over."

"Well, they're in school right now. How about this weekend?"

"That's fine, no hurry."

Bogie left the kitchen and went to the back room to put away laundry. She was the kind of woman who shook her head a lot. She shook it yes and she shook it no. She had been in the United States for years, yet it seemed to me as if she didn't speak a word of English. I always thought that if you were going to go to a foreign land, that was great, but if you were living there, then you had to learn the language. We were the land of immigrants, and what kept us strong was the assimilation of immigrants. Alex's parents had emigrated from Lithuania. They learned English and assimilated into the community. It was expected.

"Mom, I was wondering if I could talk to you about something," Alex said.

"Of course you can."

He went on with trepidation. "Mom, my bills keep getting higher and higher for my medical insurance. We're reaching a point where I just can't afford it anymore."

"Can't you get new insurance?" she asked.

"No, mom. I have no cap on this insurance; every other insurance now has a cap on it. It pays for my nursing, and it pays for my hospitalization. I have to pay the premiums or I'll end up in a home."

"Alex, I don't know vat to tell you. You know I have expenses too. I have two homes I'm paying for. It's not cheap. I pay for Bogie. I have six children. I don't think that I can help you. I'm sorry."

I wasn't there, but I am sure the silence was rife with despair.

Alex rolled back down the street a despondent man. He wheeled into the house and into the kitchen and it was written all over his face.

"What's wrong?" I asked.

"Kiss, kiss, kiss. Stab, stab, stab. I asked her if she could help with the insurance and she said she couldn't afford it."

Speechless. That's exactly what I was. I knew better, and not only did I know better, I knew that if his father were alive, Alex would never have felt the constant feeling that he was teetering over a cliff.

"What did you say?"

"I said , are you fucking kidding me, Mom? I'm going to lose my nursing. Do you want me in a home?" He looked at me, despondent. "Gail, you should just leave me now. You'll be better off without me."

Once again, I had to let it settle. I did not jump on things immediately. I needed to think about them and let them ruminate.

That day, Alex's agitated state started to increase immediately. He had less patience than before he'd gone to see her, and his eyes looked straight ahead as he bit on his lower lip and jutted his chin out. He leaned back in his chair and raised his feet. There was always a noise coming from his electric chair, so you knew when he was reclining, raising his legs, and rolling around. I knew what he was thinking about. He didn't know where he was going to live. Or how he was going to deal with not having nursing.

Healthcare was and would always be the most important thing on his mind. Everything else was secondary. He did not have the luxury of choice. Nursing was as necessary as breathing to him. Without it, he couldn't get out of bed in the morning. He could do nothing on his own: he couldn't do his morning toileting, he couldn't shower nor could he get dressed, and he knew it. And with two small children, I couldn't help, and frankly, I didn't want to. It was hard enough to keep the family together as it was. He was focused on staying alive. I was focused on keeping him alive and getting the kids through life in a healthy mental state.

What you learn about depression when someone you love has it is that it permeates like mold. It grows and it can be overwhelming, and if you don't address it, it takes over and you will suffocate from the toxins. I didn't think I could fix anything. But for him, there was Wellbutrin. For me, well I just felt I had to stay the course.

It would take a few weeks filled with fear and angst, but in the end Molly realized that she needed to help with the insurance.

19. Diversion Therapy

The lack of control dominated everything. But I knew I needed two things: one was some kind of optimism, and the other was a way to relieve my stress. I began to troll what was then called the world wide web with my new computer. The claim was that everything would be on it. I continued to look into what was going on in medicine, as far as discoveries around spinal cord research were concerned. I began to discuss it with Alex.

"Alex, maybe someday there will be a way out of this."

His response was, "Please don't talk to me about that. I don't want to hear it."

"Fine, I'm still going to look," I said.

And so I did. Friends were kind. Whenever someone heard something promising they called us, they gave us names with phone numbers. Lee and Brad were still living in Philly and Lee had told me that there were promising new studies with mice, using regeneration.

"Of course, studies in mice doesn't mean anything," he had said. "It's a long way and many phases until you can treat humans. First there is a phase I trial, then phase II, and then phase III trials."

But the fact that someone was working on it, and that there was now a huge focus on it, baited my enthusiasm. It was exciting and fascinating, and at the heart of it all was a new term that became a lightning rod: stem cells. I knew that Christopher Reeve and his wife Dana were supporting stem cell research. Eventually, they would spearhead a foundation to fund scientists to help find a cure. The theory at the time was that you could get stem cells only from an unborn fetus, and how could you possibly re-create that without the use of a fetus? Enter the righteous religious zealots, who wanted to put a stop to all government funding of stem cell research.

When I wasn't shuffling the kids, making dinner, going to the grocery store, or taking care of Alex's needs, I called and spoke to doctors, scientists and anyone I could about what the possible options were in the future. When visiting my mother one year I drove to Miami, where an entire center had been opened in 1985, called The Miami Project. Dr. Barth Green and Nick Buoniconti, an NFL legend and sportscaster, helped found it. Nick's son Marc had suffered a catastrophic injury when he was tackled playing college football. He, too, was paralyzed and a quadriplegic. From his pictures I could see that he was on a vent, and needed constant care.

I did as much investigation as possible, and at one point I went up to New York with Michelle to see someone speak about Schwann cells, a different approach to regeneration than stem cells.

After our afternoon at the Waldorf Astoria in midtown Manhattan, we were both depressed. "It can't be that far away," Michelle said.

"Seven to twelve years. I don't know if I'll make it." That is what they had announced, that it would take that long to bring these cells into human trials.

"Listen," she said, "it's not going to be that long. But in the meantime, I have been going to this trainer in Margate. He's really tough and I think you should go. It will take your mind off of this, and he's really helping me get into shape."

"Why do I need another trainer?" I asked innocently. I had stopped using Lisa and had just started to run.

She continued, "His name is Darren and he's tough. Amy uses him, and I know she likes him too."

"I suppose," I said.

So after we came back from New York, she handed me the personal trainer's phone number. "Call him, he is a very good trainer and he has helped to put me back on track." Michelle and her husband David had separated, and it didn't make any sense to me, nor to her I imagine.

The thought of leaving the house to go somewhere besides the grocery store and school was overwhelming. Alex's accident had reduced my travels to friends' homes, doctor's appointments, the grocery store, school, and children's activities. But I knew one thing: exercise was therapeutic and I needed therapy. I guessed this would be my way of re-entering the earth's atmosphere. Breathe in. Breathe out. Breathe in. Breathe out.

I called Michelle's personal trainer, Darren, and we set up an appointment on a Sunday. I met him at a small gym in Margate, on Ventnor Avenue. I had dropped the kids off at Sunday school, so I had an hour where he could judge how weak I really was. I parked my car in the side lot and went inside. A tall young man with bright green eyes and a closely shaved head greeted me.

"Hi. I'm Darren," he said cheerfully. "You must be Gail."

"I am. Thank you for coming in to train me on a Sunday. Do you always do that?"

"Well, if I have a client that can't fit me in on any other day, I like to accommodate them. I just need you to fill out some health forms and then we can get started."

I followed him to the front desk. As he reached over to grab the clipboard and a pen, pulled back his arms, revealed his incredibly well-toned biceps that bulged halfway through the short sleeves of his shirt. *Breathe. He's a baby.* He must have been right out of college. No wonder Michelle wanted me to make an appointment with him. Diversion therapy. It was number one on my list of escape techniques. Here it was, right in front of me. He caught me staring at his arms. I looked up, feeling a warm flush on my face, and wanted to apologize. But I said absolutely nothing. Holy crap-and-a-half! I am not dead! I had just been awakened from a deep impenetrable sleep by a set of biceps. Praise Jesus!

He began to ask the usual questions. "So, what have you been doing for exercise?

"Lately, I've just been running. I guess I need something else to tone me up a bit."

He responded, "Don't worry, Gail. Together we will work really hard to get you where you want to be. Let's start with your legs and we will work our way through the gym."

"Okay," I said.

And so we began the routine of me following him like a little puppy dog.

"Do you work?" he asked.

"I'm a freelance copywriter right now."

"So you write ads?" he asked.

"Yep. That's what I do."

"Well maybe I'll let you write a classified ad for me one day."

I just smiled. I had learned to say very little. I liked the anonymity of meeting someone who didn't have a clue as to what I was going through. I could pretend I was normal, and I did that whenever I was in an area where no one knew me. Should I say, hey I used to be one of those ad women on Madison Avenue, (actually Third Avenue, if we were being honest). I wrote commercials for Procter and Gamble, and Richardson Vicks, as well as doing radio and print. Oh and by the way, my campaigns were national. I even won an award for increasing revenue in a declining market! Nope.

I also realized that he was one of the first people I met who had no clue to what was going on in my personal life. He knew nothing about me. I had thought that in Tiny-Town everyone had an idea of what you were going through, because here…people talked. Of course, no one really ever knows what you're going through… it's so 'whisper down the lane.' He had no idea I was a quad wife with two little children and 24-hour nursing. I liked it that way.

I realized that I was being completely defined by the injury—not like Alex was, but like an accessory to the crime. I would have to work on that. I would try to be two people in one body. I looked at him as he talked about the muscle groups and what we needed to focus on. Then I thought about home for a brief minute, and me, the exhausted facilitator using every drop of energy trying to keep our world turning on its axis. But out here I was going to be someone else altogether. What I was going to become, I had no idea.

As I began to work muscles that hadn't been used in years, I initially felt like overcooked pasta. But at least I wasn't thinking about the constant, life-threatening emergencies that were bringing us to the edge. I was thinking about my very small new world. And when I was finished, I was a mess, sweaty and tired, and I needed a nap. I drove home in a daze, grateful that my body worked. I was unable to sit on the toilet for two days. I had no idea that I had those muscles back there.

After that, I was hooked. I made an appointment for twice a week. By the time the following summer would arrive, I would be in great shape physically. That, and a little lipstick, and I would have the perfect camouflage.

On the way home, I picked up the kids from Sunday school. By that time we had another new nurse, named Mike. Since we already had a Mike D at the time, he became Michael M. His wife was a doctor in Atlantic City and he had an affinity for playing the guitar. He was a tall, thin, athletically built African-American and he would encourage the kids with their sports.

Adam was one of those kids who could care less about sports. He had absolutely no interest. When he started on the soccer field he would get distracted by a butterfly, and instead of focusing on the game, he followed the butterfly. We had tried basketball, which he had no interest in, then soccer, and as he entered Belhaven, he would try baseball. What we noticed about Mike M. was that he was a good coach. He was one of the most encouraging boys I had ever seen. He was not in it to win. He was in it for the camaraderie.

Mike M. thought that Danielle was becoming a natural at soccer. Her assertive personality was played out on the field with a competitive intensity that I found fascinating. We were not competitive people; she was an anomaly in our family.

In addition, she was an eater. When Mike would make an omelet he would say "Danielle, Adam, you want anything to eat?"

Danielle's appetite was something I had not seen in a child her size. She was a still a skinny little girl, with wavy, light brown hair and natural blonde highlights. She had big brown saucers for eyes, flanked by the same black lashes her father had. And she ate everything, as opposed to Adam, who continued to only eat white food- Frosted Mini-Wheats and Special K, plain bagels, plain pasta with a little butter, and absolutely no green flecks of garnish.

"Yes, I'll have an omelet, too," Danielle said. "Thank you."

"No problem, sweetheart." He looked at me. "Would you like something, Gail?"

"No thank you." I sat there, dripping leftover sweat from the gym.

Adam looked at me and said, "Mommy why are you all red?"

"I worked out Adam, and it was really hard. I have a trainer and he made me do a lot of things, things that I have never done before."

"Well, I don't want a trainer. I couldn't work out like that."

"I don't blame you. I didn't think I wanted to work out like this either."

Michael had replaced Warren, who had moved to New Mexico with his wife Anne. Warren had taught Alex how to transition into a world that was foreign, as well as into someone who navigated a wheelchair with confidence.

Michael seemed so mellow I thought he was drugged half the time. Maybe it came from seemingly being laid back, and from playing guitar in his spare time. Maybe it was that his kids were grown and out of the house, and he could relax. Who knew? Once in a while, Michael came over with his best friend, Cliff, and he was an artist in every sense of the word. One look at him and you felt like you were flashing back to the sixties. He wore a beret and sported a goatee, and even his jive talk was a throwback. He painted complex, layered abstract oils on large canvases. Cliff believed that everything inherently came from a circle, the circle of life. So the basis of his paintings sprung from circular formations.

I took the kids to look at his paintings one day at his home, where he lived with his wife Tee. She was warm, friendly and "ever so sweetly brewed" as Cliff would say. Cliff had been raised in the projects of Newark, and somehow he'd survived his violent surroundings to blossom into a man with a nurturing intent. He would become an important influence in our home, especially with Adam. Cliff would be forever welcome.

"Hey buddy, how you doin' today?" he would say to Adam.

"Good," Adam would respond.

Adam was goofy around his friends, but quiet at home. We thought he was shy, but we would turn out to be very wrong.

"Hey Adam, I saw some of the art you did at school. You're very good."

"Thanks, Cliff." Adam left for the backroom to play video games.

It was in around fourth grade that Adam had made one of his best friends who wasn't part of his Hebrew Academy days. His name was Dori Deen, and he was Sri Lankan. His mother was Dr. Swarna Jaysingher, an extremely dedicated cardiologist, and they lived about a block away. Dori had an older brother named Bahti, but since Dori's parents were divorced and his father lived out of town, and his mother worked all of the time, he would come to spend a great deal of time at our house.

The one thing I learned about having more kids in the house was that it enabled me to feel more like a normal mother. And I learned what was going on in my kids' lives from their friends, some more forthcoming than others.

We loved Dori for many reasons. He was one of the most polite young men I would ever encounter.

"Hi Mrs. K. Hi, Mr.K. How are you doing today?"

"Adam, is he for real?" Alex would ask.

"Yeah Dad. He's for real."

"Thank you for having me," Dori would say when he left the house.

"Thank you for coming," I would respond. "I can't believe that kid is making me more polite."

There had to be something else out there, other than stem cell research. Something more expeditious. The web was filled with information, but it was still in its infancy.

My next call was to the National Institutes of Health (NIH), one of the largest biomedical research institutes in the world. I spoke to people on the phone, some helpful, some not. I wrote down names of the heads of departments, called them, got more names, more advice, and hit more dead ends.

From all the research, the common thread of opportunity seemed to point towards stem cells. NIH also had a list of clinical trials—these were studies that you could be a part of. They were in every medical category, and you could sign up for them in their database. I looked religiously at what was on the boards. Phase I, Phase II, and Phase III clinical trials were the options. I was told that first the preclinical research had to be approved by the FDA. Those studies were the studies that involved mice. Sometimes after that they used monkeys or dogs, or even cats. I did not want to think about that, because I did not believe that anything should be tested on animals. I was a hypocrite, I guess. I didn't mind the mice, but I couldn't stand the thought of monkeys, dogs or cats being used in that way.

Anyway, if the preclinical research seemed to be effective, and not harmful, it was approved by the FDA. Then researchers could move on to a Phase I clinical in humans. The point of that phase was dosing- the timing and side effects of the dosing. If that study was not harmful, you could proceed to a Phase II study. A Phase II study was more detailed, and regarded the safety of the dosing and how well the treatment worked. And Phase III of the clinical trials was to take a promising new treatment and show its efficacy in comparison to the standard treatment available.

For us, for Alex, there was no standard treatment. We were hoping, or I was hoping, that there would be one on the horizon.

At that point, there wasn't much at NIH. I continued to research online; I joined a group where Bio-research papers were published from all over the world. I had absolutely no clue what I was reading. But it made me feel like I was doing something. As I looked at the text in front of me on the computer, I felt like the language barrier between me and the science-speak was the Great Wall of China.

I continued to scour the web, reading every article that was relevant, looking for some kind of hope. I knew that living like this was insane. I also knew that people outside of the injury thought that you get used to it. You don't. You deal with it, you hate it, you have frustrations and fears that don't go away, but the injury owns you. At least it owned Alex and his body, in the sense that it took control of him physically. The spasms, the blood pressure, the dysreflexia, the medicines he took. I watched Alex. He definitely became adept at managing the dragon, but he never stopped wanting to stand, or to jump up, or to use his hands, or to make love, or to go for a run or a bike ride, or even to hold my hand.

It was that inside ache, that he had and that I had for him, that seemed to deaden me a little as time went on. I noticed that I was becoming numb—not the initial numbness of the injury, which was more like shock, but a calmness that was pervasive in my actions and reactions. I no longer got angry, or felt the intensity of feelings that

I used to. I didn't feel joy either. Was I submerged in emotional molasses? It seemed as if I was.

There was no getting used to it. There were so many intrusions. 24-hour nursing was a blessing and a curse. Since the nurses were on 12-hour schedules, I didn't know who was coming and who was going. Some of them, not all, did not understand that they were in someone else's home. They didn't understand that I was raising children and they needed to respect the fact that this was their home. The nurse's room had been the playroom, and now there was no room for play.

20. 2003

One day, I was reading an article online about a man whose daughter had been paralyzed at a similar level as Alex. Her name was Erica and she lived in Detroit. Her father had been scouring the world for a cure. He had come across a doctor in Lisbon, Portugal whose name was Dr. Carlos Lima, and he worked with stem cell grafting.

In the United States, stem cell research had continued to be a political hot button. The right-to-lifers had helped to put Bush into the White House and there was no way he was going to disappoint them. They had their voice all the way at the top. The initial theory was that stem cells had to come from the embryo, which was *life* and had the potential to become a baby. To me, an embryo was not a living breathing human being, so why should it have more value than a living breathing human being? It didn't make sense. They did not want all those potential babies destroyed in order to aid those who were actually living and suffering on a daily basis. Therefore, funding on research for embryonic stem cell treatments was cut.

But Dr. Lima had discovered a way to harvest stem cells from the olfactory mucosa, and transfer them to the site of the spinal cord injury using a technique called the olfactory mucosa autograft.

I implored Alex to call the man in Detroit. "Don't you want a chance to walk again?" I asked.

He was depressed. His spasms were getting worse, he was missing everything about his Before Injury life, and I was trying to fix it. Life lesson: Some things are not fixable. But I nagged, and cajoled, and then nagged again.

And one day he picked up the phone and called Detroit. The man in Detroit was positively optimistic. His daughter had received the transplant with no adverse side effects. But the most important thing, he said, was the physical therapy afterwards.

"She works out four hours a day in a rehab facility that I built for her."

"He must be some kind of auto executive," Alex said after he hung up the phone. "He invited me to come look at the facility in Detroit and meet his daughter."

"You should go."

"I'll think about it. He said that I should talk to his daughter. He was very encouraging."

"Alex, no one wants their loved ones to suffer like this. Between the spasms and the constant dysreflexia, I'm not saying you would walk again. But maybe you could get your fingers back, or the use of your hands. Even bladder and bowel or sexual function, anything back would be amazing."

"IF I do this, I'm doing it for you. Not me."

"Just investigate it, that's all I ask."

"He gave me Dr. Lima's number in Portugal," he said.

"Are you going to call?" I asked.

"I will call. First let me talk to his daughter."

"Thank you. I love you."

"I love you, too," he responded.

I kissed him on the cheek and sat down on the edge of the bed. We all need optimism, and I needed it as much as he did.

"Did he tell you how much it would cost?" I asked.

"Yes. Forty-four thousand for the operation. But then you have to spend an additional amount on rehab when you return. It doesn't work unless you have intensive rehab."

"If you have the surgery you could go away somewhere for the rehab. You could go to Detroit."

"I am not leaving the kids for three months. I already did that, and I am not doing it again."

"OK, let's just take this one step at a time," I said. "Let's continue to look into it. And see where it goes."

And so began the journey of a cobbled road to Lisbon. The next time we were in Cleveland, Alex made a side trip to the outskirts of Detroit with his nurse, Michael D.

He met with Erica, and she told him that the procedure was not that difficult. She didn't know whether it was worth it or not yet. But she was standing. And that was something she hadn't been able to do before. Within a few weeks, they became phone friends. And I was glad. He needed to talk to someone that wasn't me. He needed a friend that *got it* and she was that friend. He came home satisfied.

So he called Dr. Lima, and they began to make arrangements for the trip abroad. He was to be the twenty-fifth patient to have the surgery. I thought that twenty-five could be a lucky number, but I had to make plans for the kids. I called our babysitter Adina, someone I knew I could feel comfortable leaving the kids with. She and her sister Elise would stay and take care of them. I was confident that they were in good hands.

21. OLA' PORTUGAL

When we left for Lisbon a few days before Memorial Day weekend. Tim M. was the nurse who traveled with us. He had been with us for several years at that point and had gone on to another job. But he came back as a favor to Alex. We flew out of Newark International and all I could think of was *will they speak any English?*

When we arrived, a man was waiting at the gate with a manual wheelchair. Together, he and Tim transferred Alex and I pushed him to baggage claim. He was tired and needed to drain his leg bag. We went to the street and found a drain, where I helped him empty the bag. Then we waited for an accessible van for about half an hour. We knew it was coming because Dr. Lima's staff had made all of the arrangements. I would be staying in a hotel about a half an hour away from the hospital.

We were all exhausted, but the van took us directly to the hospital. Lisbon was a beautiful port city speckled with homes that had orange tile roofing. It was a hilly drive over cobblestoned streets. As we drove around one of the many twists, turns, and curves cut out of the hillside, the van lurched, and I was grateful that Alex was strapped down. Off in the distance you could see the ocean.

When we arrived at Hospital Egaz Moniz, the nurses checked Alex in and took him to a room. They spoke very little English and we spoke absolutely no Portuguese. We just smiled and said "Hola." It was Spanish, but it would have to do.

Tim and I followed the young nurse who took us to the neurological wing of the hospital. There we met with Dr. Lima's staff. They asked if we were hungry, using the few English words they knew, and we nodded and said "Si."

"You like meat? Fish? Fish is good."

"OK," we all agreed, "fish would be good."

One of the women returned within twenty minutes with three trays of freshly cooked fish, with the head, tail, skin and bones still intact. There were fresh green beans and freshly sautéed potatoes to accompany the fish.

When she left, I looked at Alex and Tim. "First of all, have you ever been in a hospital where they asked you if you were hungry? Secondly, this is fresh. Maybe even fresh from the ocean, fresh."

"Looks like we're not in Kansas anymore, Toto!" Alex said. "I have never been served food actually made to order in a hospital before."

"It's delicious," Tim said. "This is amazing. Real food."

I added. "Did you notice it's quiet here? It doesn't sound like an American hospital either."

"And the nurses are so relaxed, they're really nice and friendly," Alex said..

"Look, I'll admit it," I said. "I thought this whole thing seemed a little scary."

"It still does," Alex said.

"Well maybe when you meet Dr. Lima, you'll feel better."

"Maybe when this is over, I'll feel better." I felt his not so subtle anger directed at me.

Tim had gotten Alex situated on the bed.

"I'm going to have to make sure I don't get any skin breakdown here. These beds aren't water beds, I'm glad I brought my straps." Alex had a list for every time he traveled: towels and straps for turning him, a bucket for his night bag to rest in at night, medications, Fleet Bisacodyl enemas, and Metamucil to keep his bowels moving. He had a separate medical bag. He also traveled with a gel pad for the airplane, so he wouldn't get skin breakdown in transit. It was a lot of work. Traveling was something that he got very nervous about at least a month in advance. Even though his body had its own unnatural responses to things, he felt safer at home. But there we were, trying to see if his nasal cells could help him get something back.

When Dr. Lima finally arrived, he walked in looking very Mediterranean. Dark hair, dark eyes, and a casual stance seemed to belie the persona of a medical renegade. His khaki pants and polo shirt said more about his relaxed style.

"Hello, you must be Alex." He held his hand out and Alex lifted his to shake it.

"Hi, Dr. Lima. It's nice to finally meet you. This is my wife, Gail and my nurse, Tim."

"A pleasure," he said. "Well, now that you are here, we may as well get started. Let me tell you what the protocol is and how and when we will proceed. Tomorrow we will run blood tests, and you will take a psychological exam to make sure you are emotionally stable. It is important that you know the risks. Remember this is experimental.

"Let me explain how this is going to work. There is a sub-population of cells in the nasal area called olfactory ensheathing glia (OEG). These cells have rather unique properties. Their job is to support continual regeneration of nasal (olfactory) receptor neurons throughout life. What is special about OEG, and the reason I and other neuroscientists continue to study them, is that olfactory receptor neurons originate in the peripheral nervous system (PNS) but are able to extend axons into the central nervous system (CNS) tissue of the olfactory bulb, in the brain. There, the axons connect upstream with other brain neurons. In all of human biology, it is quite rare for axons to cross from the PNS into the CNS. Since we know that PNS nerves will regenerate while those in the CNS will not, the olfactory system could be the only cells to enable a connection. Possibly bringing back sensation or movement. We have been very optimistic, but most importantly, after surgery you will need to follow up with rehabilitative measures. Have you found a facility at home?"

"Well, I am thinking of buying the bike, or there is a rehab facility near me that has one that I could use."

"That is good. It is very important to follow through with the exercise program. Do you have any questions?"

"Not right now," Alex said. "I guess I'm really tired. It's been a long day."

"Well then, I will see you tomorrow. Get some rest. I see you've already gotten something to eat."

"You know, Dr. Lima, the hospitals are very different over here," Alex said.

"I know, it is more relaxed. It is better for the patient. It is also less expensive."

"Why is that?" I asked.

"We don't have the lawsuits here that you do in America."

"People don't sue their doctors?"

"No, they don't."

"Wow, that's pretty incredible," I said.

"Not really. I think there is a great deal of respect for the medical profession, and part of it may be that medicine here is socialized. The government is paying for your care to begin with, so no matter what your feelings on the matter are, you can't sue the government." He began to walk towards the door, carrying folders in one hand. "Have a good evening."

I looked at Alex. "Alex, I'm tired. Do you mind if I go to the hotel and get situated?"

"No, I want to go to bed. But I'm a little scared."

"Of the surgery?"

"No. No one speaks English. How am I going to communicate? Will you stay with me?"

"Alex, I promise nothing is going to happen to you."

"Why can't you stay with me?"

"Let me just get a good night sleep. I'll be here first thing in the morning."

"Fine," he said.

All I could think of was that we were all tired and needed to sleep. If I stayed there, then I wouldn't get any sleep. We were all a little on edge. Sleep fixed everything. I just needed to get some.

I kissed him goodbye, and he looked as if I had given away his favorite bicycle. I found my way down the corridor to the elevator and out the front of the building and caught a cab to the center of town.

My hotel had once been a palace, literally. The grounds were immaculately groomed, there were cobblestoned pathways, a spa, and a beautiful dining room with hand-painted ceilings and mirrored walls. It was simply majestic, and the transition from the hospital to the hotel was akin to walking into air conditioning on a hot sticky day…what a wakeup. *Blend in, Gail. No one here knows you're a quad wife, with insides that feel like they were mangled in a trash compactor.*

I found my room and opened my computer. At least I could read what was going on in the world. Spain had been attacked in March by terrorists affiliated with Al Qaeda. They had once again gone after transportation as a mode of mass casualties, this time commuter trains. Almost two hundred people were dead, and eighteen hundred were injured. Yet, when you walked around the city, there was no angst written on any one's face. They seemed at peace, sitting in cafés drinking wine or sipping on coffee. Where I came from, everyone would be on high alert. Life stopped in the states after 9/11. The horror was felt and spoken of continually. Maybe it was because I didn't know what anyone was saying, but the people of Lisbon seemed to take it in stride.

I emailed Michael G, Christina, Michelle, and my family. I also emailed Robert so he could tell the rest of Alex's family how things were going. I called Molly to tell her we'd arrived, and told her I would call again after the surgery. I was tired, so I showered and slipped into bed. It felt like a solid block of cement, with very nice sheets on top, not very royal for a palatial hotel.

The next morning I awoke to the birds chirping outside my window. I got dressed and remembered to bring a sweater for the hospital. Alex was going to have his psychological testing done. *Really*? What were they going to do if he failed, send him home on a plane? I ate a croissant with jam by myself, enjoying the scenery and the delicious coffee. I watched a crowd gather by a gentleman who was eating breakfast. Apparently he was a soccer star staying at the hotel. He was blonde and well built, and considering that the interruption was so early in the morning, he was being very gracious. Futbol was big in Europe, and I had absolutely no appreciation for it. I had no appreciation for football in the states either. But I had met enough hyped-up-on-winning steroidal parents to know I needed to steer clear of them.

By the time I got to the hospital, Alex had already been given his psychological exam. They were just finishing up as I walked through the door.

"So did you pass?" I asked.

"Yes," he said with a wry smile. "I cheated," he went on. "They just want to make sure I don't want to kill myself."

The nurse who administered the questions said to me, "Excuse me, but I think he will be fine having the surgery."

"Thank you," I said. After she left, I looked at Alex. "Well, what line of crap did you feed her?"

"I was very nice, you would have been proud of me. I told her I was a fighter, and that they didn't have to worry. I have two beautiful children at home. You know, stuff like that, oh and this injury sucks."

"Ain't that the truth."

He continued, "She said she was going to talk to Dr. Lima, and then they would probably schedule the surgery for within a day or two."

"Do you have anything else to do here?" I asked.

"I don't think so."

"Do you want to see if we can get you a ride into the city and we could walk around and have lunch?"

"Sure. I would like to see what Lisbon looks like."

"Me too."

"You'll have to push me," he said.

"I know."

After the van dropped us off at Comercio Square, I pushed Alex around over the cobblestoned street onto the square. As I looked ahead I could see cafés and boutiques, and my urge to shop bubbled up like Old Faithful. We came upon Rua Augusta and knew that it was time for coffee. Alex needed to tilt back, so I sat at an outdoor table and pulled the back of his wheelchair to an angle where he could rest his head on my chest.

"Oh the perks of a manual wheelchair." He rubbed his head into my breasts and smiled.

I was holding on to the back handles of the chair in order to help maintain the balance. "It's really pretty here. The architecture is so beautiful, look at the mosaic pavement...only in Europe."

"What do you want to do?" he asked.

"I want to go shopping. I'm in Europe. I may as well buy something."

When we were done drinking our cappuccino, he said, "Can you check my leg bag?"

"Sure." So I pushed him toward a drain in an inconspicuous area, and emptied the leg bag in the drain.

Afterwards we found a Zara, where I bought a spectacular crimson red dress, which was a stretch knit, long sleeve, off the shoulders number, that was so tight I knew I wouldn't be able to eat whenever I wore it. But I didn't care. Whenever Alex had surgery or went into the hospital, I lost weight.

"Okay, I'm done." I put the bag on the handles on the back of his chair and began to push again. Within half a block there was a liquor store.

"Port," Alex said. "Everyone said this is the place to buy port."

"Do you know what port to buy?" I asked.

"No, but I bet they can make a recommendation."

It was not accessible so I went into the liquor store without him and came out with three bottles. "The guy inside said that this was an excellent choice, for the money."

"Yeah, well how does it taste?"

"He said that it was one of their finer ports. Are you going to know the difference?"

He shook his head.

"Me neither. Do you think I can put them on your lap?"

"Yeah, I'll carry them."

"That's good, because I can't push and carry." I placed the bottles, in their brown paper bags, strategically on his lap. "Got it?"

"Yep, got it."

I began to push again, and for some reason Alex started to fix their positioning. A bottle dropped and smashed on the cobblestones. "Oh, my God, I'm sorry," he said.

"It's okay. It's just one less bottle for Gary to drink."

I picked up the damp brown bag of broken glass and took it to the nearest trashcan. "Alright, time to meet the van, let's go back to the hospital," I said.

When Dr. Lima walked into Alex's hospital room, wearing another pair of khaki pants with a button-down shirt, all neatly pressed, with shiny oxblood leather loafers, I thought, "This man has style."

"Alex," he said, "tomorrow is the day. Your surgery will be early in the morning. All the blood work is complete, and your chest X-ray is clear, as is your urine. So we will proceed with the next step. Do you have any questions?"

"Yes, do I get to do my bowel routine in the morning? And, will the nurse didge me?"

"Yes, Alex. We know how important the bowel routine is in keeping your blood pressure in line, and whatever you need we will help you to do so."

"Oh, thank you Dr. Lima."

"I can assure you, it is no problem," he said with his sexy Portuguese accent.

"So tomorrow is the day," I said. "What time should I be here, Dr. Lima?"

"We will begin at 8 a.m. Mrs. Kiejdan, you do not need to arrive until between 10 and 10:30. The procedure will take several hours. It will be done in three steps. Alex, you will be put under general anesthesia with an endotracheal tube. We will administer a prophylactic antibiotic before we begin the surgery. I believe they will give you an oral one this evening. We will use morphine to anesthetize you. Then your head will be stabilized and we will position you on your side so we can access the damaged part of your spinal cord with a standard incision—it is called a posterior laminectomy—and opening of the dura mater. Then we will carefully remove the scar tissue from the lesion. After that, we will close the surgical wound temporarily. Next, a very established colleague of mine who is an otolaryngologist will use a transnasal endoscopic and instrumentation approach to harvesting your stem cells from the olfactory mucosa. Here we will gather enough tissue to fill the spinal cord cavity. We will pack your nose to avoid excessive bleeding. Your nose will be packed for several days, and the nurses will change the packing as needed. The transplantation of the olfactory mucosa into the site is last. We extract it, put it in a petri dish, keep it sterile, and then plant it in the previously prepared area. Then we close you up, and you are transferred to post-op for recovery." "So," he said as he looked at Alex. "Do you have any questions?"

"Not at the moment," Alex replied.

"Well then, I will see you first thing tomorrow morning."

After Dr. Lima left, I looked at Alex. He was pensive.

"Did you understand what he was saying?" I asked.

"Yeah, they're going to chop the shit out of me. Why don't you go back to the hotel? I'll see you tomorrow." Tim was going to stay with him that night, and get him up for the surgery in the morning.

"You OK?" I asked.

"Really?" he said with disgust.

I knew it then: he was still not on board. But who would be? It was elective surgery, in the hopes of fixing something deemed unfixable.

It would be a long time until he stopped being angry at me. I felt it then, and I continued to feel it for many years.

I kissed Alex goodbye and went outside to see if I could catch a cab. There weren't that many, but eventually I caught one and stared quietly out the window as we returned to the Palace. It was a relief. My nerves were frayed, much like the fringe of a pillow's tassel that had been worn away.

When I finally made it to my room, I sat down on the overly firm bed, weary and frightened. Where had all my optimism gone? It had vanished like vapor. Just keep moving. Take a shower, and in the morning you'll eat breakfast and head back to the hospital.

22. THE EXPERIMENT

When I arrived in the morning, I went straight to Alex's room. It was empty. I turned to walk towards the nurse's station and one of the day nurses greeted me and asked me to follow her. She would show me where I was to wait. Tim was already sitting there.

I sat next to him. "Hi Tim. How was he this morning?"

"Well, he was apprehensive, but he was also making his usual sick jokes."

"Glad I missed that part. How long has he been in there?"

"They took him in about an hour-and-a-half ago. They think it will be another hour-and-a-half to two hours."

"I guess we just wait here, then," I said.

We took turns napping, and at about 1:30 p.m., Dr. Lima came out, to tell us that everything had gone well and there were no complications.

"He is in recovery. Gail, you can see him in about an hour. Things went as expected, and at this point only time will tell."

Within the hour I was by Alex's side. I kissed him on his cheek; I could see the packing coming out of his nose. He was in a morphine haze, but I squeezed his hand, and he said with a raspy-throated voice, "I can feel my middle finger."

"You can? Wow. That's amazing."

"It feels so good to feel my middle finger. It was worth it."

"Oh my God, I am so glad to hear that."

"I'm tired, I need to sleep."

"I'll wait for you in your room. Go back to sleep, Alex. I love you."

"I love you too," he said. And he was out.

I waited in his room for him to be wheeled back. It was a private room without a view. I looked for the portable DVD player that Mark Dannenbaum had lent him. I didn't have many choices in movies. *Scarface*, Alex's favorite. I didn't get that stinkin' movie, where the word fuck was used over 170 times. Let's see what else is here. I flipped through *Master and Commander, Changing Lanes, The Last Samurai*... No comedies. Really, where the hell was the levity? Isn't life about laughter? Ahh, there was something funny I could watch, *Gangs of New York*...no blood in that one. I continued to flip through the limited selection and finally found something suitable...*Van Wilder*. The opening scene alone was hilarious. Childish humor, the perfect carpet ride away from here. So as I sat there laughing to myself, I forgot about why I was there. I was cautiously optimistic when I finished the movie. Was it Ryan Reynolds? Possibly.

Fade back in. Alex had gotten through the surgery. He had what seemed to be an immediate feeling in his middle finger, and maybe, just maybe, he would get more.

By the time they rolled him back into the room with two IVs— saline and sugar and morphine—I was jealous. I am not a drug addict, but there is something appealing about morphine. Not morphine as a lifestyle, but as a test. But the good girl wins out more often than not, and I continued to wonder what kind of high morphine would give. I stuck to what was legally available, a shot or two of really good tequila. Fortunately, the only addictions I had at that point were shoes and chocolate.

It was late, and when the nurse came in to check on Alex she said, "Mrs. Kiejdan, it's time for you to go. He had a long day, and he is going to sleep through most of the night. You need to rest yourself."

"Thank you," I replied. I looked at Alex and stood up, I went over to his bedside to kiss him goodbye. Tim would be here soon.

He opened his eyes, they fluttered a little; he smiled.

I said, "Hi, I love you. It's over."

And he closed his eyes and went back to sleep.

When I got back to the hotel, I cracked open my computer and started to send everyone updates on Alex's condition. First to both our families, then to Christina, Michelle, and Michael Grossman. Michael had become one of my confidants. I talked to him all the time. He truly cared, and I was grateful for his friendship. As time went by, there were fewer and fewer people who even wanted to hear about what was going on in our lives. Maybe it was the intensity with which everything happened. We were riddled with emergencies. Blood pressure issues, possible strokes, bladder infections that made him go dysreflexic, impacted bowels that made him go dysreflexic, a continuation of health issues that, when not addressed, could become life-and-death situations. It was insane. Michael got it. He understood the loss, so he was right up there with Christina and Michelle, when it came to compassion. I emailed them next, and then I went to sleep.

The next few days were trying. I couldn't wait to leave. Alex was in excruciating pain at the posterior surgery site. I learned that a posterior laminectomy was the breaking of the bone, so his neck was broken…again. He was miserable and angry. *And it was all my fault.* I was tired, and I was running out of patience with him. He had no patience for me whatsoever.

I tried not to snap, I felt my jaw clench so hard it brought out my TMJ. "Honey, what can I do to make you more comfortable?" I asked him.

"Fuck, this pain is ridiculous. They took me off the morphine."

"I can tell. Where's Tim?" I asked .

"He went back to the hotel to get some sleep. He was up all night with me, helping me to turn. I can't talk to the nurses here. They don't understand me. I want some water. Ask the nurses for some ice."

"Okay." I limited my conversation with him. I just did as I was told, and kept my mouth shut. Breathe in, breathe out.

Within a few days, we were on our way home. Within days of returning Alex's nasal passageway started to hemorrhage; he had a mother of a nose bleed. We could not get it to stop.

"Who do we know?" I asked. "We need an ENT." I started making phone calls. I explained over and over again that he had had surgery abroad. There wasn't a doctor in the area that would see him after they that found out. We called Michael Gottlieb and he told us to use Afrin. "That stuff is great," he said "It's magic 101." It was immediate relief.

But Alex still had to have it looked at, so finally, we called his cousin Ira Trocki, who was a plastic surgeon, and he was kind enough to see him immediately. He looked at it and put something up his nasal passageway to cauterize it, then he packed it, and we were on our way.

Things began to settle down. Dr. Lima called a few times to see how he was doing. There were no other changes that we could see. Alex had ordered an exercise machine so he could work out near the kids. He put it on the second floor of his family's office building, and tried going there to work out. It didn't take long before his hips began to bother him. Dr. Graciani had him get an X-ray.

After reading the report, she said to him, "Alex, unfortunately, your hip has undergone a substantial amount of osteoporosis. Because you haven't been weight bearing, it has become brittle and the pain you are having is a symptom of the fact that you haven't used it in a quite some time. My recommendation for you is to not use the bike that you purchased. It will only inflame the matter, and unfortunately it will most likely cause you to break something. Then you'll need surgery."

When Alex came home, he stopped in the garage to have a cigarette. Somewhere along the way he had become a smoker. He was not allowed to do it in the house, so he would stay outside in the garage and have a smoke and a Diet Pepsi. There he would talk on his cell phone to friends, doctors and Blue Cross Blue Shield of New Jersey. But for the moment, he just leaned back in his chair, raised the legs, and smoked. Then he finally came in the house to tell me he could no longer use the hand-propelled bicycle that we had purchased.

"So what does this mean?" I asked.

"This means that it's the end of the road for me as far as any kind of recovery is concerned."

I sat down, "That sucks." I responded. "Are you upset?"

"What do you think?"

"I think it seems like you've gone to hell and back for nothing. But I also think you're going dysreflexic a lot less, too. So maybe, the surgery did something for that somehow."

"And my fingers have lost their sensation again," he added.

"I'm sorry," I said.

"Yeah, me too."

There was no shortage of apologies in our house.

23. And the World Came Tumbling

The phone rang. "Gail," Gary said. "Mom had another accident."

"Shit! What kind of accident? When did it happen?"

"Well, it happened this afternoon. She was having lunch with the Minoffs, and when she walked to her car it happened. She was getting into the car and I guess she tripped on something and fell. They ran over and asked her if she was okay and she said, "Yes, I'm fine. See you all later." But she wasn't fine. She drove over to our house and honked the horn because she couldn't get out of the car on her own. So we went outside and saw that her color was off. Andrea called the hospital and we took her to Hillcrest. Her pubic bone is broken."

"Oh God," I whispered to myself.

"She should be in the hospital for about a week and then they'll probably put her in Montefiore for rehab." Montefiore was a rehabilitation hospital in the suburbs.

"She keeps tripping. Do you think there is something more that's wrong with her?" I asked.

"I don't know. I was talking about that with Andrea. You know this isn't the first time she has fallen."

"Besides when she was here?" I asked.

"Yes. She just keeps going and going because she doesn't want to bother anyone."

"Our very own Eveready Bunny. Did you tell Diane?"

"I'm going to call her after I'm done talking with you," he said.

"What's wrong?" Alex interrupted.

I told him.

"Shit," he said. "Does she need surgery?"

"I don't know. Gary, does she need surgery?"

"No. I guess she was lucky."

"Well we all know what real luck is- an accident that happens to someone else."

Fern volunteered to help watch the kids, so I could visit my mother. Andrea picked me up at the airport, as she would for most of my future visits. After this fall, I began to make an effort to see my mom at least every six to eight weeks.

At Montefiore, we walked up to the front desk and asked for her room. I sensed that smell that greets you when you are visiting a waystation for the aging and the injured-aging.

"Hi Mom." I bent down to kiss her soft, lightly freckled cheek. She had the kind of natural cream-colored skin that people envy and pay big money to emulate. I hoped that I had inherited her skin.

"Hi honey! Welcome to Cleveland."

"Well, you look really good," I lied.

"I'm fine. I want to go home. They want to put me in a wheelchair."

"For good?" I asked.

"No, just until I finish rehab. Then they said I will need a walker."

A walker isn't so bad," I said.

She smiled. She was always smiling. No matter what the situation, she managed to smile. She also always put an optimistic spin on things. The glass was always half full, with another glass on its way.

Andrea interjected, "I was talking to Gary and we were thinking that she has a long walk to the elevator from her apartment and it may just be too much for her."

"Well I'm not moving," Mom said indignantly. "I like my apartment."

She was living at The Village in Beachwood, a nice gated community with single family homes, apartment buildings, and town homes.

"Mom, how about if while you are here, Gary, Andrea and I look for an apartment closer to the elevator. Then you won't have to walk so far. It could still be in The Village. I promise it will be a nice two bedroom place."

She looked up at me. "Well, as long as it's in The Village it should be okay."

"It will be every bit as nice as the apartment you have now, but a little bit more accessible."

"Diane called," she told me. "She's going to try and come in with Randy and Brandon in the next few weeks."

"Well that's great," I said.

The television was running on mute, and as I looked out the window to see the parking lot. I thought about how two of the strongest people in my life were now disabled. Life was truly a test, and I had felt as if I was failing, but I needed my energy for those around me. There were many times I thought that we were either here to learn, or here to teach. And at this point I had no idea what my category was. It was obvious that I had much to learn, as does everyone. I was not gifted in predicting the future or the present, or even reassessing the past. But it was one of those rare occasions, A.I., after injury, when I indulged in thinking. I normally focused on what had to be done. It was the only way to survive all of this. Just keep moving, and don't overthink it.

As we left Montefiore, Andrea told me that the doctor had taken a CT and has diagnosed my mother with Cerebellar Ataxia.

"What is that?" I asked.

"Well, it's when the cerebellum begins to atrophy. It's the part of your brain that controls motor function and balance, as well as coordination and equilibrium. That's why she's been falling. There are several kinds of ataxia. The one that she has, well, they tell you in the pamphlet to get your things in order. It's progressive."

"Shit," I said.

"Hers could progress slowly, you never know. They gave her a pamphlet on it. It's back in her apartment. I have to go to work tomorrow. I guess you and Gary can stop by your mom's apartment and pick it up."

"I guess tomorrow we should also start looking for a new apartment for her," I said.

"I think that's a good idea."

The next day, Gary went for a run and I ran on the treadmill in the basement. I couldn't believe that with the world falling apart, I was lucky enough to be in a basement on a treadmill watching television. I was watching as the war continued to rage on in Iraq and Afghanistan. Someone once said that somewhere, someone always has it worse. Truer words were never spoken.

Gary and I spent the day looking at what was available at The Village. We found a place on the fourth floor of a very nice apartment building. It was the second apartment from the elevator, and it was bright, airy, and empty. I asked about the possibility of removing an unnecessary wall in front of the walk-in closet, and the real estate agent said she would look into it.

"That would be great." I turned to my brother. "Gary, we don't know how long she is going to be in a walker. She needs to be able to navigate things more easily. Eventually, I'm guessing she will be in a wheelchair."

"I know," he responded. "I was thinking about that. She's also going to need assistance."

The real-estate woman interjected. "The beauty of this apartment is that there are two bathrooms, with two showers. And if need be there is a second bedroom, which some tenants use as a den, and others use as a second bedroom."

"That's good to know," Gary said. "Can we call you and let you know our decision in a day or two?"

Of course, here's my card. I really don't think it will be a problem to take down that wall, I have no idea why it's there."

I took a last look at the master bathroom to make sure a wheelchair could eventually be maneuvered into it, so my mother, who didn't need the help yet, could eventually be transferred to a commode chair.

As Gary and I quietly rode down the glass elevator, I turned around to see the lobby fast approaching. There was a fireplace and two separate seating areas. It was filled with bright green plants and traditional furniture in floral patterns with jewel-tone hues. We walked out towards his car, and I felt the warm sun on my face.

"I think she will like it here," I said.

"Yeah, me too. The grounds are pretty."

"Esthetics! An important ingredient," I responded. "I won't be able to help you with this that much," I confessed. "I feel guilty."

"Don't. I know your hands are full."

"I wish you could count on Diane a little. But she really has never been that available."

"I know. I don't expect anything from Diane."

"The consummate realist. Do you have any idea how annoying that is?"

"I know it annoys you. But for me, it serves my purposes. No use in wasting time with things that will never be. Look," he said, "Andrea will help with Mom. And we will move her."

"Thank you," I said.

"Gail, you don't have to thank me."

"Yes I do. I appreciate it."

"What? You appreciate the fact that I love Mom?"

"No, that's not what I mean. I appreciate the fact that I don't have to worry. That I know she's in good hands." He smiled and for a second I saw my father. Quiet and confident, but at 6'3" Gary was taller.

"I'm not like Alex's family," he said. "Five siblings and you can only count on one or two."

"Let's not talk about them."

"By the way, how is his mom doing?" he asked.

"She's fine. You know, the normal daily complaints. "This hurts, that hurts, it's no fun getting old. You shouldn't know my pain." Other than that, she's great, still going on cruises, playing cards, going out to dinner. You know what Mom says about her?" I asked.

"No" he answered.

"She says that she enjoys ill health. I just think half the time she needs the attention. Or, maybe it's just become a way of life. To make sure she is still heard and relevant."

When I returned home, I felt like what was left of the world I knew was forever gone. And what I had learned from Alex's injury thus far was that control was an illusion. I needed a life raft, a place to feel secure. I didn't know it, but it was time to fight.

I went to work out with Darren, and he took me upstairs to a part of the gym that was an open room with a heavily shellacked wooden floor. He was carrying mitts with him, and a set of boxing gloves.

"Today we're going to see what you are really made of, Gail."

"I'm made of chocolate. It's all I eat."

"Really?"

"Kind of. Actually, it's my drug of choice. I have had chocolate every single day of my life since Halloween 1931."

"You're not that old."

"That was my other life. I had a rebirth but I'm still eating chocolate."

"Here, let's put on these gloves." He was helping me with the second glove. They were large black boxing gloves and the moment I put my hands in them, I realized I could not move any of my fingers. They were stuck in a C formation, much like Alex's. And there it was: this is what it is like to not be able to move your hands. This is what it is like for them to be paralyzed. Not to be able to hold a fork, or knife or spoon. This is what it's like…except when I'm done I get to take the gloves off.

"Gail!"

"Oh, sorry."

"Where did you go?"

"The Bahamas."

"Well, next time let me know. I'll come with you." He smiled down at me.

I thought, I don't think I'd know what to do anymore. But I said, "Okay."

Then Darren said, "Put your hands up by the side of your face, like this," and he showed me. So I followed the instructions and then he said, "Look at these mitts; you are going to learn to jab them. I will teach you how to do an uppercut, a jab, and a hook. Now let's get your feet into position. The left foot is in front, and right one is back a little. Show me how you can move around a bit."

"I hope you know I have no balance."

"You'll be fine. Just space your feet like this, there you go. Okay, I'm going to put mitts on. Keep your hands up protecting your face—always protect your face."

"You're not going to hit me in the face, are you?"

"No, I am not."

"That's good, because I'm not paying to get hit in the face."

"Set your feet, Gail, and try jabbing at the mitts. Bring your right arm back and jab it into my left mitt."

I was following directions, and my hand to God, after hitting the mitts a few times, I thought, "oh my God, I have violent tendencies! I like hitting!"

But it wasn't just hitting, it was hitting with force! All the force I could muster...years of buried rage came bubbling up to the surface. It was like I had just struck oil, and the ugly black crude was spouting from an untapped well of anger. All that bottled-up stuff was being projected right out of my arm and into a pair of gloves.

"Now, we are going to learn a few moves, right, left, uppercut and hook, cross and duck."

"Duck? Why am I ducking?"

"You're ducking so you don't get hit in the face. Right is one, left is two, uppercut is three, and hook is four. I will throw out the numbers and you will jab the mitt with the corresponding move."

"I'm going to have to think?"

"Just in the beginning, then hopefully it will come more naturally to you."

"Doubt that," I said.

And there it was, my first exposure to boxing. When we were done, I was drained. "Thanks," I said. "That was fun."

"You're welcome. We'll try it again next time."

I only had the energy to shake my head and smile.

Spring brought a change in my workout routine: a new trainer and a new gym. The trainer's name was Trevor and I was surprised to find that he had his arm in a sling. *Well, we all have challenges,* I thought.

This new gym was in Linwood, literally two minutes away from where I lived. I didn't have to pay a toll to go over the causeway and get to the island. If you live in Margate or Ventnor, they call Linwood the Mainland. Mostly because Atlantic City, Ventnor, Margate and Longport were all barrier islands, connected to the mainland by bridges. I laughed every time someone called Linwood or Northfield the Mainland. It is definitely not Hawaii. So, when I joined Mainland Fitness, I was thrilled. It offered a huge space that was clean, had great locker rooms and a juice and shake bar. It was the nicest gym that I had ever belonged to. But for whatever reason, I was stuck with a one-armed trainer. Not judging.

"How did you hurt yourself?" I asked.

"I dislocated my shoulder while wrestling. It shouldn't stop me from training, though."

"How long are you going to be in that sling?"

"A couple more weeks," he responded. Trevor was compact, and since I was an arm person, I looked for his one bicep, which was unavailable for my viewing pleasure. More importantly, I was wondering how the hell I was going to box with a one-armed trainer.

"Well, when you are better, do you think we can box?" I asked.

"We'll see," he answered.

We'll see? I said to myself. *Asshole, you better box with me. I need it.*

"Well, I really need to box," I said. "It's important to me."

"Gail, let's just start out here." He pointed to all of the machinery and the indoor track lane. "And we'll see how you do, and where we can work our way to."

"You know, I'm not a newbie, I have worked out before."

"And that's fine, but I need to see what you can do."

"Alright," I said. When I was finished I thanked him, and scheduled workouts for two days a week. This is my therapy, I thought. But he is not a good therapist.

I went home and called Christina. "OK," I said. "I just met my new trainer, and I don't like him. He's a little condescending, and he's not sure if I can box yet. He has a dislocated shoulder, so now I have to wait until he gets better."

"Calm down, missy," she said. "Just give him a chance."

"Why?"

"Because I hear he is a good trainer, number one, and number two, you are used to someone else, so allow yourself to transition. I have a new trainer, too."

"Can he use both his arms?"

"Yes."

"Well, you're ahead of me on that one."

24. CODE RED

It was February, and my mother's decline had been as slow and steady as the snow piling up outside. She had difficulty keeping her head up and was wearing a soft collar around her neck. She could no longer stand and was now permanently in a wheelchair. She was cared for by an aide named Toni, along with several other women. They took turns with day and night shifts. My mother's aides were not covered by any kind of insurance, and were paid strictly out of pocket.

Toni, who was a churchgoing soul, was about 5'10", with a large girth and a low voice. She was also a little hard of hearing; you had to repeat everything to her at least twice. But when it came to Edith, Toni was a mother hen and a night watchman all rolled up into one. She was a long and lasting presence who made sure my mother was clean and fed. She showered her every morning, and treated her like a china doll. My mom's diminishing size enabled Toni to transfer her to and from the wheelchair with ease. Not everyone was that lucky with in-home care. We heard the horror stories.

Edith still had her faculties, though she was slowly losing her ability to speak. On my visits we had begun to spend more time in her apartment, watching movies that I would rent from Blockbuster.

She watched the news with the same constancy she'd always shown. Except now, there were more news shows on television. The news show category just seemed to grow like Jack's Beanstalk, as did the tongues of those whose opinions were continuously filled with an acidic bite. I knew that sparring made for great theater, but on this visit I was not in the mood.

"Why don't we watch the cooking channel, Mom?"

She looked at me, nodded, and smiled.

"Great." I picked the remote up from her side and changed the channel. An hour passed, and she began to nod off. The snow outside continued to fall. I looked out the fourth-story window, down to the street below. The hushed silence of the snow created a feeling of peace inside me. Maybe it was from my childhood memories, the ones where I went out after dinner to make snow angels and pour warm maple syrup in the fresh drifts to make hard maple candy. Now, as sad as the scene inside the room was, there was a calming sense to the drift. My mother's struggle to eat and to talk was silenced by sleep.

I turned around and kissed my mom on the forehead. She opened her eyes and smiled.

"Mom, I have to go now. I think the driving is going to be pretty bad. You know they're calling for a total of twenty-one inches."

She smiled and said slowly, with a raspy tone, "Be careful driving."

"My plane leaves in the morning. If it's cancelled or delayed I'll be back tomorrow. If not, I will call you when I get home. I love you," I said.

"Love you too," she responded slowly.

And I walked out towards the hallway, said goodbye to Toni, and slowly made my way back to Andrea and Gary's.

By May, it was time for Alex to get his baclofen pump replaced. It was done every five years, because the pump runs on batteries.

His physiatrist at the time was Dr. Virginia Graziani, and she would remain one of the greatest and most helpful doctors that he would ever have the pleasure of receiving care from. Complications were a given with his injury, so it was no surprise that prior to the pump replacement surgery he was having blood pressure issues. One minute his BP was high, the next minute it was low. This fluctuation was called labile blood pressure, and it was an uncommon side effect of being a quad.

The doctor who had previously replaced his pump had passed away, so Alex went to someone new to him at Liberty Hospital. I was in the waiting room until it was over, and within an hour or so I got a phone call that he was in recovery.

I was relieved, because as I knew from years of my father telling me, "Surgery is no laughing matter. It's serious business. Even the smallest surgeries can have complications." Fortunately, it had been an uneventful procedure, and since Alex was stable and the doctor was in the midst of another procedure, we were able to leave without speaking to him.

Within a few weeks, Alex's blood pressures became unstable again. If he sat up in his chair, his blood pressure would go to 40 systolic, and if he was reclined, it was 70-80 systolic. Normally, he could bring it up with a Diet Coke, or additional salt, but these remedies just weren't doing the trick.

Alex called Dr. Graziani. "I don't know what is going on, Dr. Graziani. My BP just keeps getting lower and lower. And I am having spasms right and left."

"Do you have a fever?" she asked.

"No. No fever."

"Okay, I want to run some tests. We'll do a workup. Urinalysis, neck MRI, a CBC with differential, and a comprehensive metabolic profile. But the first thing we have to do is get your blood pressure stabilized. Do you have a cardiologist?"

"Yes. She's one of my son Adam's best friend's mother. Dr. Swarna Jaysinger."

"Can you call and make an appointment?"

"I can do better than that—I have her home number, and Dori can give me her cell number."

"Great, tell her what has been going on, and see what she recommends."

"Okay. Thanks, Dr. Graziani."

In the meantime, Alex was put on a steroid that helped stabilize his blood pressure. He also started taking one Ativan a day. His incision healed properly and Alex called Swarna, who called him back as soon as she got his message. She listened to what was going on and then told him she would like to put him on Florinef and ProAmatine. Both the Florinef and the ProAmatine were ways to bring his blood pressure up. In addition, he would raise his legs in the chair to bring the blood flow back to the heart. That, he had been doing for years. Or if his blood pressure was too high, he would lie back in his chair to lower it.

His tests came back normal, but as per Dr. Graziani's instructions, the nurses started to monitor his blood pressure even more closely. Looking for problems in a quadriplegic is not easy. It could be anything. Alex was sleeping on and off most of the day. He was being treated symptomatically.

By this time, I was getting ready for Danielle's bat mitzvah. Adam had entered high school and joined the rowing team. Crew would soon become an invaluable part of our lives, removing us from the stress at home and enabling us to put a focus on an all-encompassing sport. It was something to be grateful for.

By November, Alex's symptoms had become severe and his blood pressure was completely unstable. In addition, he started to spasm more than ever. The spasms in his trunk made it impossible for him to move without having contortions. Small movements seemed to throw him into convulsive fits. The spasms were sending his blood pressure up.

One night in November, his blood pressure went up to around 219/190. Mary, the nurse on duty, had put on nitropaste so he wouldn't go dysreflexic, but it continued to get worse, to the point where she couldn't control his blood pressure with medication. They called Dr. Graziani after midnight on her cell phone—she was always available, no matter what time of day or night.

She said, "You need to go to the ER. You can't handle this at home."

Mary said, "I think I can manage this at home." And eventually, she was able to get his BP down to 110/80.

During the next phone call, Mary told Dr. Graziani, "He's been itching at the top of his head and on his arms, as well as having the trunk spasms."

"Mary," Dr. Graziani said, "he may be having intrathecal baclofen withdrawal. You need to start him on oral baclofen, 20mg every two to three hours, as long as he tolerates it. So that would be at 12:30 a.m., 2:30 a.m., and 5:30 a.m." Mary administered the baclofen as directed.

At 7 a.m., JoAnn came on duty. By mid-morning she was having difficulty controlling Alex's blood pressure. She called Dr. Graziani, who at this point insisted that he go to the ER. JoAnn called 911 for an ambulance to take Alex to Seaside Hospital. I drove separately in my car.

When I walked into Seaside's ER, I was told to go back to the small treatment areas, with a bed in each and curtains used as partitions. There I found Alex, who was already being hooked up to monitors. They had changed his leg bag into a night bag. He looked worried.

"Hi. Have you seen anyone yet?" I asked.

"No. Not yet."

"How's your BP?" I asked.

"Gail, it's all over the place. I don't know what's wrong with me."

"Maybe you have a urinary tract infection?"

"I really don't think so," he said. "But they are doing a urinalysis. They are also going to scan my bowels to see if I have an impaction."

The standard rule is, blood work, urinalysis, bowels. Check those three things first. Because in a quadriplegic, it's usually one of them. That was why Alex also had to be strict with his bowel medication: Senna for pushing and emptying, Colace for softening if needed, and Metamucil to add bulk.

By the time he went for testing, it was about 2:30 in the afternoon.

The hospital nurse walked in and said, "So far, you only have a small UTI." I thought, *a small UTI doesn't cause head itching*, but I kept my mouth shut. She continued, "We're going to take you for an X-ray to check on the integrity of the catheter, as requested by your doctor."

I said, "Alex, I'm going to have to pick the kids up from school soon, will you be OK?"

"Don't worry about me, Gail. Just get the kids and tell them I'll probably be home tonight, and that I love them."

"I will." I kissed him goodbye, said goodbye to JoAnn, and went to get the kids. Adam was a freshman at Mainland High and Danielle was at Belhaven Middle School. Every year, I wondered if Alex was going to make it through to see his kids reach their milestones. I was waiting on death. It always seemed to be lurking around corners, getting ready to pounce. I was living with it, and no matter how often I felt its presence, I knew there was no preparing for it.

The isolation of feeling that death was not far off in the future made me realize that some of the people I could relate to were those in physical trouble, or those with loved ones in some kind of physical or emotional crisis. The rest of the world looked happy, from where I stood. I knew it wasn't true, but most people seemed to have a handle on things. At least they got to make plans.

I thought Alex would be coming home within a few hours, but that didn't happen. It was Friday afternoon, and when I called to see what was going on at the hospital, I was stunned. The nurse had put Valium in Alex's IV to bring his pressure down. They had refused to give him his nitropaste. When he was telling one nurse what to do with his blood pressure, she walked away.

"God damn it, I know my body, I know what I need," he had said.

"I will not be spoken to like that," she had replied, and she left him with a BP hovering near 250/ 140.

I called Christina. "Hi, Alex is in the hospital, they don't know what's wrong with him, and his blood pressure is fluctuating and not responding to any medication. Adam is out to dinner with Dori and his mom for Dori's birthday, and he is going to sleep over at their house tonight. I know it's getting late, but is there any way you could come over a little later and stay with Danielle?"

"Of course," she said immediately. "Do you want me to come over now?"

"I'm going to go back to the hospital in about an hour. Could you come then?"

"Absolutely."

"Thank you so much."

"Gail, you don't have to thank me."

I had fed Danielle, and she had assumed her position on the couch in front of the television. Then Christina came over and I left for the hospital.

When I arrived, Alex had been transferred to a private room. His nurse Karen, who was always on the nighttime shift, was sitting in a chair reading the notes. I could see Alex's spasms from the doorway as I walked in.

"Hi," I said. "How are things going?"

"Not good," Alex responded.

"Looks like you have a few tremors leftover from an earthquake," I said.

"They don't know what's wrong. They wouldn't give me my Metamucil, so if I'm backed up it's going to get worse."

I looked at the monitor. His heart rate was up to 130 and climbing. I knew that it shouldn't have been higher than 100. His blood pressure was still very high.

"Did they put nitropaste on you?" I asked.

"Yes, then I bottomed out. The nurse in the ER was a bitch. She left me there with nitropaste on my head. What kind of nurse does that? Thank God JoAnn was there to wipe it off. Where are the kids?" he asked.

"Adam is with Dori, Danielle is watching TV and Christina is watching Danielle. Have you been seen by a doctor?"

"Yeah, the ER doctor. I asked him if he knew what autonomic dysreflexia was, and he said yes. I didn't believe him, I asked him what it was and he got irate."

"You're questioning his knowledge as a doctor; he was pissed."

"If I didn't question what the people around me did, I would be dead already."

I looked at the monitor again. Everything was going up. His heart rate was at 150, and his BP 260/130.

"Your pressure is way up. Shouldn't you put the nitropaste on?"

"I can't. I can't take any medication from home, now that they've admitted me. Now, they have to order everything from their pharmacy, and I have to wait for it to come."

"Did you call Dr. Graziani?"

"Yes. Since she's not on staff here, she is talking to Dr. Gualtieri."

Alex had two hot female doctors- one a beautiful Latin American, and the other a beautiful Italian with a pale, creamy complexion and pale blue-green eyes. They both had great bodies, and no matter how sick Alex was, even if he was at death's door, he always made an inappropriate comment, such as, "Look at how pretty my doctor is, Gail."

I would reply, "You're a lucky guy, Alex, you're always surrounded by sugar."

Now, a nurse hurried in with a sense of urgency. She had seen the monitors from the nursing station.

"Hello Mr. Kiejdan. I can see we are having some blood pressure problems. Have you had this before?"

"Yes," he said. "I've been getting spasms a lot lately, which sets my blood pressure off."

"Well, I spoke with Dr. Gualtieri, and she said that she had already called in all the tests that needed to be done and everything has come back negative so far. I'm going to give you another shot of Valium, maybe that will bring down the BP."

I threw my coat over a chair and pulled it up to the bed. I put my hand on Alex's arm and began to stroke it gently. I thought this might calm him a bit, but it did not. For the next few hours, as his blood pressure and heart rate rose to frightening new levels, the nurse vigilantly worked to bring it down.

"I need my nitropaste," Alex kept insisting.

"I can't give you nitropaste right now." She buzzed the nurse's station and said, "I need you to get in touch with his urologist."

"It's Schutz, Mike is my urologist."

"He's not on call tonight," she responded. "His partner is."

The phone rang, and it was Dr. Schutz's partner. The nurse explained the problem she was having with Alex's blood pressure and heart rate. His spasms were completely out of control, and I had a horrible feeling that there was no one here to help him. There wasn't a doctor on the floor, and this poor nurse was doing her damnedest to keep him alive.

When she got off the phone, she said the doctor was going to come in and see what he could figure out.

It didn't take him long to arrive, given the fact that we lived in Tiny-Town.

"Hello Alex," he said, "I hear you're having some problems, and I can see by the monitor that we need to stabilize your BP."

The nurse interjected, "I have been trying for hours to bring his BP down. We did a scan. He's not impacted."

As the doctor was listening he was putting on gloves. He reached under the white blanket and went in for some personal information with his finger. Then he felt Alex's abdomen and looked at his super-pubic. He could see the spasms, but he didn't seem concerned about them.

"No hemorrhoids, your catheter seems fine, your urinalysis was normal, I really don't know what's wrong, but I'm pretty sure it's out of my domain."

There it was in a nutshell. Specialization. If it's not your area of expertise, than you're shit out of luck. "Although," he continued, "I did recently read in a medical journal that belladonna suppositories could help with phantom pain. They have been using it in patients such as yourself. I know it will most likely help with your spasms, and hence bring your pressures down. I'll order you the suppositories from the hospital pharmacy." He snapped his gloves off and threw them in the wastebasket.

They did not have the suppositories in the pharmacy, and the pharmacist went above and beyond by going out and picking them up at CVS. By the time Alex got his suppository, it was after midnight.

I called Christina to let her know that I didn't think I would be back and to ask if she would sleep over with Danielle.

"Whatever you need, Gail. I'm here."

"Thank you again, I really appreciate it."

"Don't thank me. Please give Alex my love."

"I will."

By 2 a.m., the belladonna, the Valium, the extra baclofen, and the baclofen from his pump were all circulating in Alex's system. His spasms were gone, and he fell asleep. I looked at the monitors, which told me that at this point, I could stop worrying. Since the beginning of his injury I had learned to self-soothe by breathing. I began to do it. Breathe in, breathe out, I told myself. Breathe in, breathe out.

By 3:30 a.m. I thought I should go home. "Karen, I'm going to go home to get a few hours' sleep. I'll be back in the morning."

She looked at me and smiled. "I think that's a good idea."

I got home at around 4 a.m. Christina was sleeping on the couch. She was a professional worrier, but she was hiding it well. It was dark in the house, but I tried to be quiet so as to not wake her. Danielle was in bed, and once she fell asleep, the rest of the world could explode and not wake her.

Christina woke up and saw me. "How is he doing?"

I told her about Alex's ordeal. "Oh God, Gail. I'm so sorry. What else can I do?"

"You did it. You stayed with Danielle. You have no idea how much I appreciate it."

"Don't be absurd, I will do whatever you need."

She got up, we hugged and kissed each other goodbye, and she went home. Fortunately, she only lived a block away. I went upstairs and took a quick shower, feeling the numbness rinse over me like the water. When I was done, I climbed into bed and slept for a couple of hours.

The next morning, a Saturday, I got up early. Danielle had a bat mitzvah to go to. I made her breakfast and arranged for her to be picked up and returned. After all, what better excuse to get out of a carpool than "my husband's in the hospital?" It was right up there with handicapped parking. One must look for even the smallest perks in life.

I threw on clothes and was putting on my shoes when the phone rang. I thought about ignoring it, but then thought it could be Alex, so I picked it up in the kitchen. It was not Alex. It was Dr. Gualtieri,

"Mrs. Kiejdan?" she asked. "This is Dr. Gualtieri."

I just want you to know that Mr. Kiejdan had a very, very, bad night. I just spoke with the nighttime nurse and I'm heading over there now. I really am so sorry to tell you this, but Mr. Kiejdan is very, very, sick. He's in grave condition. I really don't know what happened yet."

"Well, I was there until 3:30 a.m., when he seemed to stabilize. I'm heading over there now, too. I will see you at the hospital."

I jumped in my car and headed to the hospital. I called Gary and Andrea and Andrea picked up the phone. I had Bluetooth, so she was on speaker.

"Andrea, I just got off the phone with Alex's doctor and she said he's in grave condition. I'm flipping out."

"What! What happened?"

"Well, after I spoke to you last night, his heart rate went up to near 200."

"Oh my God, was it a sustained heart rate?"

"I don't know. All I know is things aren't looking good."

"Gail, just focus on your driving and call me when you find out what's going on." After that I called Robert and Christina. By the time I made it up to his room I had the runs and bee-lined it for the bathroom. Shit! Literally. From there, I went to Alex's room.

I was greeted at the door by a cardiologist whom I hadn't met.

"Mrs. Kiejdan?"

"Yes," I responded.

"I am so sorry. I really don't think he is going to make it."

I was stunned into silence. I looked passed him. Alex was surrounded by Dr. Graziani and Dr. Gualtieri, and I was half expecting him to be dead.

When I reached his bedside he looked at me and said, "Hey Gail, don't I have two of the hottest doctors?"

"Yes you do, Alex,"

"Dr. G., show Gail your shoes."

Definitely not dead. Even on his way out, his libido was intact.

I looked at Dr. Graziani's shoes, which were an expensive pair of ankle-height cowboy boots with beautiful hand-stitched detailing.

"Love them," I said. *Am I really talking about shoes when my husband is at death's door? Absolutely.*

Dr. Graziani had driven down from Villanova to see what she could do to help. Dr. Gualtieri began. "Last night, Alex's blood pressure went from one extreme to another," she said with her Latin American accent. "I'm afraid this morning his BP has bottomed out. Now it has dropped to a systolic of 50 and a diastolic of 39. This is very dangerous. We have run all the tests, and have not come up with anything."

I was nauseous. Historically, the first thing to go when my nerves are fried is my stomach.

"Well, since we're in the hospital, does anyone have anything for nausea and bowels doing the thirty-meter dash?"

"Yes, I will find you something to settle your stomach," Dr. Gualtieri said. Within seconds she brought me a liquid cup of crème de menthe-flavored Maalox.

"Thank you," I said, "Cheers!" And I chugged it like a shot of tequila.

"Maybe it's gas?" offered Dr. Gualtieri.

"The best way to figure that out," I said, "is to didge him like they do every morning."

So that is what the nurse did. They turned him over and didged him. The gas came out but it did not change his blood pressure much. It went up a little from the manual stimulation, but then he bottomed out again.

Either way, Alex was still able to talk. "Gail," he said under his breath, "you have to get me out of here. I am going to die here."

I nodded in total agreement. "I'll be right back."

I walked into the waiting area and found Robert there with Christina and Gary.

"How is he doing?" Robert asked.

"Not good." By then it was almost 11 a.m. "I have to get the kids over here to say goodbye. I'm also going to call Swarna."

I used my cell to call Adam to come to the hospital. He was still with Dori, and Swarna said she would pick up Danielle and bring them all to the hospital.

When they arrived, Swarna said," Gail, why didn't you call me last night?"

"It was Dori's birthday, I knew you were out to dinner and I didn't want to bother you."

Swarna, who was Sri Lankan, always repeated what you said to her to make sure she was 100 percent accurate. I appreciated this, because often I could not understand doctors from foreign countries; their accents were sometimes heavy and miscommunication was unavoidable.

Swarna looked at Alex's charts and walked over to me. "He needs to go to Philadelphia, Gail. I am going to try and get him on a helicopter to either Jefferson or Presbyterian."

She went to work the phones, while I waited with Alex and the kids.

"Guys, why don't you say goodbye to Daddy. We are trying to get him out to go to Philly."

One by one, they kissed him goodbye and told them they loved him. First Adam, who said, "Love you dad," then Dori, who said, "I love you Mr. K.," and then Danielle, who said, "I love you so much, Daddy."

I could see the tears welling in Alex's eyes. Then Robert came in and said goodbye, and so did Gary and Christina. At this point, they wanted to put a port in Alex so he could be transferred. Dr. Graziani had called the neurosurgeon Dr. Strenger to see if this was intrathecal baclofen withdrawal, but after Dr. Strenger had evaluated him, he said the pump seemed to be in place.

Death was lurking again. A doctor had just given me his condolences. I had just told the kids to say goodbye to their dad, and both Alex and I were thinking it was for the last time.

Then I felt someone tug at my sleeve. It was Swarna.

"Gail, they wouldn't take him at Jefferson, I think their beds are full, so I got him into Presbyterian. I know the cardiologist there, he is very good. I want Alex to go now, because he is somewhat stable. I don't know what can happen in the next hour or so. His heart has been through a lot. I don't know what kind of damage has happened. So, after they stabilize him, I would like him to get a cardiac catheterization."

"Thank you, Swarna," I said. "Thank you for bringing the kids to the hospital. And thank you for getting Alex on that transport."

"It is no problem, Gail. I hope you don't mind that I brought Dori. Alex is very important to him."

"Dori is important to Alex too." I hugged her, and the kids left with her.

I looked at Alex, not knowing whether I was going to see him again. "I love you," I said.

"I love you too," he responded.

243

I kissed him and hugged him. "I'll be up there in a little bit. I just have to go home and pack a bag."

He looked frightened. I had not seen that look in a long time. It had taken him years, but he had tried to seize control of this injury by being the sole proprietor of his body, even with a non-stop cycle of nursing by different nurses, some better than others.

I picked up my purse, and threw on my coat and headed out to the waiting room.

"What are you going to do?" asked Christina.

"I'm going to go up to the hospital. I have to go home and pack an overnight bag." I turned to Robert. "Robert, do you think Fern could spend the night with the kids?"

"I'm sure she can. I'll call her right now."

I hugged Gary and Christina. And I could tell by the looks on their faces that they could see my world crumbling.

When I got home, I went into our closet to pick out some clothes to pack. I looked at the accessible shelving that I had put in and thought *he's never going to wear these clothes again. He's never going to be in this house again.* I was feeling a pre-widow angst. Then I thought, *so I guess Alex is going first, and then my mom.* There had been times when I thought it would be my mom first. But now, I wasn't sure.

Robert was going to pick me up shortly and take me up to the hospital, but I felt I was leaving my body again, and I was watching myself from the outside. I had a few phone calls to make. I called Andrea and Gary and asked them to call my mom and tell her what was going on. Then Robert honked the horn, and I got in the car to head up to Philadelphia.

On the way up I said to Robert, "I have to call your mom and let her know what is going on." Molly and Bogie were in Florida.

"Do you want me to do it?" he asked.

"No. It's better if I do." So I called Molly from my cell, and when Bogie answered the phone I tried to calm my voice. Do you come out and tell an 83-year-old woman her son is dying? No. *What the hell am I going to say?* The phone rang as I prepared myself to….just tell the truth. "Hi Bogie, it's Gail. Is Molly there?"

"One moment," she said in broken English.

Molly came to the phone and said, "Vhat goes on, Gail?"

"Molly, I just wanted to let you know that last night Alex had a very bad night. His blood pressure was all over the place and they couldn't stabilize him. It doesn't look good, so they put him on a helicopter to Philadelphia."

"Oh Mine God," she said. "Oh mine God. Where are you?"

"I'm in the car with Robert, he's driving up with me to the hospital."

"Vhat hospital?"

"Presbyterian."

"I'll come home. Call me ven you know vhat's happening."

"I will."

25. MOLLY 101

By the time Robert and I got to Presbyterian Hospital it was late afternoon. We found our way to Alex's room in the cardiac unit and were told to put on cover garments and a mask. His room was sealed with a glass wall and a door looking out to the nurse's station. He was sleeping. I immediately looked at the monitor. His blood pressure was stable, but low. Whatever they had done in the time it took us to get there, it worked.

Robert and I pulled two chairs around Alex's bed. He opened his eyes and went back to sleep. We both watched him sleep for a while. Around dinnertime, Alex's nephew Sid and his wife Stav stopped by. They lived in Philadelphia and both were physicians at Jefferson Hospital. I remembered what my mother always said: "Good news travels fast, bad news travels faster."

We stepped outside the room to greet them, as Stav was reading Alex's chart.

"Hey, how is he doing?" Sid asked.

"He's stable right now," I responded.

"We brought you guys something to eat," Stav said.

They had brought two large bags filled with Greek food. Stav was originally from Greece, so she knew her way around a good spanakopita and horta vrasta. But all of this was over the top.

"Wow. That is so nice of you! Thank you so much." I hugged them both.

"You don't have to thank us, Gail. Where are you staying tonight?" Sid asked.

"I have no clue. I packed a bag and just left."

"Stay with us," Stav insisted. "We have a blow-up mattress. We'll take you to our apartment and you can walk from there back to the hospital, or Sid can give you a ride in the morning."

"Oh my God," I said. "That would be perfect. Thank you so much."

Robert said, "I'm going to drive home tonight, Gail. I'll be back tomorrow."

"Okay, Robert. Thank you for everything."

"You don't have to thank me, Gail."

"Yes I do."

When I came back from Sid and Stav's the next day, Alex was awake and alert. I kissed him hello. The first words out of his mouth were, "Gail, on the helicopter ride up, I felt like I was fading, like I was really on my way out, and you know I was OK with it, and honestly, I don't think I would have lived had I not been greeted by the most beautiful nurse at the helipad. I was ready for all this to be over, I'm sick of it, but this nurse, she was so magnificent. I know I'm shallow, but, I couldn't do it. She kept saying, 'Stay with us, Alex.' And all I wanted to do was to stay with her. Her beauty kept me alive. I swear."

I chuckled to myself, knowing that when it came to women, the water didn't even reach his ankles.

Later that night, when I was back at home, I received a phone call from Molly.

"I'm home," she said. "Will you take me to the hospital tomorrow?"

"Of course, Molly. I was planning on going in the morning after I take the kids to school, Alex is having a cardiac catheterization tomorrow, I don't think it will be until around 11 a.m."

"That's fine; pick me up at 9:30."

When I picked Molly up, her hair was done and she was wearing bright pink lipstick. She always dressed well when she left her house. And she always wore an abundance of jewelry. She was smaller than I remembered. Aging does that to you. Her petite frame made its way to my car, and no matter her size, you couldn't underestimate the lifetime of toughness that came with it. She had survived the Holocaust, after all.

She got in the car and I kissed her. "Hello," I said.

"Hello." She always said hello, but rarely said, "How are you?" The pleasantries were not a part of her vernacular.

I backed out of the driveway and headed down the street towards the NJ Parkway.

"Tell me, Gail," she started. "How did Alex get to Philadelphia?"

"They had to fly him in a helicopter. They only had a small window, because they couldn't predict what was going to happen with his blood pressure."

"Who is going to pay for it?"

Wow. Front and center. Nice jab.

"Molly, I don't know. I don't think anyone was asking that question, they were just trying to save his life."

Silence.

"Vhy is he getting the heart test?"

"Because his cardiologist is afraid that after everything that happened, he might have sustained some damage to his heart."

As I turned on to the parkway entrance she began her story…one that she had told me before. But war stories don't get old, and neither does the memory of them. They were painfully seared in place.

"You know during the war I was with Pina. We had left the barn because the Russians were coming; I said 'Let's get out of here, they're going to kill us here,' so we went to a Jewish cemetery. We went way, way back up to the hill and we laid there for two days. It was quiet, and then I asked a peasant woman to give me a piece of bread, I said, 'he's sick and he has to eat.' She said, 'I didn't know you were Jewish. You speak such good Polish. You don't have an accent.' I was educated in their schools. No one knew I was Jewish because I spoke with a perfect Polish accent…" She looked out of the window as her voice trailed off. Then she began again, but she and Pincus were somewhere else.

"We jumped from a window, we jumped on to dead people. Everybody was dead. The whole camp was dead. And then we escaped the camps. We were hiding in a basement, my uncle Joseph, he was there, he made a hiding place. He made a false wall. We smeared it with our waste. The stones are still there. When they came to look for us, they couldn't take the smell, and they left. March 27th, they killed the children. In June or July they came to shoot us. Everywhere was machine guns. July 27th, no, April 27th, 1944. And still the war was going on in Germany. We were liberated in '44 by the Russians. They were liberated in May '45. What do you kids know? Nothing." She trailed off again, and the car was quiet. "I tell you something," she began. "I gave a Gentile woman a ring, a wedding ring. I told her you walk ahead of us, if dey ask for papers

I'm going to turn around and go back, you know. And she went ahead, and dey didn't look for papers, so I gave Pina a shovel. His head was shaved, so he had to have a hat on his head. And as we walked there were tanks, machine guns, everything. I wore a peasant skirt, a crocheted skirt and boots, and I looked like a peasant. I walked on the sidewalk. I walked to my house for miles. I thought let's go in my neighbor's house. When I walked in there, there was SS laying all over there. Just go straight, I said to Pina. Make believe nothing. The SS didn't bother us and we went to the field out to the river, and next to the river my teacher had a house. And I went into my teacher's house and she said I'll feed you. So she gave us food. She fed us. But she said you cannot stay here because the Germans told everybody to evacuate. You know what I did? I turned from her house. There was a gate by the fence. I knew it went to my house. I used to live there. First we went out onto the balcony in my house. Everything was burning around us. The fences, everything. I said Pina, let's go hide in the hole in the ground. There was a gate by the garden and I went into the garden. There's a hole dere. So we went to lay down, and two women came there, and we all laid down. And then the Russians came in and we thought we were liberated. And we got up, and I said in Russian, 'we are live people.' And the Russians said sit, sit, we won't bother you. All of sudden we hear boom, boom, boom, boom, boom. And the Germans are back. And the Germans are sitting with us. In the same hole. And one, he was eating sardines, and he said 'here, eat some.' I said 'No. Danka schoen.' And I asked the Germans, 'do you hear the bombs?' 'Yeah, don't worry. It's going to hit further down.' So then I asked the same German, 'please, I have a bunker in there. Can I go in my bunker? It's an ice cellar.' I hear them screaming, 'where are the loiter, de loiter?' Loiter is people. And then he says before that, 'petera, papers, petera.' Vas is das? So, the Polish woman says to him, their house burnt, 'da pirra in da house, it burnt.' Things were burning, and there was a barn and in the barn there were two floors, one they put in the ice and ice cellar, you go down, and you go down lower yet. I know we had a larder, down there, a root cellar, we used to keep the butter, and the sour cream down there, cabinets were made of metal. That you put in the ice. We had a grocery store. Okay? So, we went in there, and from there we went into the ice cellar. They didn't know that in the floor, in the floor there were cement flaps that cover the floor. All of sudden I hear, the Germans are screaming, 'A letter to his mother.' The Germans are on top of us. He was wounded, they didn't know that there's a basement there. You understand what I am saying? You pick up with a handle and you cover the cellar, one side there is the ice and a pick, the other side, we had the storage. They were laying down screaming, and all of sudden it was quiet. We went up from the cellar, and I stuck my head out, just my head. And I saw the Russians were walking the streets with machine guns. I saw a dead cow, and a dead horse, we used to have gates, big gates, so I stuck my head out and I saw everything that goes on. Pina says to me 'we can out.' And I say 'un-un, Pina, I'm not going.' And then I said 'Pina, I'm not going to the city. I'm going back. The Russians are coming there, instead of going to the city, I am going back. Where Russians are coming from.' There was a kitchen there. I asked them for food, they didn't have any food. You know the buckwheat, that's what they ate. They used to eat black kasha, they had a kitchen, I asked a soldier and he pulled out his pocket and said 'that's what I have. Bread crumbs.' They were so good. The people are good. The regime, the government is not, was bad. But the people were good. And they would eat tobacco together with breadcrumbs. They didn't have what to eat too. Then I went back to my house after a few days.

And I went to the neighbor's yard and I pulled up some rhubarb, and I picked some beets from the garden and I found two bricks, and a pot some place, and I made a fire, and put some water on the pot. I made a fire, I washed the beets and rhubarb and I ate dem. Would you do that? Would you understand to do that? No. OK? I saved his life. I hid him. If not for me he'd be dead. He'd have no place to go. Miriam's father in the kitchen he put a separate wall, they used to bring in the pocket bricks. He made a separate wall and they crawled in there. His sister, Miriam, and the other sister. And, the mother jumped the fence, She left everybody to die. Yankel jumped the fence with her. And then after liberation I said 'we are going back to the city,' and the soldiers was still on the mountains the Germans shooting. And I went to the camp, you don't want to know what we found in the camp. I won't tell you. And Jack was standing by the camp, screaming, 'Are you alive? Are you alive?' You know Miriam is alive, and her mother is alive, but I don't know where the father is and the other sister is. The sister was killed by the Germans and the father, they find the father without a head. They cut his head off with a grenade, and Pina's sister was buried someplace out there. That's where we find ourselves, by the camp. Who was alive was alive and who was dead, was dead. That's the story of my life. And we went back to my house. I sold my house. It was a big house. They give me 100 rubles in gold. And I knew what was going to happen. I wasn't going to stay there. You want to buy it? He gave me the gold, 100 rubles, I said to him, I moved away to the city, Vilnius. I lived in the city with how many people in my apartment? Three people, another two people with children, and I stayed in a little room. And then we went to Poland. I was born in Poland, not Lithuania, and from Poland I went to Berlin. And then to Hanover, and then to Bergen-Belsin, a camp. They gave us a mattress from straw, some clothes, some clothes for Michael, and later a room. With a couple blankets. I washed my clothes, whatever little I had. When Riva was liberated from the concentration camp she found out where we were, and came to Bergen-Belsin, from there she took us all to the Swiss border. They have a house where the Germans used. Ven they get wounded, they would stay in dat house. It's like, raverous heim. We lived there for three years. Then we came to the United States. I came to the United States in 1949. Then we ended up on a chicken farm. Yula, Pina's mother, said 'Pina bring the money we bought a chicken farm.' We were the only ones who had money. Bring the money. She took the money, I lived in the attic for three years."

By the time she was finished, we were in Philadelphia and I was pulling in the garage at Presbyterian. I was always fascinated by her stories. She was living history. Her memory was a treasure trove of information. Sometimes the pieces didn't all fit together, but it was her memory.

We stopped at the front desk and asked for Alex's room. He was no longer in CCU. He had been moved down to the surgery floor and from there he would be taken back to a new room. When he was wheeled in, he was still groggy. He opened his eyes and saw his mom.

"Mom, I didn't expect you to come."

"Of course I came," she said as she bent down to kiss him. "How you feeling?"

"Tired."

"I know, I know. Life makes you tired. I'm tired too, mine kin."

253

26. The Debacle

We waited for the doctor and the results of Alex's cardiac cath. Later in the day, Jon Ashner and Mark Dannenbaum stopped by. Jon was down from Boston and these two lifelong friends of Alex's seemed to be filled with trepidation. Alex was lucky, though. After twelve years with this injury, his friends still visited. I was sure that they thought this was *it* for him. *It* had been perched on our shoulders for a very long time. So I understood.

"Hey. What brings you guys here?" Alex said as he perked up. Fake-mode was turned on. When people were around I saw fake-mode, obvious only to me and one other person, Christina.

"Have you seen the doctor?" Mark asked.

"No," I answered.

"Not yet," Alex said.

"Hi Molly, how are you doing?" Jon asked.

"My son's in the hospital, how could I be doing?" she replied.

They hung out for about a half an hour, then Jon said he had to catch a train back to Boston.

They hugged and kissed him and said goodbye.

Within the hour, the doctor stopped by. He introduced himself and said, "Mr. Kiejdan, you are a very lucky man. Most people who went through what you did would have had some damage to their heart. You, amazingly, did not. There were no abnormalities of the coronary arteries and you had a normal ejection fraction and normal left ventricular function. Your heart is very strong. Do you have any questions?"

"Yes," I said. "What caused this?"

"It was caused by autonomic dysreflexia."

Alex and I looked at each other, knowing full well that autonomic dysreflexia was a symptom, not a cause.

"But dysreflexia is a symptom," I said. "A reaction that something is going wrong somewhere in your body. It is the body's response system to a bowel problem, a bladder infection, or some other kind of infection or internal problem that the patient can't feel. It is also a warning system, you know, like…an alarm."

He looked at me and smiled. Not the condescending smile that we had gotten so many times…just a regular smile. "It was from the autonomic dysreflexia," he repeated.

"OK. Thank you so much, doctor."

"You are very welcome." He shook my hand and left.

It was not lost on me that most doctors spoke to me instead of Alex. I wondered if this was common. I wish they had spoken to him and made more eye contact.

They discharged him, and fortunately, he would be home before Thanksgiving.

By the time Alex got home he had begun itching again, and he felt like bugs were crawling all over him. Eileen, his nurse at the time, called Dr. Graziani, who recommended that Alex take 20mg of oral baclofen and 5mg of Valium. His blood pressure continued to go up, as did his heart rate.

Dr. Graziani said, "You need to go to the ER at Liberty Hospital. I am worried that you might be having ITB withdrawal."

We were supposed to go to Robert and Fern's for Thanksgiving. I went downstairs and told the kids. "Look, we have to go back to the hospital. Something is still wrong with Daddy. I called Aunt Fern and you guys are going to go there without us."

"We don't want to go without you," Danielle responded.

"Can't we just stay home?" Adam asked.

"It's Thanksgiving. You should have turkey. Uncle Robert will pick you up around 4:00. And, I will call you from the hospital when I know anything."

Alex was itching like a man who wanted to rip his skin off. Eileen got him ready and I switched the car seat over in the van so she could drive up to Philadelphia. They really didn't want to admit him because it was Thanksgiving. But not everyone can avoid the hospital on a holiday. Note to the uninformed: Do not go to a hospital on a holiday or holiday weekend. Short-staffed, no doctors, just residents; that is what you will find. Patient care over the phone is to be expected.

After they admitted him to Liberty Hospital, we waited. And as far as I was concerned, it was too dangerous to take him back home. He was unstable and it was unmanageable.

Dr. Graziani had called and spoke with a neurosurgical resident, and told him to look for ITB withdrawal. After Alex was situated in his room, he said, "Gail, go home. It's Thanksgiving. Go be with the kids. But before you go, can you just scratch my head and my arms, your nails are better than mine."

So I started to scratch—"harder" he said—and scratch—"my neck," he said. I worked my way around: "top of the head, yeah, that helps." All the topical creams in the world could not help him.

"Can you just give me the buzzer, I need the nurse, I can't take this." He rang the nurse. Eileen and I waited until the nurse arrived, and then I kissed him goodbye in the hope that I could spend a little time with the kids on Thanksgiving.

"I love you," I said. "I'll be back tomorrow."

"I love you too," he said. Then Eileen and I headed for the door.

That night they had to give Alex an IV with morphine, to help with his itching. The next afternoon, when I walked into his room, he had a frightening look on his face. He was in bed and his electric wheelchair was in the corner. His eyes were popping out of his head, like someone who was deranged. He was an animal caught in a trap, agitated and angry.

"Hi," I said with trepidation.

He started with, "You wouldn't believe what assholes they are here."

"What happened?" I looked at his monitor and noted to myself that his blood pressure was moderate and his heart rate was normal.

"First of all, let me say that my nurses are beautiful. I told them they were beautiful and I think I scared them. All I did was ask, 'Are you wearing a thong?' I said my wife wears them."

"Maybe that was a bit inappropriate, Alex."

"I told her she was beautiful. There are two of them that are beautiful. But I think they're a little green. They seem new to me. Like they're still in training. But after one of them put me on the pot, she left without didging me. I couldn't go. So I asked her to didge me and she said, 'We don't do that here.' What the fuck is that?"

"OK. Calm down," I said. "Did they run any tests on you?"

"Yeah, they did a nuclear study."

"Did they find anything?"

"I don't know."

"What tests are next?" I found that changing the subject helped to defuse the situation. I couldn't pinpoint it, but there was something really wrong with him, and it had nothing to do with blood pressure or heart rate. I knew they were trying to get to the bottom of the labile BP, and the heart rate problem, through a whole workup.

"I'm scheduled to see a gastroenterologist and a urologist, and someone from rehab. My neurosurgeon was here early this morning but he didn't stay because I was in the bathroom. He said he would come back. Fred and Mindy were here earlier. Fred gave me the name of the COO. He told me to use it if I needed anything. And I'm going to use it. How can they not didge me? That's just wrong. My blood pressure could go through the roof from not going to the bathroom." His voice was escalating, and the wild look in his eyes was scaring me.

I said it again: "Alex, please calm down." There was no reaching him.

Just then one of the nurses walked in. She was very young and beautiful, with shiny dark hair and a dark almost Indonesian complexion. She was also very uncomfortable.

"This is my wife" Alex said as he introduced us.

"It's nice to meet you," I said. "What kind of medication has he had today?"

"He had morphine last night, he had a shot of Valium, he had his belladonna suppository this morning and he is on 20mg of baclofen every four hours," she responded.

Disregarding the conversation completely, Alex said, "Isn't she pretty? I told you my wife was pretty." I thought if he could have gotten out of bed he would climb the walls.

She left as quickly and quietly as she came in.

"Are you hungry?" I asked. "I could pick up a falafel for you; there is a great falafel place around the corner."

"Oh, yes. I need to eat something decent. The food sucks in here."

"Well, it is hospital food," I responded.

"I love cafeteria food," he said. "I love the overcooked green beans from a can. I love the mashed potatoes from a box, with the canned gravy. I just can't eat that crap right now."

"OK, let me run out and get you something to eat."

"Can you bring me back a Diet Pepsi too?"

"Yes, I can do that."

What transpired while I was gone was something that I could never have imagined happening. Liberty Hospital had a reputation as being one of the top medical facilities in Philadelphia, and to this day it still is. But even in the best of facilities, things can go wrong if no one is reading the signs, or the charts. And between Alex's threats of calling the COO, so he could get didged by a nurse, and his overall manic behavior, I knew in my gut that something was wrong with him. By the time I returned with the food, he was quiet and in tears.

"What happened?" I implored.

"My neurosurgeon came back. He shut the door behind him. I thought he was going to examine me. But he didn't. He yelled at me and said that he had never seen such bad behavior in a patient. That he never should have let me be admitted. And that it was a mistake and he was kicking me out. I have to leave by tomorrow morning."

"But what about the rest of your tests?" I asked incredulously.

"He said I could get them done somewhere else. He also said that my nuclear tests were normal, the pump he had put in was fine, just as he suspected. And then he went on to say that I had insulted his nurses, and behaved like an animal, and I was not welcome back at this hospital."

I gave him a hug, and sat down on the hospital bed. "Alex, we will figure this out. I don't know how, but we will." I pulled the rolling table over his bed and put the food down on it.

"I'm not hungry," he said. "He scared me. I couldn't speak. I couldn't answer him. I don't know what I did," he said with tears in his eyes.

"I have never in my life heard of a doctor yelling at a patient, let alone kicking him out," I said.

"I guess I have to call Dr. Graziani, and tell her what is going on," he said.

"Let me call Robert, maybe he can pick you up in your van in the morning."

When Robert picked Alex up in the morning, he made sure to sign a complaint that his brother was being released against his wishes. It went nowhere.

After the debacle at Liberty Hospital, Dr. Graziani decided to do the necessary testing from home. It was up to Alex's nurses to keep him stable with Valium, an extra 20mgs of baclofen and BNO, the belladonna suppository, if needed. Alex was drugged most of the day and night, and took long naps. When he was awake, he was pretty oblivious to our daily life. For months I continued with life and this new normal, pretending that everything was fine.

In the meantime, Danielle had started to ask for a dog. She begged and pleaded, and I told her, "I am not emotionally or physically capable of taking care of a puppy right now."

"Mom," she said, "I will do all of the work. I need a dog. I will give him a bath, feed him, walk him, anything he needs. I will take care of everything."

"Danielle, a dog is a lot of work, especially a puppy. You're in school all day. You have no idea what you're asking of me. I don't think I can handle a dog on top of everything else."

She didn't hear one word. "You can get one for Hanukkah and it will be our Hanukkah present."

"So now you're saying that Adam wants one too?"

She nodded. "Adam wants a dog, Mom, he's just not as vocal."

I knew in my heart that getting a dog in our situation was probably a step closer to insanity. But sometimes you just need to add a little crazy to the chaos for things to make sense.

Christina was on Danielle's side. She had been begging me for a couple of years to get another dog. But I was in over my head. When would I ever not be in over my head?

Danielle continued her negotiating tactics. "Mom, you grew up with a dog, didn't you?"

"Yes, Danielle, I did."

"How could you not want me to have that same childhood experience? Besides, I know you don't believe that I will take care of it, so here's a contract that I wrote up. It says right here in writing that I will fully take care of the dog."

She was good. I began to look online for dogs. We needed a lap dog, so the dog could sit on Alex's lap. I also thought that if by some chance Danielle bailed on her promise, it would be less excrement to clean up. Adam was allergic to so much that the dog had to be hypoallergenic. That narrowed the field.

I had settled on a Maltese when I saw these two adorable pups up the street at our neighbor's. Small, white and fluffy. I began to make phone calls. By the time Hanukkah arrived I had found a male Maltese puppy who was a couple of months old and would be ready to be picked up by Christmas time.

"When was he born?" I asked.

"September 2nd," the breeder responded. That was the date of Alex's accident. A year didn't go by when we felt the shivers of change down our backs. But this was a sign. This was supposed to be our dog. He was going to change that day into something besides negative reminiscing. He was going to make it a celebration of life. It was perfect.

We would visit my family for the holidays and pick the dog up on the way home. The breeder lived in Stroudsburg, Pennsylvania and told me the dog was priced to sell.

"Why?" I asked.

"Because I'm just selling him for a friend. He's not one of mine. My dogs are beautiful; Google me and you will see a picture of the dogs I breed."

And so I did. The dog in the photo was perfect. He showed me a picture of the dog I was about to buy and I saw the difference.

Did I care? Absolutely not. You love what you get. His snooty voice was not lost on me, but I needed a male Maltese by the holidays so I agreed to pick him up after Christmas on our way back from Cleveland, and his name was going to be Riley.

After the Christmas holiday came and went, I drove with the kids and picked up our new puppy. He was as feisty as he had been described, and loving and adorable. We all fell in love with him, as he refocused the family's attention to him. The injury still loomed large, but our new little fluff ball loomed larger.

27. TREADING WATER

In the next few weeks Alex was hospitalized three more times for abdominal spasms, itching and labile blood pressure. At that point Dr. Graziani said, "I realize that the opinion is that it is not the baclofen pump, but what they teach us in medical school when we are learning about the pump is that if the problem continues to occur and there are no other answers, it's the pump. Alex, I think you need to have the catheter to the pump changed. I spoke with Dr. Strenger and he agreed, along with Dr. Hooper."

Alex's response was, "I can't take this anymore, I don't want to live like this."

So in February, Alex had his catheter replaced at Seaside Hospital. The catheter is a thin tube the size of an ink chamber inside a pen, except for the fact that it is soft and malleable. It stretched from the pump in front of his lower right abdomen and was fed up through the cerebral spinal fluid to an area where the medicine was released every several hours.

I sat by myself in the surgical waiting room, feeling jittery. This time there was no autopilot. I had no idea why. I picked up a magazine and started reading. Then I put it down. Then I picked up again. Christina called to check up on me.

"It's a waiting game, nothing is new, until I see the doctor." I looked up. Robert and Fern had walked in. "Robert and Fern are here. Let me call you back when I know something."

I stood up, "What are you guys doing here? Fern, it's your birthday, you shouldn't be in the hospital. You should be going out to dinner." It was 6:30 p.m.

"Birthdays are no big deal anymore, Gail," she responded in a low undertone.

"You guys are gold. Thank you."

By the time Dr. Strenger came out, another hour-and-a-half had passed. He walked right over to me and shook my hand. We had not met before and I truly appreciated his decorum.

"Everything went fine," he started. External sigh, from me. Robert and Fern moved in closer. "I will tell you, I did find a significant kink at one of the connectors. I don't know for certain if that what was causing the withdrawal-like symptoms, but it could certainly be a contributing factor. I replaced the catheter with one that doesn't have connectors. It is continuous line, so hopefully these symptoms will abate. Do you have any questions?"

"When will he be able to go home?"

"He can probably go home tomorrow if he does well overnight."

The next morning I came to the hospital with Alex's nurse, Michael D., who would help to take Alex home. Alex's body was bruised. He had black and blue marks with a few yellow patches.

"What happened? Did they drop you?"

"I don't know, maybe it happened while I was under anesthesia. Plus, I can't feel anything anyway." By the time we got home, his lower right tibia area was swollen and discolored. We would soon find out that it was fractured. That particular tibia would be fractured in three more incidents. It would turn into a major source of arthritic pain and discomfort. The problem of feeling only pain magnified yet again.

I focused on Adam's crew schedule: crew meetings every Tuesday night, and carpooling every day. I also shuffled Danielle back and forth to synagogue so she could continue to prepare for her bat mitzvah, which was in April. My mother was getting progressively worse, so I knew in my heart that she would not make it to the beautiful religious affirmation of Danielle becoming a woman. I kept wondering, *who is going to go first?* I was in constant preparation to lose someone I loved, and I carried it around my neck like an albatross. I made an appointment with the florist, and the caterer. I called the DJ that we'd used for Adam's bar mitzvah, and I began to get the list together. I was not concerned with the details that every other Jewish mom frets about. It was just something else to get through.

Danielle, though, was very specific. She wanted a cake with fondant frosting, and an entertainment booth where they could do something fun. I hired dancers, and used an entertainment company so the kids could make their own CDs. Then I had to order gifts for the kids to take home. I went up to Cherry Hill to pick out the menu—Danielle had decided on a Hollywood theme. I ordered life-size cardboard cutouts of her favorite actors, and named the tables after them.

It was the beginning of spring, and I spent every Sunday at the Schuylkill River in Philadelphia. Adam rowed in the freshman boat. It wasn't the Freshman Eight, the top freshman boat, but the work was every bit as difficult. Crew was all-consuming, and I was in awe of those who ran the program. It was a program funded and supported by the parents, and they were committed. Everyone got a major assignment, from storing and cleaning the trailer where all the food and supplies were kept, to shopping for the food at Sam's Warehouse, to selling the uniforms, sweatshirts, T-shirts, and sweat pants. All I could do was manage to bake banana bread every week. I felt the ugly rearing of Jewish guilt telling me that I wasn't doing enough.

In our house, we were used to swinging from tree to tree, or maybe it was from hospital to hospital. Alex couldn't go to the races because his body, which had been stabilized, was floating in and out of a drug-fueled haze.

"He is on the baclofen titty," I would joke, but I had no idea how long it was going to last.

It would go on for a total of six years. Thank God for living in the present. I was far from Zen, but thinking about the future did me no good. I would listen to the conversations of those around me discussing their travel plans, and their family plans. I would smile and nod. But I felt that I had a cloak of invisibility wrapped around me.

Where did I go? The only places I went were the hospital and the gym, where I continued to box with a new trainer named Juan. The only family plans we made were with Robert and Fern.

Eventually, I became a little more vocal at crew. The parents would line up close to the edge of the river and scream for the Mainland teams as they raced by. It was such a beautiful sport. Young men and women rowing in unison, like flocks of geese taking to the water as if it was air. It was visually majestic, even calming... except the parents really knew how to scream! "Go Mainland! Go Mainland!"

I was not a screamer. I didn't think that I had a scream anywhere inside. I had plenty of silent screams. I had them every day. But I didn't have that voice or those vocal cords, I silenced my sneezes! I was not a noise maker.

At first I spoke the words, "Go Mainland." No one was paying attention to me, which was good. They were looking at the boats rowing by. I went a little louder. I could actually hear myself. Then someone blew the horn, the big green horn that reminded me of an angry moose. I started with a low-grade shout, and then a 'Go, go, go!' It took a while but finally I got my scream out, and it felt weirdly liberating.

As Danielle's bat mitzvah approached, Alex seemed to stabilize. It was looking like he was going to make it through. Since my mother couldn't travel, I reached out to her rabbi to see if Danielle could do a second bat mitzvah in Beachwood at Fairmount Temple. The rabbi there was very accommodating, so I made travel arrangements for us to fly in one weekend after her first bat mitzvah, and for Danielle to have a small service and reading of the Torah and the Haftarah.

That weekend we stayed at Gary and Andrea's in Orange Village, a small community that was part of Chagrin Falls. It was May and the crocuses were starting to bloom. The grass was a lush green and the beauty of the suburbs of Cleveland was that land was plentiful and the yards, for the most part, were deep and bristling with foliage from the abundance of maples, oaks, buckeyes, and arborvitaes, all deciduous to the area. We met my mom and her aide, Toni, at the synagogue. My mother had invited some of her closest friends to join us. She was wearing the soft, cream-colored collar, about seven inches wide, to hold up her head. She still had to look upwards from the downward tilt of her head and it made me so sad that I felt a tightness in my chest. But I didn't let on.

"Hi Mom!" I said as Toni rolled her in her wheelchair down the aisle towards the bema. "Hi Toni." I bent over to kiss my mom hello, then gave Toni a hug.

She smiled and squeaked out a hello. Danielle came over and gave her Nana a big hug. "Hi, Nana."

Nana was beaming! She couldn't help it. She was getting to see her granddaughter's bat mitzvah. Her friends came to share in the celebration as Danielle went up to the bema for the mini-service. It was a beautiful day, completed by having two Mitzvahs in one. There was a small Kiddush after the ceremony, which was made all the more special by having my mother's friends there.

Over the next few months, I would travel back and forth on my own to visit my mother. By July she could no longer swallow without choking on her food, so we decided that a liquid diet would be best. Toni pureed her food and it looked absolutely disgusting. She pureed chicken with vegetables, and meat with potatoes, and to me it all looked like some form of regurgitation.

"Mom, is there something else we can do so you don't have to eat this crap?" Of course, she couldn't answer. So I asked Andrea.

"We can talk to the doctor, Gail, but I think he is going to suggest a feeding tube."

"Well, if that's the case, I think we should ask my mom. I'll talk to Gary first."

Together we decided that it was time for an end-of-life plan, so we went over to my mother's apartment at the Beachwood Village and sat down with her, while she was in her recliner/push-up chair. The chair was pretty cool. It pushed you up if you couldn't stand on your own. Then we could stand her and pivot her to her wheelchair.

"Mom," I started, "Gary and I have a few questions to ask you. Gary?"

He looked at me.

I smiled. "You're the attorney."

He began with, "Mom, I know your estate is in order. But there are other questions that we need to ask you."

She nodded and smiled.

"Like if you can't eat anymore, would you like a feeding tube?" I added.

In a grumbly voice she answered, "Yes."

Well I was wrong. I had thought she wouldn't have wanted that. But not having a feeding tube means that you are going to starve to death. And she was still very cognizant. She watched the news morning, noon and night. And even though Gary and Andrea had taken over her finances, she was still aware of what was in her accounts. She could no longer write; her hands were so clenched that she could not even press the buttons on the phone, and since speaking was down to a minimum, we would call her and do all of the talking.

I thought about the past couple of years. Alex and I would come to see her at least a few times a year with the kids. I flew with the kids and he drove with one of his nurses. It was difficult for him to travel, but he never batted an eye.

Gary continued. "Mom, is there a point you can think of when you would not like us to resuscitate you?"

She stared out the window. Her eyes were not blinking like they used to. All her muscles were in atrophy mode. Her nose ran consistently. Her bowels had their own ideas. She had had several UTIs this year, and a bout of C-Diff, a bacterial infection. "Is there one of us who you would like to be the one who decides?" Gary asked.

She shook her head. "No."

Gary and I looked at each other.

"Well, it's not going to be Diane," I said. Diane had become so removed from what was going on with my mother that there was no way for her to make an educated decision.

"I would like to talk to the rabbi first," she said with a grainy mixture of whatever was caught in her throat.

"Okay," we responded in unison. "I'll have Andrea call him and see if he can come out," Gary said.

After we left that day I looked at Gary and said, "Why do you think she wants to talk to the rabbi?"

"I have no idea."

She would end up spending an hour with the rabbi, and we were sure what she needed was peace of mind. After they finished, she seemed ready to commit to the conversation. It was not something that needed to be written down. Gary and I trusted each other implicitly. If at all possible, we would do it together.

Andrea set up an appointment for my mother to get the feeding tube inserted. It was in August, on her birthday.

"Mom, are you sure you want to spend your birthday that way?"

"It doesn't matter. It's fine," she said in her scratchy voice.

"Well, we'll all come in for your birthday, so I will go with you."

"Okay," she said with a smile. With all of the muscles that were failing, she always managed to have a smile on her face. It was a small and consistent remnant of who she had always been.

When we went to Cleveland in August, Alex drove in with JoAnn in the van and I drove with the kids and Riley. With all of Alex's equipment, there wasn't room for another passenger. I wanted my mother to meet Riley; I thought she would love our "little white glow stick of love," an affectionate phrase that Adam had used for him.

Diane and her son Brandon flew in from Atlanta to Canton, and she had hired a driver to pick her up. She was becoming more and more removed. She decided to stay at a hotel again, and let Brandon stay at Gary's and hang out with his cousins.

Gary and Andrea had a new puppy named Grady, still in crate training. He was an adorable golden retriever, friendly and sweet, but when he met Riley he didn't quite know what to make of him. Two puppies, one curious…the other one not.

"I think we'll take Riley down to Judy and Pedro's," I said to Andrea after Riley started vomiting from too much puppy-play..The ramps that Gary had ordered had come in handy for both Alex and my mother. My mother could no longer go out to eat; it was too difficult. Her right arm seemed frozen to her side, from a fall that she had ignored while living on her own in Florida.

Her head was bent over as she strained to look up. It was like her entire body was slowly moving to a fetal position.

When Toni dropped her off, the puppies ran to the front door to greet them.

Toni said, "You know I don't like dogs. They scare me."

"They're just puppies Toni," I said.

"I don't care what size they are, they all got teeth."

I picked up Riley. "See how sweet he is?"

"You can keep your sweetness to yourself. Call me when Mrs. Desberg needs to be picked up. Goodbye everybody."

"Thank you for bringing her over," I said.

I wheeled my mother into the family room and helped her onto the couch.

"Hey Edie! How ya doing?" Alex said.

"Fine," answered my mother with a shake in her voice.

"You wanna swap spit?"

"No thank you," she said slowly. Riley jumped on the couch and started licking my mother's face.

"He's cute," she said.

"He has germs, don't let him lick her face. Her system is compromised," Gary interjected.

"OK." I pulled Riley into my arms and let him kiss me. A true bundle of love, and he had done more to bring our family together than any therapist ever could. He had helped to change the focus of the family, uniting us in a way that only the love of a dog could. He was our new world, and he had brought joy back into our home.

We ordered dinner in from the Winking Lizard, and Judy and Pedro joined us, along with Andrea's parents Art and JoAnn. Gary brought out the beer. He had gotten more and more into the craft beer scene. Of course, he was getting into fine wines too.

"You want a drink?" he asked me.

"No, thanks," I responded.

"I have wine. Red? White?"

"I'm good."

Alex rolled his chair closer to my mother's. "You're lookin' fine, Edie."

She smiled. There is always a place to find entertainment, and she found hers in him.

In a blink of an eye he lifted his hand and went to feel her chest, and with the same speed she blocked him with her good arm.

"What the hell is wrong with you, Alex!" I screamed.

"That's what you call a gag-reflex," Pedro, Andrea's brother-in law added. We all started laughing.

Andrea's mother JoAnn looked at me and smiled, and then said, "I think your mother appreciates his humor."

"Did I make you pee in your pants, Edie?" Alex asked.

"No," she responded.

"You wearing a diaper? You know just in case…I am. You never know what's going to slip out."

No response. Her nose was running again. We put a thickener in her water so she could drink it without choking, and we fed her as best we could.

The next day was her birthday, she was going to be eighty years old and get her feeding tube. What a birthday gift!

We had seen her friends dwindle, just like we had seen some of our own friends fade into the woodwork. Not all of them disappeared, but you really don't find out what people are made of until they are put to the test. Friendships we thought we would have forever, crumbled and blew away like dust. Others surprised us. Some friends grew the wings of angels.

And so it went with my mother. A few of her closest friends were dedicated to the very end, and many were not. It was no different with family. You can imagine that all of your offspring would be there for you, but that's just imagination.

28. QUIET GRACE

Danielle was getting ready for high school and Adam was going into his junior year. They were growing up despite the situation around them. I was continually amazed that years had passed, when I spent so much time wondering how I was going to get through the days. But that is the beauty and the curse of time. It doesn't stop for you to catch your breath.

It was time to start looking at colleges, but Adam was not interested.

"I need your input, Adam," I told him.

"I don't have time. I have schoolwork and I have crew, and I have to take the SATs. I just can't think about it."

"Adam, the point of all of what you are doing *is* for college. Are you just going to pick a random school? Don't you want to know what a college campus looks like?"

"Yes," he responded flatly.

"I have an idea," I said. "Why don't you decide what direction you want to go in. Think about whether or not you want to be in the Northeast, the Midwest or the south. You can't go out west because it's too far. As a matter of fact, you can't go past the Mississippi River."

"I want to go south. I want to go where it's warm."

"OK, that's a start. When you have a weekend off from crew, we'll go look at a few colleges."

And so it began. I went to the bookstore to investigate books on college options. There was one book that I was told was the most succinct, *371 Best Colleges and Universities*. It would become my Bible. I would read it at night in bed and memorize information about the schools. But Adam's SAT scores would be the final indication of where he could and couldn't get in. He had taken his PSATs and started to receive invitations to visit schools that I never thought he would get into. Washington University and the University of Chicago were a couple of them. WTF?

"Alex, do you think Adam can get into either of these schools?"

"I don't know. How are his grades?"

"They're good, 3.6 or 3.7. They're not exceptional, though."

Even in his baclofen haze, Alex brought things down to its base level. "They probably just want the application fee. It's a numbers game, just like with everything else."

"Well, he should go to the best school he can get into." It was up to me to take him, but he wouldn't have an opportunity to start visiting until early in his junior year.

In the middle of October, the phone rang. It was Andrea. "I just wanted to let you know that Edie is in the hospital," she said.

"Shit. What happened?"

"Well, Toni called us last night, and she said that she had a fever. Because she has an indwelling feeding tube, my first thought was that it might be an infection. Plus, Toni said she wasn't urinating very much, so since that's never a good sign we took her to the ER. We were there all night, and they're still running tests."

"Say no more. I will be on a plane tomorrow morning. Let me just get some back-up for the kids."

"You don't have to come in, Gary and I can handle this."

"I know. I want to be there."

"OK, I'll tell Gary."

I hung up the phone and turned around to talk to Alex. "Alex, my mom is in the hospital. I have to go home."

"OK, use points, it will be cheaper."

"Who can take the kids to school? Holly?"

Holly lived across the street. She was the mother of one of Danielle's best friends. Holly had two brothers on the street and they were a closely knit family. I knew I could ask her, and even if she was already carpooling with one of her brothers or their wives, they would somehow make it work. Small town, small favors, big relief.

"Do you think Edie can pick the kids up after school?" I asked. Out of all the times Alex had been in and out of the hospital, I could count on his sister Edie for school pick-ups.

"I also need someone to drive for crew. I'll go to the grocery store so you have food in the house."

I just started rambling the list out loud and all Alex said was, "Don't worry. Gail I will make sure they get picked up. I can make their lunches at night."

"But they have Hebrew High on Tuesdays, and normally I have to pick them up from crew, shove food in their mouths and take them to Hebrew High. Then I have to go to the Tuesday night crew meetings, which of course you don't have to do."

"So if they miss Hebrew High, what's the big deal?" he said.

"Well, they're only allowed to miss so much. After a few absences you get in trouble."

"Who is going to punish them, God?"

I felt the uneasy feeling of losing the small amount of illusory control that I had told myself I had.

"Just pack," he said.

"OK."

Is this it? I thought. *Is this the end for my mother?* I wasn't ready. Is anyone ever ready? Some people are ready to go. Some want to go.

I had started to believe that there was more to this world than just the concrete evidence we had before us. I had gone to my share of psychics, thinking I could gain some optimism or insight as to what the future looked like. Was I always going to be treading water? Would I ever be happy again? Would I ever feel that genuine happiness that you have when you are young?

Thank God for Riley, my little glow stick of love. He brought me joy. He licked my face and snuggled in when I felt like crap personified. "I'll call the airlines and change points into a ticket," Alex said.

"Thanks, Alex."

I got to Hopkins Airport the next day at noon. Andrea picked me up. "How is she?" I asked.

"She still has a fever. They put her on an antibiotic. Toni spent the night with her. She's so attentive. I'm so happy we have her. Gary had to go to work this morning, he's going to meet us at the hospital later when he finishes up. They must be really busy, because they put her in a waiting area all night. When we left this morning she still didn't have a room."

By the time we got to the hospital it was around two p.m., and she still hadn't gotten a room. I pulled the curtains back and kissed her hello.

"Hi Mom. How are you doing?"

She opened her eyes and smiled. And there it was, one of the things I appreciated and loved the most, a ready smile with grace and dignity, under a fading light. She was amazing. I sat down with her.

Andrea smiled and said, "How are you feeling, Edie?"

She literally couldn't answer.

"Do you think you can look at her chart?" I asked Andrea.

"I don't think so. Even though I'm on staff at the Clinic, I really wouldn't want to overstep my bounds. I can look for her doctor, though. Maybe he'll know what's going on."

I sat down besides the gurney that my mother had been on since last night. I held her hand and smiled back at her. "I love you, Mom."

She closed her eyes, and I knew her body was failing her. This insidious disease was like a slow leak, drip by drip, taking over her physical abilities and her energy until it was almost gone. But it wasn't gone yet. She no longer had the ability to communicate, but she was still there.

Andrea walked back after seeing the doctor. She said, "I think they are going to keep her overnight again."

"What do they think is wrong?"

"She has had an infection for a while, and it hasn't cleared up. Now she has C-Diff again, so they want her on an IV. She's also dehydrated, so they want to give her fluids."

"I'll stay with her tonight. I know you and Gary are tired."

"Gary will be here after work," she said. "I think I'm going to go home and take a little nap."

"OK. Well, I'll be here."

It was getting dark outside when we finally got a room. I went upstairs with my mom as they wheeled her through the hallways and the back corridors into the elevator and up to the fifth floor. I sat there quietly, as she slept.

When she woke I asked her if she was hungry, and she shook her head. The nurse had brought a liquid that she fed her through the tube. The IV was hydrating her. They gave me those yellow sponge lollipops, so I could stick them in water and then let her suck on them to keep her mouth wet. Toni had brought lemon flavored dum-dums to help quench her thirst too.

At about eight p.m. a nurse came in and told me I had to leave.

"I'm not leaving."

"Visiting hours are over, and we are very strict about that."

"That's fine," I said. "But my mother can no longer communicate, and if you need to communicate with someone, I will be able to answer your questions."

"I see. Well, I guess you can stay then."

"Thank you," I responded.

I was grateful that my mom didn't have a roommate. I pulled up a chair from the other side of the room and put it together with my chair to make a little leather quasi- couch. My chair reclined a bit, so I pushed it back. I borrowed a pillow and a blanket from the unused bed and made myself as comfortable as possible. This was not the first time I had slept in a makeshift bed, and it would be the last. I was so used to staring at the heart monitor that it was odd for me not to worry about it. But I stared at it out of habit. I had noticed that she had been taking more and more naps the last time we were in. This time she seemed even sleepier. It could have been the infection, or it could just be part of her battery winding down.

The nurses came in at midnight and took her temperature; it was escalated. They came back at 4 a.m. and took her temperature; it was down. She was still not going to the bathroom. They had catheterized her, and there was more urine in her bag due to the IV.

The indignities of getting old were not lost on me. I thought about my dad, who had died of metastatic cancer. It had started in one of his lungs and progressed throughout his body so quickly. He was gone in three months. Was it a shock? It's always a shock. Even if you see it coming, there is a big difference between death and dying.

It's such a mixture of emotions. You hate seeing the person in front of you suffer; yet you don't want to lose them. But you want what's best for them. Are they living the life they want at this stage? Do they want it to be over? The delicacies involved overwhelm the mind. You pray they are comfortable. By the time my dad passed, dementia had taken over his brain. They said it was from the cancer. He was angry and screaming, and in and out of rationality.

Fast-forward. I looked at the peaceful way my mother was lying there.

By morning she seemed to be awakening.

"Hi Mom. How are you doing?"

She smiled and mouthed the words "good."

Never a complaint. I knew plenty of people who could learn that lesson.

"Mom, Andrea is on her way over. Gary came last night but you were sleeping. The doctor poked his head in. You have a pretty bad infection. But the antibiotic should be kicking in shortly, if not already." I continued, "It's around 8 o'clock. The nurses switch over to a new shift at 7 a.m., so I guess we'll be seeing some fresh faces."

A woman brought in a tray for breakfast. "Hospital food," I said. "And you don't have to eat it! See there… a perk for having a feeding tube."

The doctor was making rounds at around 9:30, and by then Andrea was there.

"How did you two sleep?" she asked.

"Well, my mom slept great," I said. "Me, not so much."

The doctor poked his head in and said, "Hi Mrs. Desberg," to my mother. I introduced myself as Edith's daughter. He already knew Andrea.

"Well, what's the verdict?" Andrea asked.

"She has a urinary tract infection," he told us, "which will hopefully respond to the course of antibiotics that we have given her. I think it would be ok if she went home today. Her temperature is normal this morning. I think we have nipped this in the bud."

My mother was home by 1 p.m., resting comfortably in her own hospital bed at her apartment.

I wasn't ready, and I didn't have to be. Breathe in. Breathe out.

Gary came to my mom's after work. She was more alert and he kissed her on the forehead when he came in to her bedroom. "Hi Mom, you gave us a scare."

"I'm sorry," she mouthed.

"It's OK," I said. "When life gets boring, we like to go to the hospital. Alex is doing his own Zagat book on hospitals. Who has the best food, the most attentive nurses, the nicest doctors, who's the cleanest. So far, he has had experience in Southern New Jersey and Philadelphia. I, for one, am not looking to add to his experiences."

My mother closed her eyes again; she was tired. I kissed her on the forehead and walked with Gary towards the kitchen. Toni was doing the laundry, and the apartment had taken on the smell of Pine-Sol.

"What time does your flight leave tomorrow?"

"I think it's at 3. I'll be able to visit Mom in the morning and then we can head to the airport."

And so it went. I got on the plane the next day with such trepidation I couldn't focus. But as they say, there is no rest for the weary. From the moment I got home I was in fast-forward motion with crew, school, and Alex.

29. LOVE AND LOSS

On the 5th of November I received another phone call, Gary telling me that mom had another UTI and had gone septic.

"Do you want me to come in? I can get on a plane tonight." I walked with the cordless phone and sat down on the couch. Riley jumped next to me. He sensed what was going on, as all dogs can.

"No, not yet," he said. "But what do you want me to do?"

"What do you mean?"

"I mean it doesn't look good. We're at the hospital, Toni is with her. And we have spoken with the doctor. He's put her on a very strong antibiotic, and we are waiting to see if that works. He said it could go either way, I guess we just have to wait and see. Andrea said there are other measures we could take."

"Why, Gary? She didn't want to be resuscitated. She has no quality of life. She can't eat. Her body is almost curled into a fetal position. She's not living. She's existing."

"I know," he said quietly. I was quiet too. We both sat on the phone, not speaking, just breathing.

"I'll call you back when I know more," he said finally.

"OK. I'll be here. Did you call Diane?"

"Not yet. I will."

I sat on the couch and turned on the TV. I couldn't move. I didn't want to move. Riley wiggled his way onto my lap, and because my legs and feet were up on the couch, he was able to sit in between the crevice of my legs. He was acutely aware of the emotional reaction in my body.

"How bad is it?" Alex asked as he rolled into the family room.

"Bad. I think this is it."

"I'm sorry, Gail. You know how much I love Edie."

"I know. She loves you too."

"What can I do for you?"

"Figure out dinner for the kids."

"No problem, I can always order pizza."

Pizza had become a mainstay in our house. It was practically the only thing that Adam would eat. Pizza, peanut butter and jelly, plain pasta with butter and no green flecks, and plain chicken. Boring as hell and there was nothing we could do about it. I was told by many friendly, advice-giving mothers to just make what I wanted for dinner and if he didn't eat it, *too bad*. Eventually he would get hungry enough and eat whatever I made. But I didn't have the stomach to watch him suffer. It wasn't a matter of wills, it was a matter of won'ts. And we made accommodations for everyone else in the family— why shouldn't we make an accommodation for him?

At about 9:30 that night, Gary called back to tell me the doctor didn't think the antibiotic was working.

We were both silent.

"What do you think I should do?" he asked.

Silence…. "Let her go, Gary."

"Yeah, I know," he responded.

In the end, he was the one who would have to tell the doctors what to do. I was grateful not to be the one that had to do that.

"I love you. Will you give her a kiss from me?"

"Of course," he said. I could hear him getting choked up over the phone. "I'll call you whenever," he said.

"OK." I hung up the phone and didn't move. Danielle was sitting on the couch with me watching television, and Adam was upstairs.

"Danielle, I think Nana is going to die tonight."

"I'm sorry, Mommy." She came over and hugged me.

There is nothing more comforting than a child trying to make their mother feel better with a hug. It gives that sense that things truly do come full circle. It was a welcome relief, when those we have spent so much time nurturing return the kindness. I hoped I had done that for my mom. She was so strong, and she had supported me on so many levels. I knew then that she would always be with me, as I knew that I had passed a part of her down to Adam and Danielle.

When the pizza came, Adam made his way down the stairs and saw me on the couch. He came over and asked, "Are you okay, Mom?"

"Yeah, honey. It's just that Nana isn't doing very well. Uncle Gary called; she's back in the hospital and I think this is it for her."

He sat down next to me and looked at me with such a sad face.

"I'm sorry," he said.

"Grampy always told me, 'Death is a part of life,'" I said. "We were all lucky to have her."

"You should eat something," he said.

"I'm not hungry. That just means there's more for you."

I sat on the couch until 11 p.m., watching television and waiting for the phone to ring. It didn't. So I went to bed.

At about 7:30 a.m. the phone rang.

"Hi Gail, Mom passed away last night."

"What time?" I asked, as if it really mattered.

"Around 3 a.m. Andrea and I were there until midnight. We were both so tired. Toni was with her. So we went home to get a couple hours of sleep. And Toni called us around three in the morning and said she'd stopped breathing. I feel bad I wasn't there."

"Gary, you have nothing to feel bad about. She probably waited for you to leave."

"We had to go back and identify her body and sign some documents. You know, before she died her body looked so stressed. Her hands were clenched, she was approaching a fetal position, and her neck was in that soft brace. And after she was gone, everything relaxed. It was like all the tension was gone."

"She's free from her body," I said. "Being a prisoner in your body is just a constant struggle. When do you think the funeral will be?"

"Why don't you ask Alex how soon you can get here? I'm thinking Thursday."

"I'll go talk to him and I'll call you back. I love you."

"I love you, too."

I got out of bed and walked down the hall to the master bedroom. Alex was sleeping in our bed, and snoring so loudly it sounded like he had a microphone. I woke him up by pulling the covers down from over his head.

"Alex."

"What? What? What?"

"Alex, my mom died last night."

"Oh Gail, I'm so sorry."

"I just got off the phone with Gary. If we leave tomorrow, the funeral can be on Thursday. What nurse can you take?"

"I'll find someone, don't worry."

But I did worry. Our traveling always depended on if we could find a nurse to go with us. Most of them wouldn't travel. Some we didn't want to travel with, because it is truly a lot of work, and there were those who acted more like queen bees than worker bees.

"The kids have off for NJEA so they won't miss any school," I said.

"Who cares if they miss school, Gail? Their Nana just died."

"Can you get me three plane tickets?"

"Yes. Let me get up, and while I'm on the pot I'll work on it."

"Thank you."

"Come here," he said.

I sat down on the bed and he opened his arms for me to lean in and get a hug. I leaned in and he pulled me close to him as I lay down on his chest. I felt the warmth and I put my hand on through the thick patch of hair on his chest. He kissed my head.

I wasn't sure what it was, but I had no need to cry. Was I emotionally vacant? Was I spent from years of worry and wonder? I had no idea. But as I lay there, I felt the comfort and love of someone who was focused on me. I hadn't felt that in such a long, long time.

But I couldn't just stay there and ruminate, I had to get up and make phone calls.

"Thank you," I said.

"Gail, you don't have to thank me. I loved Edie. She was a good woman." And then he imitated her smile. He used to do it all the time; it was so wide it was almost as if the corners of her mouth reached her ears. She did it with her mouth closed, and it was pure Edith.

After the funeral we went back to Gary and Andrea's house to sit Shiva. The Jewish custom was simple: bury the dead as soon as possible, so the soul can have peace, and because leaving the body out to decay is disrespectful to the dead. Then you are to sit Shiva for three to seven days, depending on how religious you are. Shiva means seven, but less religious Jews sit for less time.

So we sat for three days, not including the Sabbath, because that is the holiest day of all. My mother's friends and our friends sent trays of food and desserts in to Gary and Andrea's house so we wouldn't have to focus on cooking or doing anything other than mourning.

One woman, who I had never met before, came up to me and introduced herself. She said, "I'm so sorry, for your loss. Now you are an orphan."

I looked at her. "I don't really see myself that way."

"Well, you don't have both parents. So you are an orphan."

I nodded in a manner that said, 'I see what you mean.' But I did not. In my mind, an orphan was a child. I was in my forties. I had known the love of my parents throughout my youth and until my father passed away when I was in my thirties. I was no orphan...I continued to feel the love of my parents after they were gone.

If this was a way to compartmentalize my losses, count me out. I knew in my heart that I was lucky. Not everyone got to feel the love from both parents. I had a wonderful brother, a great sister-in-law, and yes, a sister who was slowly stowing herself away. I would continue to reach out to Diane, but eventually the brick wall I would hit would start to hurt me. She had been putting deflector shields up for years, and they were invisible, so I really didn't know that they were there until it was too late.

Diane and Brandon left for Atlanta sooner than we expected. "I ordered a car to take us to the airport tomorrow," she said. "Brandon has to get back to school; he has a lot of homework."

"OK," I said. "Do you need a ride back to the hotel?"

"That would be very nice," she said perfunctorily.

I borrowed Gary's car. They all hugged goodbye, and we left for the hotel.

"Diane," I said once we were in the car.

"Yes?"

"We have to come back and go through Mom's stuff. Her apartment is filled with things that we need to figure out what to do with."

"I could probably come in February, when Brandon has President's Weekend off." Brandon just sat quietly in the back seat, not saying a word. "He could stay at Elaine's." Diane added, referring to a friend from Atlanta.

"I'm not bringing the kids," I said. "They can stay at home with Alex. It's going to be all work."

"I know, she has a lot of stuff in there," she replied.

"Think about what you might want. We could give Andrea and Gary her silver; all the silverware has a D engraved on it. I'll have Andrea store her jewelry somewhere safe until we get back."

"OK," she responded.

I pulled up to the Marriott, where Diane and Brandon were staying. We all kissed goodbye and as they got out of the car I wondered how often we were going to see each other now that my mother was gone.

As I drove back, the sky, which was almost always gray in Cleveland, looked like it was going to snow. Flakes started to come down minutes after I was back at Gary's.

"Gary," I said, "Alex is leaving tomorrow. Adam is going back in the van with him and I am going to put Danielle on a plane. I spoke with Cliff, he said he would pick her up at the airport. I will stay so we can figure a few things out. I also want to spend your birthday with you, cause it's gonna suck."

"Yes, it is," he said.

30. The Normality of Numbness

Re-entering the earth's atmosphere is always a challenge, but never more so than after my mother's death. I was a ghost who wore lipstick. If you wear lipstick, everyone thinks you're fine. It is part of the camouflage that I developed while in emotional hiding. Since I was pale Gail, the shade had to be just right. Nothing too bright to draw attention; something muted with a pale rosy brown tint to it. Lipstick could hide a variety of maladies. You could look polished when you were not, emotionally stable when you were not, and together when you were not. For me, it belied the feelings underneath. For most, it was an enhancement of one's personality. Bright pink screamed "I'm here! Now stop what you are doing and look at me!" At least that's what I heard when I saw someone wearing a shiny fuchsia shade. But since I had no desire for anyone to stop and look at me and really see me, I picked something that would maintain my invisibility, while looking like I cared about putting myself together.

And what was really odd was that the feeling of not feeling was becoming my companion. There was definitely a vacancy where I lived. Who the hell was I anymore? Everything I did seemed perfunctory.

Except boxing. I needed to box. I needed to feel the physical pain, and know that I was alive. Plus, I had to get my shit out. Nothing unloaded my baggage like a conveyer belt to the emotional claim area of a faux boxing ring. I remember once feeling that Darren had cracked one of my ribs: it was pain I could define. I had difficulty breathing, but I knew that at some point it was going to go away. It could be managed. And I was free to unload my anger and frustration on someone who could take a beating. It was my small window to sanity. And, on top of everything else, I didn't feel helpless. It was an exercise in empowerment. I felt alive while I was boxing, I was high on hitting someone, and I didn't feel the least bit guilty. So as drained as I was, when I got behind the glass-enclosed room at Mainland Fitness, where they held all of the classes, I was ready to fight.

31. BACK IN THE FRAY

Two months after my mother passed away, conditions at home seemed to be deteriorating. Alex was fine until February, then he began to itch, and spasm, and shake uncontrollably. Movement sent him into spasms. The worse he got, the more evident it was that something had to be done. It had been almost one year since his catheter had been replaced. In that time he'd had no major health issues.

After my mother passed away, I was somewhat removed from everyone, including myself. But by February, I had to re-engage.

Alex's blood pressure was once again labile. Dr. Graziani put him on 20 mg of oral baclofen every three to four hours. The thought was that he wasn't getting enough from his pump. He was getting a new physiatrist, who was affiliated with a new hospital, Edison Medical (an alias). And since he needed someone who could manage his pump, Dr. Graziani recommended a doctor there whom she knew very well and spoke very highly of.

Alex was initially very worried, but since Dr. Graziani had decided to retire from medicine and go to law school, he had no choice.

"What's up with that, Dr. Graziani? It's not enough to be a doctor?" he had asked in his last appointment.

"I will tell you, Alex, the way you were treated at Liberty Hospital a little over a year ago infuriated me. You were helpless, lying in bed, unable to move, and a doctor you trusted laid into you in the most unprofessional way possible. You just had to sit there and take it. What happened to you has been ruminating within me for a long time. It is clear that there is a need for a patient advocate. Someone who understands medicine as well as the law. You had no way to protect yourself. You were stuck there. You couldn't get up and leave. You were going through withdrawal, and no one picked up on it. Even criminals don't get thrown out of the hospital, and you're no criminal." She smiled at him. "I will still be here if you need me. You have my cell number. You have the office number."

"But does this mean you won't be my doctor anymore?"

"No, it does not," she replied. "I will always be your physiatrist. Just not while I'm getting my law degree."

"Dr. Graciani, I don't think I could live without you in my life; you have saved me so many times."

"I'm not going anywhere. You can still call me."

He was scared. Dr. Graziani was his commander-in-chief as far as his health was concerned; she was the other woman in his life, and I, for one, was glad. She had interceded so many times on his behalf he couldn't remember them all. When Blue Cross wanted to cut his nursing, she spoke to them to make sure he retained it. The worry of losing his nursing was always on the back burner, unless they told him he could no longer have it. Then it was burning front and center until the danger passed.

"Alex, I promise you will like Dr. Spewel (an alias). I know him well and he is a very nice man, as well as a good doctor."

Dr. Graziani was the one drug he didn't need a script for. She always knew what to do, and she was always there to talk to him and his nurses and walk them through whatever emergency was presenting itself.

So when Alex met Dr. Spewel, it was with trepidation. Much to his surprise, Alex liked him. But by the time he started with Dr. Spewel, there seemed to be another problem with the mechanics of the pump. Several things were going wrong. He had uncontrollable itching, and his spasms had taken over his body again. Every time he spasmed, his blood pressure went up, and so he would need to increase his baclofen.

The spasms were so violent that the doctor had to give him a remote for his pump. It was called a PTM, Patient Therapy Manager, so he could give himself a dose to get him through his bouts of increased spasticity and itching. He was drugged all of the time. The more baclofen he got, the more tired he became, and the sleepier he would get. He slept at night, and he napped a lot during the days. There were many days I couldn't talk to him about anything. His words became slurred and he sounded as if he was drunk. Another side effect, another thing to adapt to.

I didn't know what was going to come out of his mouth, so I had stopped listening to him talk. Did I know what effect this was having on the kids? No. And I wouldn't until years later, when it came up at the dinner table as a period where their father was on the baclofen "titty." A drug addict without the option of rehab. So I continued to function without his input. I took care of everything in the house, and the kids. He was too tired to do anything. But the kids kept me in line. Their needs superseded all. Riley kept me sane, and feeling loved. And boxing kept my inner turmoil abated.

At some point we had all had enough: he and I, the kids, and the nurses all knew it was time for a different kind of management. It was time for surgery. A new pump was the only answer, and given the fact that the last physician who replaced the pump had kicked Alex out of the hospital, there was no returning to the scene of the crime.

Dr. Spewel picked out a surgeon at Edison Hospital in the northeast part of Philadelphia. Alex went up to meet him with JoAnn. They both thought he was fine. There were no red flags. Alex continued to sleep all of the time. The doctor set a date to have the pump removed. Then it was pushed back a month. Then it was pushed back another month. We were both confused as to why there were so many delays for a surgery that was supposed to be a simple fix. By the time the doctor finally decided on a date and adhered to that decision, it was June. The surgery was set for late August.

I said to Alex, "What is the big deal? Is it an omen? Dr. Graziani said that it was a fairly simple procedure, I don't get it." When I thought back to what happened at Liberty, with the veil of shock lifted, I wondered how it was that no one had identified the problem. How do you not see withdrawal when the madness of it is staring you in the face? I had known something was desperately wrong from the fierce expression in Alex's eyes, filled with rage and angst at the same time. He had acted like an animal in a trap, threatening one minute, spewing swear words the next. But that was almost three years ago. And since then he had survived another one of his pump's catheters being replaced. So despite the continual rescheduling, I was cautiously optimistic.

By late August it had been at least seven months since the initial surgery date. In the meantime Dr. Graziani had been weaning Alex off of his intrathecal baclofen, so he wouldn't go into the withdrawal that we had seen a few years ago.

Surgery day was a beautiful warm summer morning. The surgery was going to be performed at an Edison affiliate hospital, part of the Edison Health System. Alex went up early with JoAnn and I followed separately in my car. The kids were old enough to be left home alone for the day. I never used to think that would happen, but somehow time kept moving on.

When I got to the hospital, Alex had already been taken to a waiting room

The pre-surgery room was dirty, and the one thing I had learned about hospitals was that if you weren't sick when you went in, you could be sick when you left. Hygiene was not at the top of the list in many cases. But we were there, and it's not like I could pull out the Clorox.

Christina walked in the room while we were getting situated and said, "Is it me? Or is this place dirty?"

"It's not you," I responded. "If you want a clean room, stay at home."

"I wonder how many people get sick after going to the hospital?" she asked.

"You know some of our friends, who are doctors, have told us to stay out of the hospital if at all possible," I said. "And it's not for insurance purposes."

Just then a male nurse walked in and said, "It's time to roll you out of here, Mr. Kiejdan."

"Ladies," Alex said to us, "I will see you when I see you."

We both got up and kissed him good luck.

"Gail, if anything happens to me, you know what to do."

"Yes, I do. I'll get a boyfriend before your body is cold."

"Alex, nothing is going to happen to you," Christina said.

"Christina, Alex says the same thing every time he thinks he is going to die. It's his mantra. He starts sentences now with "When I die…""

"I just want to make sure that you are taken care of," he interjected.

"Now, now, Mr. Kiejdan, everything is going to be fine," the nurse said. "Just relax and you can enjoy the drugs that you will be getting as soon as we get you down to the surgery unit."

"You'll be fine." I kissed him goodbye again as the nurse started to roll him away.

Was I sure he was going to be fine? Never. I always thought that he had one foot in the grave. I didn't know why. Maybe because he told me he did and I believed him.

"Where should we wait?" I called after the nurse.

He told me there was a waiting room on the second floor, and Christina and I picked up our bags and walked to the elevator.

"You OK?" Christina asked.

"Yeah, I'm fine. It's just another surgery. I can't even tell you how many he's had already. I guess I've stopped counting."

As we approached the waiting area, we saw our friend Mindi sitting in one of the chairs. It was nice to have company, and I was forever grateful for those who were still a part of our rickety old lifeline. With this injury, it was not easy to maintain friendships. But that's how you learn who is made of what. It had been a long road, filled with energy-draining dramas, and bigger emotional crashes than the stock market the prior year. If it was an endurance test, we would all be champions…champions without gold medals. There are, after all, no medals for those who are ravaged by the storm of life.

Mindi asked about Alex and I gave her an update, then she turned to Christina.

"How is your son?"

"He's OK. He has his ups and his downs." Justin had been struggling with Crohn's disease since he was a little boy. It had taken two years to diagnose, and there were times when we were all afraid of what it was going to do to him. But he had an excellent pediatric gastroenterologist affiliated with the Children's Hospital of Philadelphia, who had kept him as healthy as possible. Justin knew daily pain and he was a champion at not complaining. He was another Olympian without a medal.

By the time the surgery was over, it was 2 p.m. The surgeon came out and spoke to us. "Mrs. Kiejdan?"

"Yes, that's me," I said as I stood up.

He walked into the waiting room and came over and shook my hand. I introduced Christina and Mindi as my friends.

"Everything went very smoothly. Alex is in recovery and you should be able to see him in about an hour. They are going to take him back to the room, so I guess that is where you can wait for him."

"Thank you so much. I really appreciate it," I said.

"You're welcome," he responded. We all walked back to the room and waited for Alex to be wheeled in.

He was sleeping as they rolled him in on his hospital bed. "I told you the drugs were good," the nurse said to me.

"I know, I wouldn't mind an IV drip of whatever he's having." I could have used a little sedation myself, just to kill the permanent edge that I'd had for the past 13 years.

"Shoes and chocolate, Gail. With a chaser of tequila, that's what you need," Christina added.

"Everyone's drugs are different," Mindi said.

Alex began to open his eyes. He smiled. "This is a great hallucination, I'm surrounded by beautiful women, IF I have died, I'm good with it."

"You didn't die, Alex," Christina said. "Well, now that I know you survived I'm going to head home."

"Yeah, me too," Mindi added. "I'll call Fred and let him know you're OK."

"Thanks for keeping Gail company," Alex said in a groggy voice. They kissed us both goodbye and walked out of the room.

"So, you made it," I said.

"I know, and I feel good; I can't believe it."

"When are you allowed to put your head up?"

"They said slowly. They don't want me to get a spinal headache." So we waited together and soon an orderly came in to move him.

"Where is he going?" I asked.

"He's going to another floor. You can follow us if you like."

When we got to the next room, there was a note on the door: MRSA Contamination.

"Why are they putting him in here?"

"I don't know," the orderly said. "I'm just transportation."

I walked up to the nurses' station, and asked the same question. "Because he has MRSA," the nurse replied.

"I know, but it's colonized in his bladder. It's not like the skin infection of MRSA."

"MRSA is MRSA. There is nowhere else he can go."

I walked into the room and there was an elderly African-American gentleman lying quietly in the bed across from where Alex was situated. The pale green curtains were drawn and it was dark. "This is depressing," I said. "When you feel better, we have to get you out of here."

I walked back to the nurse's station. "Excuse me, how soon can he be discharged?"

"He's going to be here a few days to make sure he doesn't have any baclofen withdrawal, and then after that we'll see. At some point we're going to try and sit him up, but he just had spinal surgery so I wouldn't recommend that he try it just yet. He definitely has to be here a few nights."

Most people don't want to rush home after surgery, but something told me to get him out of there as soon as possible. I went back to Alex's room.

"I can't believe that they put you in a quarantined room. With as many times as you have been in the hospital, they have never done that before. Except when you were airlifted to Presbyterian."

As the day turned into night, no one came in the room. It was obvious that we were in the movie *Contagion*.

Normally, at some point after surgery a nurse comes in to check on you. Nothing. Not water, not a blood pressure check. Just nothing. I looked over to the poor gentleman in the other bed. I had to call the nurse to get Alex something to eat.

"Could you please get him a tray of something to eat? He had surgery this morning and he hasn't eaten since last night. He's really hungry."

"Sure hon, I'll see what I can do." She left.

"Do you want to sit up?" I asked.

"I want to try."

Slowly, we began to raise the bed.

"Stop, stop." He grabbed at his head. "Fuck, this is so goddamn painful!"

"OK, I'll put it down." I pushed the controls to put it back down.

"Jesus, can you buzz the nurse? I think I'm going to need some kind of pain killer."

"Sure." I buzzed. After a few minutes of waiting, I went out to the nurses' station. "He's having a major headache from sitting up. I think he's going to need something for it."

"Be with you in a minute," she responded.

Finally she brought Alex his pain medication. He was on another regimen too. All his meds needed to be given at certain times. He got none of them that day. He still hadn't gotten his food tray. So, half an hour later, with no meal in sight, I went back to the nurse's desk. I was very polite, "Miss, he still didn't get anything to eat. And I buzzed a couple of times."

"Hon, we've been really busy. Right now we are a little short-staffed."

"Well, can I get him something in the meantime?"

"We have juice and crackers down the hall. Help yourself."

When I got back with the juice and crackers, Alex was relieved to have something to nibble on. Within another twenty minutes the food tray was delivered. He could not feed himself. There was a flat piece of chicken on the plate and since I had always cut his food, I wondered what would have happened if I wasn't there—clearly, they didn't have time to cut his food.

His roommate got a tray too. He slept through dinner, and the woman who dropped off the trays came back to pick them up within the hour. Every so often the helpless man next to us would moan. All I could think about was this poor man who hadn't woken up for dinner. No one woke him up to help him eat, and if I wasn't there to help Alex, he wouldn't have been able to eat either. Nursing care seemed to be an oxymoron here.

It was getting late and I needed to go home to the kids.

"Alex, I have to leave."

"I know," he said. "Kiss the kids for me. I hope they let me go tomorrow."

"Maybe you could work your way to sitting up, so you can leave." We kissed each other goodbye and I went home to take a hot shower.

The next day I drove my car up and I asked Robert and Fern, who were coming up to visit, if they wouldn't mind driving Alex's van. I was planning an escape for him. My intuition was on high alert, and he needed an exit plan. We had been to our share of hospitals; the Zagat rating for this one was pretty damn low.

By the time I got to the room it was after noon. Alex, who by this time was a professional judge of hospitals, said, "You won't believe it!"

"It's good to see you, too." I tried to remember: had he always skipped the pleasantries, or just since his injury? There was always someone around him, he could never really be left alone, so hello, goodbye and please and thank you just seemed like extra energy.

"Sorry."

"What won't I believe?"

"No one takes care of you here."

"What do you mean? No one takes care of you?"

"The nurses haven't given me my medicine. I didn't get my bowel routine, and they didn't bathe me. I feel disgusting."

"Did you buzz them?"

"Of course I buzzed them. That guy over there," he looked at his roommate, "I think he went in his bed and no one cleaned him up."

"We have to get you out of here. How is your head?"

"I haven't been able to sit up, it really hurts."

303

"Look, I know it hurts, but you have to get out of here, and you can't leave unless you can sit up. So, I am going to slowly raise the bed a little at a time until you get used to it. If it hurts just tell me to stop." I began to raise the bed incrementally.

"Keep going," he said. "A little more. Wait, stop. Ahh, Ahh, no more, no more."

It took fifteen minutes for me to get the bed up high enough to alert the nurse on duty.

"Hi, I think my husband can go home now, he's sitting up."

"Let me check on him," she responded. "Oh, how are you feeling, Alex?"

"I'm good," he lied. "I still haven't gotten my meds, and I would like some kind of bath."

"I'm sorry, we have been so busy."

"I think that gentleman over there is giving off an odor, I'm guessing he could use a bath too, or at least a cleanup. Doesn't he have any family?"

"They sent him over from an old age home. Don't worry, we'll get to him."

I began to wonder if both he and Alex weren't getting the attention because they were both "contaminated." I knew Alex's MRSA had come and he had been treated, but it wasn't contagious— at least, none of us ever got it, and neither did any of his nurses. But in this unit we all wore those yellow paper gowns and hats and gloves, just in case.

"I'm going to step out while you clean Alex up," I told the nurse.

"Ok, I'll let you know when we are done here."

"Thanks."

I walked out of the room and toward the front of the building. It was a spectacularly sunny day. I went outside and the heat wrapped around me like a warm hug. I began to relax. Inside any hospital it was always so cold. And no matter the weather, I always brought a sweatshirt or sweater to throw on.

Just then I was incredibly relieved to see Alex's van pull in with Robert and Fern. They parked in the handicapped parking spot in the front of the building and got out of the van.

"What up?" Fern said with her bright pink lipstick glistening in the sun.

"I think Alex is going to be discharged," I said. "It's dirty in there, and I want to get him home."

Robert kissed me hello and walked in towards Alex's room.

"Is he OK?" Fern asked.

"He will be when he gets home. Do you think you can drive me home and Robert can take Alex? I'm tired, and frankly, I don't really know my way around here."

"No problem. I grew up around here. I know it like the back of my hand." As always, Fern was the dedicated driver. It suited her personality, her need for constant movement. Driving, cleaning, cooking, shopping, she was a whirlwind of motion. This was a busy time for her—her daughter Shayna was getting married.

Just a few days after Alex came home, Robert and Fern threw a beautiful wedding for Shayna and their new son-in-law Johnny at the Linwood Country Club. For us, it was an easy place to go because it was very accessible. And it was there that Adam ventured out further into the land of food. I watched him as he foraged his way through the appetizers. He looked so cute in the tuxedo that I'd bought him. How had he grown up so fast?

I looked over to Danielle, who never had a problem eating, despite maintaining her skinny-mini body. We were all there, and while some of the guest took for granted how lucky they were, I did not. It had been a rocky year, and we were about to be crushed by a boulder.

32. THE RED FLAG

A few days after the new pump was installed, Alex developed a fever between 99 and 100. For some, that is not much of a fever, but for Alex, who commonly maintained a temperature of 95 or 96, it was high. We ended up at the hospital, where they looked at him, gave him fluids, and sent him home. His spasticity had settled down and his blood pressure had been stable since the surgery. He was no longer slurring his words and I thought we had come to a clearing. But there was a red area surrounding the surgery site, and we all looked at it every night to make sure that it didn't get worse.

The next time he spoke with Dr. Graziani, she suggested marking the inflamed area with a pen to make sure it didn't grow towards his spine. If it did, he would have to go back to the hospital. The doctor from Edison put him on a strong dose of Keflex, for a presumed superficial infection of the skin.

The inflamed red line that had developed on top of the skin seemed to shadow the catheter that lay underneath. It was hot to the touch, and by morning the skin had begun to look puffy. Alex called Dr. Graziani and she said she was going to be in the office the next day. He was going to have to come in and show her.

Joyce took Alex in the car, and I met them at the office.

As Dr. Graziani walked in, I saw the relief on Alex's face. "You know you are my angel," he said.

She smiled and said, "OK, let's take a look and see what's going on here." Joyce pulled out his transfer board and helped Alex onto the table. Dr. Graziani unbuttoned his pants and edged them down a little so she could get a look at the skin. I looked again, and the red inflamed line had grown into a swathe of inflammation about an inch thick. It seemed to be swelling.

"I think you need to go back to the hospital and get this looked at by your surgeon," Dr. Graziani said.

"Maybe it's because I'm ovulating," he said. "They may as well give me a tummy tuck…" he continued.

Dr. Graziani took a photo of it with her phone to send up to the surgeon at Edison and waited for a response. It came quickly; he wanted to see Alex immediately. Within twenty-four hours we would be on our way to another Edison affiliate's emergency room.

"I love today's technology!" I said when we got home. "Imagine, sending a photo to your doctor and getting an immediate response? It's so…Star Trek."

Alex had been disgusted with the lack of care he had been given at the first affiliate of Edison, but hope springs eternal, and he had no choice but to return to a hospital that was in the same system, which was hopefully cleaner.

The emergency room, which was in a questionable neighborhood in northeast Philadelphia, seemed to be filled with the cases of an inner-city hospital. People were sleeping in the waiting room, and I sensed a drug addict or two amongst them. I kept wondering why we were there. We had good insurance, and wasn't that what it was all about? As we passed through the locked ER doors, the other side seemed more orderly. Heart monitors beeped away at a syncopated pace.

Our nurse Diane was with us, and she commented, "Well, it's much better on this side. The waiting room was a bit iffy."

Alex was lifted by two male nurses onto a stretcher and a phlebotomist came in to run an IV.

"I'm a hard stick," Alex explained.

The phlebotomist smirked and said, "I'm very good at this." His approach was to find a viable vein and hit it upside down, which he did with one try.

"Well, that's never happened before," I said.

Just then the surgeon walked in to look at the red swathe on Alex's abdomen, and started to talk to me as if Alex wasn't there. He must have had a tic, because he started winking and lifting the corner of his mouth in an uncontrollable fashion. I thought his face was twitching, and I began to think that something was wrong.

But he kept talking. He explained that Alex needed to be seen by an infectious disease doctor. "We have to readmit him and watch this, but he needs an IV antibiotic for his protection."

He was obviously trying to get me to understand something and it wasn't clicking.

"Why does he need an infectious disease doctor for a pump?"

"Well we don't know what's wrong as of yet. We are still trying to figure it out."

He still wasn't talking to Alex. It took me awhile, but I had learned that if a doctor doesn't talk to both of us, a red flag goes up. I wanted to scream, "He doesn't have a brain injury! He knows his body better than you do! Look at him, talk to him." But he continued to smile at me with his tic fluttering away.

Alex was carted up to a private room that felt more like a dungeon. The radiator wasn't working, the cabinet doors were falling off their hinges, and the bathroom had a big container of soiled laundry piled so high it was overflowing.

My faith had been lost in the filth. How could anyone take care of a patient in what felt like a third world hospital? I went out into the hallway to look for a nurse. I found one at the nurse's desk.

"Excuse me, do you think you could find me some clean towels? Also, there is a huge hamper filled with dirty laundry in my husband's bathroom that needs to be removed."

The nurse said, "Oh, I understand, but unfortunately the laundry workers are on strike and we don't have any clean towels."

"Not in the whole hospital?" I asked incredulously. "Not on another floor? How can you run a hospital without clean sheets or towels?"

"I know, it's horrible, but there is nothing I can do."

It was late and I had to go home. I kissed Alex goodbye and told him I would be back tomorrow. He had a distraught look on his face, one I had seen time and time again. I headed for the door, relieved that I could leave and go home to a clean house.

By the time I got back to the hospital the next day, the verdict was in: he had cellulitis, a skin infection where the bacteria can go underneath to the tissue below. It is usually caused by strep or Staph. Death knell bells were ringing in my ears. I knew that if you didn't contain a Staph infection, and you had a catheter that went up into your intrathecal space near your spinal cord, the infection could follow from the pump through the catheter up to the spine, and ba-bye!

A resident walked in. He looked at Alex with very kind eyes and said, "Hello, Mr. Kiejdan. We are going to put you on a Vancomycin

IV with Cefepine. Hopefully, this will get to the heart of the matter, and you will be OK to go home in another day or two. Do you have any questions?" He was so polite I instantly liked him.

"Yeah," Alex said. "There was another resident in here earlier and she told me that I would need another surgery, that they would have to remove the pump and replace it."

"She should not have said that. That is what we are trying to avoid. That is why you are on a very strong medication. Only time can be the judge."

"Thank you," I said.

"You are quite welcome."

Alex was on the Vancomycin IV for about a month. That's when the dry heaves started to make an appearance…daily. He was being weaned off his oral baclofen very slowly; now he was down to 5mg as needed. The surgery site still had the erythema, but it was much better. As we continued to watch the swathe of red on his abdomen, we both noticed that the catheter coming out of the pump was extremely close to the skin. Dr. Graziani came down from Villanova to look at it on one of her days off.

"It looks like it's going to come right through," Alex said to her.

"That doesn't look like any other time you had this done. What if it pops out?" I said.

Dr. Graziani said, "It's not the first time I've seen it like this on someone, so I don't think that there is any cause for concern."

"Really? Then what would I do with my time?" Alex said. "I'll have nothing to do."

"Look, the erythema has improved significantly, I think you are on your way."

"You always make me feel better, Dr. Graziani. And by the way, I like your shoes," he said.

311

She smiled and looked down at her feet. "Your husband always notices my shoes," she said to me.

She turned to Alex. "Alex, if you have any other issues or problems, you have my number."

"Thank you, honestly, I'm grateful you were born."

She smiled again, and we said our goodbyes.

For the most part he had stabilized. But within another month's time, I noticed something odd on his abdomen. I was in the habit of checking it every night before bed, and one evening I saw what looked like a giant blood clot on the surface of his skin. His nurse Mary called it a blood blister. I took a photo of it and we sent it off to his infectious disease doctor at Edison. The skin wasn't open and there was no drainage near the site. He had no fever. But the blood blister was an ugly reminder of what can lurk beneath the surface of the body.

A week later, we felt the dark clouds move in. It started with a small opening on his right flank, which was seeping a brownish-pink liquid with a slight tinge of yellow.

"I'm staying local this time," he said to me.

"Dude, you're in the driver's seat," I said. "I'm just the copilot. Whatever you want to do, we will do."

He had had it with traveling to Philly, "If I'm going to die, I'm going to do it here."

"This death mantra is getting old."

"YOU DO NOT KNOW WHAT THIS FEELS LIKE!"

I switched gears, "You're right," I said in a softer tone, "no one knows what you're going through except you."

"I'm sorry I snapped at you, I'm just scared."

"It's OK. I don't blame you. We'll get through this one too."

Alex called Dr. Strenger the neurosurgeon and made an appointment to have *it* looked at. Then Dr. Strenger sent him to Dr. Lucasti, the local infectious disease doctor, who swabbed the area and sent it out for bloodwork and cultures. Once again, the site was warm to the touch. And the open wound was over the catheter site, but not the pump.

The tests came back as Staphylococcus aureus, the most dangerous of the Staph bacteria.

In Dr. Lucasti's office, Alex was given more antibiotics, this time an IV of Daptomycin.

"Look," Dr. Lucasti said, "this pump and catheter are going to have to be removed."

"I know," Alex responded. "But I'm going to Cleveland to visit my wife's family over Thanksgiving."

"I don't really recommend that," the doctor said.

"I'm sure you don't but, I'm not going to sit here and wait for something to happen or not to happen. We want to see her family and I am making the decision to go. I have good nursing care, and they have good hospitals in Cleveland, just in case something happens."

"Obviously, the final decision is yours, but I want you to know that I am against you going."

"Duly noted," Alex responded.

None of his doctors wanted him to go. And no one in our family wanted to stay in New Jersey.

"I'll fly with the kids, and you can drive with Lynne," I said when he came home. And so that was the plan for Thanksgiving.

"Gail, I have to have the pump removed, and Dr. Graziani is going to wean me off the baclofen."

"Alex, whatever you need to do, we'll do. Is it safe for you to go?"

"Nothing for me is safe. My life is a constant series of judgment calls, and there are three people in the world whose judgment I trust: mine, yours, and Dr. Graziani's."

"OK, well, I spoke to Cliff. He's going to take Riley Monday evening, and then he'll drive us to the airport on Tuesday morning."

"And we'll be in Cleveland for your birthday," he said.

"I know, and Andrea is going to get me Cake Castle."

Cake Castle seemed to have the closest recipe to the original Hough Bakery birthday cake. It was the birthday cake I grew up eating: white frosting, white cake, with a tinge of almond flavoring in the frosting. Hough Bakery had gone out of business years ago, but someone in that city had the recipe. So the search was always on for the bakery that made cake with the original Hough Bakery recipe. Most recently, it was Cake Castle.

"I'll order the Jagielky's," he said, "and you can pick it up."

There was no shortage of sugar-shock when we went to Cleveland. We usually brought five pounds of chocolates, which would disappear by the time we were ready to head back home. Add a sheet cake and three Miles Market pies for Thanksgiving and we were good to go. Oh, and there was also Pierre's Ice Cream—the chocolate chip was the best, in my opinion. It had shaved flakes of chocolate instead of chunks, which I thought melted better and avoided the need to chew. You could just let it all melt in your mouth all at once.

Every year for my birthday I had learned to expect less and less. I began to wonder if it was situational, or if it was part of the natural progression of life. The only important gift I ever wanted was to be with my family.

33. THE CLINIC

At last it was Thanksgiving, and we were on our way to Cleveland to see my family. That alone was something to be grateful for. I always felt the easy love and comfort that came with our visits.

This time, the holiday trip was so desperately needed. We were hoping to put a brake on the mercurial pump issues that had plagued Alex for so long, if only for a few days over the holiday weekend. Andrea picked the three of us up at the airport on Tuesday, and on the Friday after Thanksgiving we were going to celebrate Gary and Andrea's one hundredth birthday. They each had turned fifty this year, and the family was long overdue for a party.

"So, we're doing the brined turkey again?" I asked Andrea, when she picked me and the kids up from the airport.

Lynne was driving Alex in his van, with sleet and snow accompanying them the whole ride. By the time they arrived there would be several inches of snow on the ground, and the hushed sounds of traffic fell along with the accumulating snow.

"Yes, we are and I just picked it up from Trader Joe's. Do you think twenty pounds is enough?"

"More than enough, especially since Pedro is cooking a ham. What else is on the list?"

"Well," she said, "my mom is doing the stuffing, Pedro is doing the ham, and of course he's making beans with chorizo, Don and Helene are roasting vegetables, I ordered the pies from Miles Market, we'll make the salad, and I already got your cake."

"And I brought the Jagielky's," I added.

As we pulled into the driveway, I could see the ramp set up at the front door for Alex. We went inside and were immediately greeted by their dog, Grady, and then their daughter Sara. David was downstairs in his man cave. Adam and Danielle descended the stairway to a room akin to an underground command center: a large screen LED, three computers with screens of varying sizes, and couches and pillows dating back to the casual decade of the 70s, with white-painted brick walls.

"I can't believe we made it," I said.

"I know. That past couple of months seem like they have been pretty unpredictable," Andrea responded.

"It's the goddamn pump. That thing has been a source of infections for the past few years. It's a baclofen booby trap."

Then Alex and Lynne arrived. "Hi! Oh it's so good to see you," Alex said as he reached out to hug Andrea. They kissed each other hello and she hugged Lynne and said, "Thank you for making the trip with Alex."

"My pleasure," Lynne replied.

And there we were. What had started as a precipitous climb just to have Thanksgiving with my family began to have that feeling of reaching a summit. As we made our way back to the kitchen, the sense of relief passed over me like a hot bath on a cold winter day. Yet, I couldn't shake the quiet unease in the back of my mind that we still had to get through the weekend, and Alex had to return to Atlantic City and face another surgery.

"Where are my kids?" Alex interrupted my thoughts. Wheeling by the basement door, he screamed, "I will not be ignored. Get your butts up here and say hello to your father."

Then, rank and file, the kids came up to say hello. "Let the bingeing begin! What do you have to eat?" he added.

And off we were on a path to gluttony. The ridiculousness of the amount of food we began to shovel in our mouths was not lost on anyone that Thursday. And of course, to top it all off, there were three pies: one pumpkin, one apple with a caramel-crunch topping, and my favorite, Fruits of the Forest—blueberries, blackberries, raspberries, and rhubarb—in addition to my birthday cake from Cake Castle, which was already half-eaten.

"Well, tomorrow we celebrate the centennial!" I said, looking at Gary and Andrea. "I can't believe you two are going to be a hundred. You look pretty damn good for not having any work done. Or have you? No, I know you're the real deal. Not that I would turn down a friendly needle."

"Well, I know we could all use some cake!" Andrea responded. She was a sugar fiend from birth. If I had ever found a fellow chocolate-lover, she was it. We went head to head when it came to Pierre's chocolate chip ice cream. And she went toe to toe with me for the candy corn and the orange colored circus peanuts. Don't even get me started on the Jagielky's. The only difference between us was that she cleansed with salads and fruit, and I did no such thing.

It was already Friday evening, and Andrea and Gary were getting ready to be one hundred. Gary's birthday was near Veteran's Day and Andrea's was the beginning of December.

It was my actual birthday, and I was starting to celebrate with a nice glass of cabernet sauvignon. Alex had been napping in his chair, and his skin color was peaked. We had tried to enjoy the day. Outside it was cold and icy. The snow that had fallen the previous two days had left a white blanket from Cleveland to Pittsburgh. The girls had gone to Beachwood Mall on Black Friday, and the insanity of that move could be measured from the number of packages they carried when they arrived home, giddy with their purchases.

It was a familial trait to be high on shopping. It came from my side of the family, but it was one of the reasons I loved Alex. He loved shopping, too. How could you not love a man who loved shopping? When other men became rabid beasts with a football game on the screen, we went shopping

"Mom, you've got to see what I bought," Danielle said.

"Sara, looks like you didn't do too bad yourself," I said, as she unloaded her bags on the kitchen table.

"Oh no you don't," Andrea interjected. "Everything has to go upstairs. We're getting ready for the party." And off they went, to unburden themselves of the heavy weight of materialistic joy.

By seven o'clock their friends began ringing the doorbell, Judy and Pedro had walked down the street; Helene and Don, Robbie and Stacie and Chris were in the living room. And Andrea's mom JoAnn had sat down at the dining room table. Adam and David were hanging out in the basement playing video games. Shelly, my BFF from high school, and her boyfriend Ben were there. It was feeling very festive.

And as we talked, Ben commented, "Alex doesn't look so good. He's kind of pale."

"I know. He's been having a few problems. Where is he?" I looked around, but didn't see him. I eventually found him in the den with Lynne. The glass doors were closed behind them and I could see that they were talking. He was recumbent in his wheelchair when I walked in.

"You don't look so good," I said.

"Actually, I don't feel that well, I'd like to go back to the hotel, if you don't mind."

"How is your blood pressure?" I asked.

Lynne answered. "The last time we took it was 70 over 50."

"Do you think Gary and Andrea would mind?" Alex asked.

"I don't think so. I'll go tell them."

When I came across Andrea, she was laughing with her neighbor in the corner of the family room. It was a clear reminder of the transitions life had to offer. I had already had two glasses of wine, and just then I thought I might need the rest of the bottle, any bottle. I asked her if she minded if Alex left.

"Of course I don't mind," she responded. "Is he OK? Let me go check on him."

She walked into the den, where the party noise trailed away. I, of course, went for the wine. We might have been celebrating their birthdays, but it was mine too. I might as well shimmy some fun in.

Andrea checked Alex then Lynne put his coat on and, as quietly as they could, they left the party and headed back to the hotel. It was cold outside. The crisp air matched the moon, in a bright crescent shape. It was the kind of night I remembered from my childhood. Clear enough to gaze at eternity in the sky.

I kissed Alex goodbye and went back for the bottle. Therapy came in many forms. And right then, that beautiful bottle of red wine was my therapist. I began to assimilate back into the carefree tone of the party. I pretended I knew about football and started to discuss the Browns and the Eagles with Andrea's neighbor and good friend,

Tim Sarac. When he discovered my end zone was empty, which took about forty-five seconds, we switched topics.

The night seemed to be flying by until the phone rang at about 10:30, and then time stopped. I could see Andrea's face scrunch as if she was trying to understand a foreign language. She walked into the den and shut the doors for privacy. I knew something was wrong, but all my senses had been dulled, so I didn't respond. She opened the glass doors to the library and looked directly at me, and then I knew that I was being pulled back to a place where the outside world didn't matter. It was a short and sobering walk to the den.

When I got there she said, "Gail, the catheter to Alex's pump has popped through his skin. I'm going to go over there and take a look at it." "

"But you can't leave your own party," I responded.

"It's almost over, and Gary will be here." She left me standing there and went up to Tim to discuss what was going on with Alex. He was a cardiothoracic surgeon at the Cleveland Clinic, and he offered to go take a look at it with her. The three of us got our coats.

When we got to the hotel room, Alex was lying splayed on top of the sheets. He was peaked, and his lips were graying.

There it was, a small section of white tubing sticking out of his flank, curled in a loop.

Tim took one look and said, "He's been compromised. This has to come out."

Andrea asked, "Should we take him to Hillcrest?" The Clinic owned Hillcrest.

"No, he needs to go to the main campus, you really need to take him downtown," he responded. And with that, Tim began making phone calls to see what neuro attending was on call.

I looked at Alex. We had a look that we shared when he was in distress and I was helplessly watching. I felt it rise within me as the adrenaline began to emerge.

Alex looked at Andrea. "Sorry, Andrea. I just couldn't stand that you and Gary were having all the attention tonight."

Andrea called Gary on her cell to let him know that we weren't returning to the party.

"I am so sorry, Andrea, I can't believe we ruined your birthday," I said.

"Well, it's your birthday too," she replied.

Meanwhile, Tim was making a call to the ER, so they knew what to expect when Alex got there. I called the house to tell the kids what was going on.

To say they were nonplussed was an understatement. How many times had we gone to the hospital in a state of emergency? Too many to count. When they were younger I had to call someone to come over... a baby sitter, a friend. Now they were getting old enough to fend for themselves, and they were with their cousins. So I didn't have to worry about that.

Lynne started to get Alex dressed as we decided who was going to drive in what car.

"I'll go with you in the van, Alex," I said. "Andrea will follow in a separate car." I thanked Tim profusely, and in his kind, simple manner he said, "I was happy to help. If you need anything else, please call me." He kissed Andrea goodbye and wished her a happy birthday. And with that, an angel in human form left.

When we arrived at the Cleveland Clinic the emergency room was quiet. I had imagined that it would be busy. After all, on the other holidays that I've spent in the ER, there were usually traffic jams from one station to the next.

The woman in admissions took our insurance card, and then said that someone would be with us in a minute. We all sat down in unison. Except for Alex. His chair was permanent. It was 11:30 p.m. And we could see the clock ticking by.

Ten to fifteen minutes later a woman walked out and introduced herself to Alex. She went to shake his hand and said, "I'm here to make sure everything goes smoothly for you." She was in her early 60's, with a swept-up blond chignon. Her bright green eyes were friendly.

Wait, smoothly? I thought. *Where am I?* This is not the meet-and-greet we were used to, but hey, we'd take it.

Alex rolled back as this kind woman, whose job it was to help us with whatever we needed, led the way. His face and lips were gray. The bright lights of the emergency room came streaming down the hallway to the waiting room. Andrea and I followed as he rolled into an area curtained off by pale blue-and-white striped curtains. We were met by a resident who introduced himself and asked Alex his name, to make sure he was alert.

Alex responded, "Ronald Reagan."

"Sir?"

"It's OK. I know my name, I was just messing with you. It's Alex Kiejdan."

The resident then asked Alex his date of birth, and asked him to explain in detail everything that had transpired up until this point.

Alex was tired, but he answered all of the questions. When he couldn't remember something, Lynne or I or Andrea filled in the blanks. They took his temperature, which was elevated, hooked him up to the monitors, and began to watch his blood pressure: 180 systolic, 100 diastolic. It had been labile all day and into the night.

I started to hum the song "Happy Birthday" to myself. When they were done taking his vitals and information, they told us that they had spoken with the Fellow who would be performing the surgery. Alex would have it first thing in the morning.

34. IF I DON'T WAKE UP

I spent the night with Alex in his hospital room. He was hooked up to the usual monitors, ceaselessly beeping away. I had long ago come into the habit of staring at his pressures, watching them fluctuate without a consistent tempo. After I had made up a makeshift bed by pushing two hospital chairs together, we held hands as best we could and tried to fall asleep.

At around 6:30 a.m. a nurse came in to check on him. It was her last round before the 7 o'clock shift took over. She told us that he would be moved shortly to pre-op, and that his surgery was scheduled for 9 a.m.

He looked at me with those bright green-and-gold eyes and I said, "Don't worry, you're in good hands. I'll be here when you wake up."

"If I don't wake up," he responded, "tell the kids I love them. I love you too," he said.

"I love you." I kissed him on the lips. How many times had he felt that this was *it*? That this was the end. Every time he went into surgery, he thought it was over for him. It was certainly a possibility.

We were interrupted by two orderlies. The nurse told me where I could wait, and said that when the operation was over, Dr. Deogaonkar would find me.

After Alex was wheeled away, I had to find someone to store his chair and the rest of his things. Then I went down to the Starbucks in the lobby and bought myself a chai latte. Just drinking a Starbucks in the lobby of a hospital made me feel a tinge better.

The Clinic was beginning to wake up. Doctors were not in abundance, but the nursing staff was. I took my chai latte and walked around the lobby. It was enormous, with stark white walls, white ceilings, and large modern black leather benches and chairs. The glass entranceway was three stories high, with wall-to-wall windows. As I turned around I noticed a projection on one of the walls, a large shadow of a tree that transitioned from a bare, lifeless gray tree without leaves to a full-blown, color-filled expression of summer, then transitioned back to a shadow of itself again. There was a sense that the wind was blowing as the leaves floated to the ground. It seemed to me to be a motif, for life, death and rebirth. Maybe my chai was spiked. The image was accompanied by slow, soft, relaxation music, the kind they play when you're getting a massage.

I sat down on the bench and focused on the changing hologram in front of me. The raw emotions of the night before ebbed away and I realized my exhausted state. Time was floating by and Alex was in surgery; the soothing sounds of chimes, a flute and a harp mixed with a calmingly slow beat, were working. The changing hologram and distant sounds of another world lulled me into a sense of peace. It was unlike any hospital lobby I had ever been to.

After zoning out for half an hour or so, I stood up to find some place to close my eyes. Behind the enormous lobby was a smaller room with a massive contemporary painting on one side and a giant flat screen on the other. This room held a distinctly different energy. I sat down and looked at my phone. Gary had texted me that he was on his way.

I leaned back to close my eyes; *Sleep, my pretty, sleep.* Why the wicked witch was there, I had no idea. She popped in now and again.

I couldn't sleep so I stared off into space, jettisoning myself into la la land.

Gary managed to find me at around 11 o'clock. I looked up as he walked into the room, the faint smiles on both our faces doing nothing to hide the sadness. He kissed me hello and sat down as we waited to hear from the doctor.

"How are you doing?" he asked.

"Holding up."

"You hungry?"

"Not really."

"How long has he been in there?"

"They took him in about 9. I'm just waiting for them to call me."

He was looking at the Rose Bowl parade on the screen, then he looked at me and said, "Let's go somewhere quieter."

We found our way to the post-op waiting area and sat down. He leaned back and I could see tears forming at the corner of his eyes. I was stunned.

"Gary" I said, "he will be OK. Really... he's been through a lot, he's very strong. He is willful, and difficult and tough. Really, you can't kill him," I joked. No matter how much Alex went through, whether it was his labile blood pressure, or a bad infection, or dysreflexia, or a myriad of other life-threatening situations, he was still here.

Gary gave me another faint smile, and we continued to sit in silence.

"Isn't there another waiting room?" Gary asked.

"I have no idea. I guess I can ask the lady at the front desk."

He was right, there was another one. So we walked over to the waiting area and sat down. It was a large area with ample seating. You could probably fit over 100 people in there. A large digital LED sign displayed the names and status of patients.

"Look Gary, they have arrival and departure times." We watched as Alex's designations changed from pre-op, to in surgery, to post-op. This hospital was a completely different experience. The screen took the wondering out of things, and I was impressed.

It wasn't too long before a man wearing scrubs approached us. He was in his late forties or early fifties, about 5'10" and medium build, with a light caramel colored skin and dark curly hair that had a few flecks of gray around the temples.

He verified that I was Mrs. Kiejdan and introduced himself as Dr. Deogaonkar, with a slight Indian accent. "You can call me Dr. Gun," he added. I imagined it was shortened for us Americans who couldn't handle the syllables of his real name.

I introduced my brother.

"Please sit down," the doctor said.

I looked at the doctor as I sat, and he began with, "Mr. Kiejdan did well during the surgery."

I felt a slight smile creep onto my face, and release of the tension that I had no idea I'd been carrying until then. He continued. "As you know, the pump was compromised when the catheter broke through the skin. What I found when I went in was a site that was completely infected. I realize that he was on IV antibiotics, and my initial hope was to put in a new pump on the left flank and feed a new catheter into the spinal column. But there was a substantial amount of purulent material inside and around the pump and it had to be removed along with the catheter. When the pump is inserted, it's placed in a small pouch under the skin. The pouch was filled with the infection as well. Honestly, I don't think I have seen an infection that bad in a long time. It is a very good thing that he came in when he did.

"My suggestion right now is that we keep him here until he stabilizes, and change his antibiotic to something stronger. And see how he does over the next few days. The only problem I can foresee is a possible withdrawal from the baclofen. After a few days, he should be in the clear. Do you have any questions?"

"Yes," I said. "Last time he had a horrible withdrawal from the baclofen, and I'm concerned that it will happen again."

"We will keep a very close eye on him, I can assure you he is in good hands."

"When can I see him?"

"Well, he's in post-op right now. He should be there another hour or so. You can peek in on him, but he's pretty sedated."

"Thank you, Dr. Gun," I said. "Thank you so much."

"This is off topic," Dr. Gun responded, "but how do you know Tim?"

Gary interjected, "He's our good friend and our next-door neighbor."

"He's a great guy," Dr. Gun replied.

I could see the kindness in Dr. Deogaonkar's eyes. He had such a relaxed manner and he spoke in a tone that was infused with compassion. He was also imbued with the silent confidence that you would expect from a neurosurgeon. His very presence calmed me.

We all stood. He said "I will be checking on him later. Dr. Bethoux will be his physiatrist. He will be on his case as well. If you find you have any questions or need to talk to me at all, please call my office…" he rattled off the number. "My staff will get in touch with me, and I will call you right back, unless I am in surgery."

"Thank you," Gary and I said in unison. "I'm so grateful, thank you for everything," I said.

"You are quite welcome," he responded.

And with that, Gary and I went to find Alex in post-op. He was asleep.

"See," I said to Gary. "He's OK." Gary was quiet. He smiled and nodded his head. I gave Alex a kiss on his forehead, not knowing whether it would wake him or not. He slowly opened his eyes.

"Hi," I said.

"Well, you did it again, Alex," Gary said.

"I know, I'm sorry. I just need to be the center of attention, I get it from my mother."

"See, not taking responsibility for his behavior," I said. "How do you feel?"

"Drugged, and I like it."

"Well enjoy!" I said. He began to nod off.

"I need to catch up on some sleep, if you don't mind," I told him. "Gary will take me home and Andrea will be here this afternoon. But Gary and I are going to grab a bite to eat first."

"OK. Love you."

"I love you, too."

"Me too," Gary added.

As Gary and I made our way to the elevator bays I noticed that there were hand sanitizer dispensers on every wall at every doorway. They were automatic, with a foaming solution. They were also at the elevator bay. I used one, then Gary used one. "These are great," I said. "This hospital thinks of everything. It has an Au Bon Pain, can we eat there?" I asked.

"Sure."

As we walked in I noted that they had the calorie amount on the various food options. And in the back they made healthy shakes.

"Wow," I said.

"I know. It's pretty healthy," Gary responded.

"Why do I feel like we're in Never Never Land?" I said as I loaded my tray.

"I guess it's because of Cosgrove."

"Who is Cosgrove?"

"He's the CEO. He's been behind a lot of the changes in the hospital. He tried to get rid of the McDonald's downstairs, but guess what? They have a lease. It's illegal to break a lease." That was the real-estate attorney talking.

"I noticed there weren't any candy machines anywhere," I said.

"Yep, you might find candy in the gift shop," he said as we sat down, "but it will only be dark chocolate."

"Really? Actually, that's impressive, but you do know that someday they will find that milk chocolate has benefits."

"If you really like it you should eat it."

"No worries, Gary, I do not deprive myself of chocolate. I'll mainline it if I have to."

"And, there is a no-smoking policy here."

"Gary, most hospitals have no-smoking policies."

"Not like the one here. They don't hire anyone who smokes. When you take your health exam they run a test on you to see if there is any nicotine in your system. If there is, they will pay for a cessation course and then they will hire you."

"So they want you to be clean inside and out. Wow." I looked at him. "Gary, I really want to say how sorry I am about your birthday party last night. I feel horrible. I can't believe that Andrea missed her own birthday party."

"That's Andrea. She wouldn't have felt right staying at a party while Alex was being rushed to the hospital. Whereas I didn't have a problem with it."

We both laughed.

"I am really tired," I said. "Let's go back to your house."

On the way out, we passed the gift store. "Ya know, I could use some therapy. Can I just look in here a minute?"

"Sure," he said. I looked around but there was no candy to be found, except dark chocolate. It seemed like a clothing store with healthy cookbooks and stuffed animals.

And then I saw it, my dream appliance!

"Look!" I nudged Gary. "They have a Vitamix! I have always wanted one of those."

"Why don't you buy one?" he suggested.

"I can't, they're too expensive. I can't spend that kind of money right now, or ever. Okay, we can go."

I was wondering how hard the withdrawal was going to be this time. Was Alex going to skate through, or was he going to roll into oncoming traffic? Fortunately, Dr. Bethoux and Dr. Graciani had begun having conversations regarding what to expect with Alex's blood pressure. Depending on the outcome of the surgery, they'd been planning to continue to wean him off of the baclofen. We would soon find out.

Andrea visited him that evening, and I went in the next morning around ten. He had been moved to a different floor, to a different kind of intensive care than I had ever seen before—and I had been in plenty of hospital intensive care units.

Each room was separated from an extra-wide hallway of glass panels and a glass door. But what elevated this NICU (Neuro-Intensive Care Unit) from the others was that every patient had his own nurse sitting at a computer directly outside the glass panes, watching the vitals of the patient that she or he was taking care of. It was comforting and frightening all at the same time.

"Hello," I said to Alex's nurse. She introduced herself and I quickly forgot her name. I had begun to lose my memory. When Alex was first injured, I began to call it the Blank Syndrome.

"If you are wondering why Alex was moved up here, it was because he was having some blood pressure issues, that were extreme."

"I'm not really surprised," I responded.

She continued, "Dr. Deogaonkar and Dr. Bethoux will be back this afternoon. Will you be here?"

"Of course," I responded.

"Thank you."

I kissed Alex hello, and asked him how he was feeling.

"I'm a little itchy," he said. "Could you scratch my head please?"

"Sure." I moved the chair over and sat next to the bed. He had the TV going.

"Are you watching anything?"

"No."

"Can I turn it off?"

"Sure. How are the kids?"

"They're fine. They're staying busy at Andrea's. Listen, I need to send them home on Sunday, they have school Monday. Cliff is going to pick them up at the airport and take them home. I just have to figure out their dinners because they have crew and they need to have food in the house."

"Where's Lynne?" he asked.

"I'm working on that, too. She wants to go home, and I don't blame her. There is no reason for her to be here, except the flights are booked because of Thanksgiving, so she can't get out on a flight until Tuesday." As I spoke, I saw that he had no interest in what I was saying.

"Scratch my head again," he said.

I began to scratch.

"Harder. Harder! Where are your nails?"

"I'm using them."

He was obviously not out of the baclofen woods. I saw his blood pressure going up, and it wasn't because I couldn't dig my nails in. The nurse opened the door and came in. She checked his urine bag, and then his IV. His blood pressure was escalating.

"Looks like we're not in the clear yet," I said.

"Yes, Dr. Bethoux is aware of the possibility of baclofen withdrawal. He was apparently fine all night and then this morning things began to change. He's been trying to wean Alex slowly since you brought him in on Friday."

"Can I have something to drink?" Alex interrupted.

"I can give you some ice chips. You're not quite ready for liquids yet."

"I'm thirsty," he said impatiently.

"OK, I'll be right back," she responded.

I looked at the monitor. His BP was 180 over 90 and rising.

"I'm getting hungry," he said.

"That's a good sign. Maybe they'll let you eat something soon."

"Can you turn the TV back on?"

"Why don't you want to talk to me?"

"Is it snowing?" he asked.

333

"Yes, it's been pretty cold and especially snowy, but you Southern New Jerseyans can't handle an inch or two, let alone a foot. By the way, I called your mother and told her you were in the hospital."

"What did she say?"

"Oh God, Oh God, Oh God." I imitated her broken English accent. We had to get our laughs where we could.

My cell phone rang. "Gail, this is Edie, how is my brother?"

"I don't know yet, Edie."

"Well I'm calling for my mother, she is very upset. Can I tell her he is OK now?

"But he's not OK, Edie."

"Please, just let me tell her he is fine."

"Edie, if you need to tell her that go ahead, but I am not going to lie to her."

"He'll be OK, Gail. Right?"

"Right, Edie."

"OK, then that's what I'll tell her."

"Do what you need to do, Edie."

Before I even hung up the phone Alex asked, "Who else did you speak to?"

"I spoke to Robert and Fern, Christina, Diane, and Michelle, and I called Michael Grossman."

His blood pressure continued to elevate. It was 210 over 105. His heart rate was going up as well. The nurse came back with the ice chips and put them on the hospital bedside table, then went outside the room and called Dr. Bethoux. He must have told her what to do, because she came back with a needle and stuck it in Alex's IV. He was starting to get agitated, and I felt a little uneasy.

334

At the time, I was reading *The Girl with the Dragon Tattoo*. It would become my escape route. When I couldn't bear to watch Alex as he ascended into a state of perpetual delirium, I would read while sitting in a chair next to him.

This first day was not that bad. There were a few bumps in the road, and when Dr. Bethoux and Dr. Deogaonkar came in that evening we were happy to see them. Gary and Andrea and Judy and Pedro had been visiting in shifts.

When the doctors arrived Alex was awake. He said, "Hi! Thank you for taking care of me."

"You are welcome," they responded. It was already about 5 p.m., and we had nuts and paper cups.

"Care for a cocktail?" I inquired.

"No, no thank you," Dr. Bethoux said.

"This is my brother Gary and my sister-in-law Andrea," I said.

"I spoke with Dr. Graziani this morning," Dr. Bethoux told us.

"I love Dr. Graziani," Alex interrupted.

"Actually, I know her. I met her at a conference where she gave one of the lectures." Dr. Bethoux continued. "She has kept me apprised of what to expect. You have shown some small signs of withdrawal, that we hope will settle down. If need be, we will put a lumbar puncture in to wean you off, but that would be a worst-case scenario."

Dr. Deogaonkar said, "The surgery went well. But the infection was so pervasive that we could not replace the pump or the catheter system, even on the other side, as I had hoped. At the Clinic, we work in teams. So, there is a specific team set up regarding your care here in the NICU, and we discuss your progress daily.

"What? No *Who's on first?*" I joked.

"Actually, we can know what's going on at all times," said Dr. Bethoux. Our system relies heavily on excellent communication."

I don't know why, but I hadn't realized that he had an accent until now. "Where in France are you from?" I asked.

"I was born in Paris."

Alex interjected, "You have a sexy accent."

"He's in touch with his inner woman," I said.

"Really, are you married?" Alex pressed.

"Yes, I have a wife and a son." Dr. Bethoux blushed.

"Alex you're making him uncomfortable."

"Aren't we having cocktails?" he continued.

"Yours is in your IV," I countered. "Back to business."

"Yes, so hopefully you will have a good night and you will be in the clear," Dr. Deogaonkar said. "Have a good evening."

"We will see you tomorrow morning," Dr. Bethoux said.

After they left, Alex was allowed to start eating. The nurse had listened for bowel sounds and he was ready for his first meal. When they brought it in, he took one look and eschewed it. "I need real food, Gail. What do they have downstairs?"

"They have an Au Bon Pain."

"What do they have?"

"They have sandwiches, paninis, soups, salads, blended drinks, stuff like that."

"Can you go down there and call me and tell me exactly what they have, and I can choose?"

"Sure."

"No, just bring me a panini and some soup, but call me and tell me what kind of soup they have."

With all his years of nursing, the one thing I could say was that Alex was, and always would be, very particular. He was particular about his nursing care, and this kept him very much alive. He wanted what he wanted, and he wanted it the way he wanted it. He hadn't always been such a pain in the ass, but before the injury he could do for himself. Given his personality, being dependent on other people made him more specific, not less.

I brought the soup and panini up and put it on his hospital bed table, then began to help him eat. He could not feed himself with a plastic spoon. I helped him with the panini as well.

"This isn't very good," he said. "Did you see anything else I would like?"

"No, I didn't. Maybe you should just take a few bites to fill up a little."

He'd stopped eating.

"They have a McDonald's," I admitted. "But I didn't think you would want that."

"McDonald's has ice cream; could you get me an ice cream sundae?"

"OK," I said, tempering my rising impatience. And off I went, leaving Gary and Andrea to entertain him.

When I returned, his blood pressure was escalating again. I fed him the ice cream sundae and that seemed to make him happy, and that was the last time I would see him like that for a while.

"Alex," I said, "We have to get the kids home. I'll take them to the airport tomorrow morning and then I'll come here on my way back. I'm going to have Cliff keep Riley, because they won't be there to take care of him."

"Ok," he said. And we all kissed him goodbye.

35. THE ORGANIZER

After I dropped the kids off at Hopkins International Airport and made my way to the Clinic, I parked my car, walked through the underground tunnel to the main building, stopped at Starbucks for a chai latte, and headed up to the NICU. Once I was allowed in through the locked doors I made a left down towards Alex's room, where I heard a commotion.

Inside, I found a new state of emergency. Alex's blood pressure was 240 over 152 and his eyes were in that animal-like state. He was pulling at the IVs in his arm. There was a nurse, the NICU doctor, and a neurologic pharmacist. No one acknowledged my presence. They were focused on his vitals and bringing his BP down so he wouldn't stroke out. I took my coat off and put my purse down.

"Alex, you can't pull your IVs out or we will have to tie your arms down," the nurse said.

"Excuse me, how long has this been going on?" I asked.

"Since early this morning," his nurse responded. "He didn't have a bad night, but this morning he woke and started screaming. We have been trying to regulate his BP, but he's been pulling at his arterial line and his IV, and I'm afraid we're going to have to tie his hands down.

"Do what you have to do," I said.

"Tell them to stop it!" Alex screamed. "Stop it. Just stop it!" He didn't want to get off the baclofen titty. "Renee! Renee! Renee!" He screamed as they begun to tape his hands to the rails.

"Who is Renee?" the nurse asked.

"It's his sister," I said. "He really doesn't talk to her that much right now."

"Renee! Renee!"

All I could do was watch the struggle of a man who was obviously delirious. He was writhing to get out of the constraints they were placing him in. His anger, and the wild look of an animal backed into a corner, snarling, reminded me of that time at Liberty Hospital, but this was way, way, worse. There we could talk to him and make some sense of what was coming out of his mouth.

"Has this ever happened before?" the nurse asked.

"Yes, but not to this extreme, at Liberty Hospital in Philly."

"What did they do for him?"

"They kicked him out."

The doctor interjected, "We won't do that here."

"Thank you," I said. "Every time we go to a hospital now, I get worried that he's going to offend someone and get kicked out."

Right now, I could see that he was going dysreflexic, and they were treating him accordingly. His BP started to go down and I felt a huge sense of relief. We were in a good place, where he didn't have to worry about directing his care, and where the clinicians listened.

Alex looked like he was starting to settle down, but he started yelling again. "Get this off of me. Get this off of me!" He was referring to the constraints.

I walked over to the bed. "Alex, you were pulling at your lines. You were trying to rip them out. They can't take them off."

"Get them off of me." His eyes were wild. I didn't even know if he knew who I was. "Just get them off of me. I won't pull at them. Just get these off of me. I won't pull at them."

I looked at the nurse and then the doctor. The nurse then said to Alex, "OK, Alex, but if you pull at your lines, then we have to put them back on."

"Just get them off of me, please."

She went to undo one of the constraints and he lifted his arm in the air and twisted it around as it was set free, and then immediately went to grab at his lines and rip them out again. It took everyone in the room to get his arm back in the constraint.

"I'll be good, I'll be good!" he implored.

"I think he needs a sedative," the doctor said to the neurologic pharmacist.

"I'll call for one," she answered. And within minutes she was injecting one in his arm.

"That was fast," I said. She smiled. And we all watched as he faded away.

"I think he's settled for now," the doctor said, and the three of them left the room to converse about their next steps.

I watched as Alex slept, and then I pulled my book out of my bag, ready for it to take me away. I sat there all afternoon, intermittently looking at his blood pressure. I knew I had to make calls to get dinner on the table for Adam and Danielle. I called Christina, Edie, and Amy B. Adam had his license, so he could drive himself and Danielle to school. And he could drive himself home, and Danielle could find a ride after football practice, where she was an assistant football manager.

I had become a cheerleader. My battle cry was, "You're going to be OK. Don't worry. Everything is going to be fine. Let's just get through this."

I began to think I was delusional. Were we really going to get through this? Alex was on the edge of a cliff again, and I couldn't control whether he was going to go over.

It was getting late. Gary and Andrea were coming in the late afternoon. Pedro and Judy had come and gone. Alex woke up occasionally to scream something at someone. And I was ready to go home, but that wasn't on my list of options.

When I returned the next day the television was on. Alex began with, "Gail, I saw the most amazing thing on TV, it's this organizer and it has snaps. We have to order one. It will change everything. I'm serious. You know how messy it always is with the mail in the kitchen?"

"Yes."

"Well, all you have to do is buy this organizer, and it has pockets for your bills and pockets for your receipts, and a calendar, and a place for recipes and snap pockets for paper clips and rubber bands. It is truly amazing. And it is only $19.95."

"You saw this on television?" I asked.

"Yes. Do you have a credit card?"

"I do, but you aren't getting it right now."

He rattled on, "Also, please promise me we are going to get another dog. I was watching this special, and it was so sad, we have to go to the ASPCA. It's heartbreaking."

I realized then that this was the baclofen withdrawal speaking.

I sat down. "We'll see when you get home."

"You have no idea what else I saw. There is this way to hem your pants now without you having to sew it."

341

"Yeah, it's called a tailor," I responded.

He went on like I wasn't talking. "It's this miracle tape."

"Is it better than duct tape?"

"No."

"Because nothing is better than duct tape, Alex." I looked at his BP on the monitor.

"Can you get me something to eat?"

"Sure what would you like?"

"Don't forget to write it down."

"What, your order?"

"No, the organizer."

"I won't."

But I knew he would forget about it within a week. As a matter of record, he wouldn't remember anything that happened that whole week.

That afternoon, I met my friend Sharon for lunch. As optimistic as I was on the outside, Alex's withdrawal was taking its toll on me. Sharon seemed as steady as a ship making its way to port. But she had had her share of loss. Her husband passed away from cancer a year after her daughter was born, leaving a gaping hole in her heart. She knew first-hand about the death that I shadowboxed with. She was knocked down and got up again. She had remarried ten years ago, and her husband was a good man who appreciated her strengths. Now we each had kids who were looking at colleges, and somehow we both had gotten there.

We met in the Clinic's lobby and she looked no different than she had in high school, except her clothes were nicer. She had a beautiful pair of black leather boots that made her tall frame shoot up another couple of inches.

"Jesus, did you grow?" I said.

"No, I have heels on."

"You look really good." We hugged hello. "You want to eat at my new favorite place?"

"Sure. Where's that?"

"Right here at Au Bon Pain."

We sat down with our trays in front of us, and she asked what everyone usually asks. "How are you holding up?"

"I'm hangin' in there." We talked about the kids and college, and then I said, "I know you're remarried now, but what's it like to be a widow? I mean, how do you handle something like that?"

"Do you think that Alex might not make it?" she asked.

"I have no idea. I never know. I feel like he's been on the verge so many times. I mean, he's not a cat. How much can the human body handle? He has blood pressure issues all of the time; one minute it's so high he might stroke out, and the next minute it's so low, I feel like he's going to just slip away."

"Well, if you're worried about how you go on, you just do. It's not like you have a choice, especially because you have kids. And the rest, well you just tuck it somewhere. It doesn't go away, it's always there."

I returned to the room to find Andrea there, discussing Alex with the nurse. It was Andrea's day off. Alex was rambling to Andrea, and I looked at the monitor and saw that his BP was 40 over 19. Usually under those circumstances you are on your way out, unconscious, and then dead. Andrea was looking at it too.

She looked at me and said, "I'm surprised he can still talk."

"I know," I replied. "You can't shut him up."

The nurse injected something into his PICC line, a peripherally inserted catheter that is used for long-term intravenous antibiotics.. "We're going to give him norepinephrine, it should bring his BP right up." Norepinephrine is like giving someone a shot of adrenaline.

Alex had not passed out, but I could see by the look in the nurse's eyes that she was rushing to help him before he sunk into an irreversible state. "Alex, can you hear me?" she asked.

"Yes," Alex said.

The unit resident walked in the room and took a flashlight to his eyes.

"Hello, sir. Do you know your name?"

"Yes," he responded.

"What is it?"

"Ronald Reagan."

The resident looked at me.

"Tell him your name," I said to Alex.

"Alex Kiejdan."

"Do you know what year it is?" the resident asked.

"Yes, 1960."

The resident looked at me again.

"Alex, please."

"It's 2010," he said.

"Who's the president of the United States?"

"Abraham Lincoln."

The resident was not amused, but Alex didn't care. He had stopped caring about what other people thought a long time ago.

"Where are you, Alex?"

"I'm in a bed."

His BP was rising little by little, and we were all more than a little relieved. Andrea and I each pulled a chair towards his bed. As his blood pressure began to return to normal, the resident and the nurse went to their computers to fill out their reports.

That evening the phone rang. It was Danielle. "Mom?"

"Hi pumpkin, how was school today?"

"It was fine. Mom, when are you coming home?"

"I don't know. Daddy is still in intensive care. He's not out of the woods yet."

"Mom, I need you to please come home."

"What's wrong?"

"I'm just a kid. I can't do this. It's scary in the house without you."

"But Adam is there," I responded.

"Adam is not helpful. He's not doing anything I ask him to, and he's leaving a mess. Please come home, Mom."

"I can't right now. Do you want me to get someone to stay with you?"

"No," she said despondently. "Just please come home as soon as you can."

"I will be there as soon as I am able, Danielle, I just can't leave Daddy now."

"I love you. Tell Daddy I love him."

"I will, honey. Is Adam there?"

"Yes."

"Can I talk to him, please?"

"Yes. Adam! Mom's on the phone, she wants to talk to you."

"Hi, Mom," Adam said. "How's dad?"

"He's still in NICU. He had a rough day. How are you doing?"

"Danielle is a pain. Other than that, I guess things are OK."

"Danielle said you're not cleaning up."

"I can't clean up, I don't have time. I'll do it when I get time."

"OK. How is school?"

"It's fine. I gotta go, Mom, I have stuff to do."

"OK. I love you," I said. "I will talk to you tomorrow and check in on things."

"OK, Mom, love you too," he replied.

And I hung up the phone with the sick feeling that I had been split like an atom. Logically, you would think that the obvious choice would be to stay and take care of the person who is in the hospital. I guess for some, it wouldn't even be a choice. But the primal instincts of motherhood have nothing to do with logic.

And depending on the strength of those instincts, the magnetic pull can be beyond your control. My kids were my life raft, they kept me going as much as I kept them going. But now I was treading water.

By the middle of the week, things had not changed that dramatically. One of the side effects of baclofen withdrawal was clear to me: shopping. I had taken Alex's credit cards away, but he would be up all night calling people he knew to get them to order him something that he saw on QVC or the Home Shopping Network.

When Pedro and Judy walked in on Thursday afternoon Pedro said, "You are a saint! I really am surprised you haven't killed him yet. And I am not kidding. I could see you knocking him out with a two by four and no one would blame you."

"I can assure you, I'm no saint." I began to think that there was a small line between a saint and a fool. "What did he do?" I asked.

"He called me at 5 a.m., and asked if I would order something that he saw on TV. I was like, 'Buddy it's a good thing I'm a lousy sleeper, otherwise I would be really pissed.'"

"What did he want you to order?"

"That organizer he keeps talking about."

"That's a piece of crap. When he's better he'll look at it and say that we were making the whole thing up. He'll say, 'why would I want that?' It's a good thing he hasn't memorized our credit card information, like me."

"That's dangerous," Judy said.

"Only in the wrong head," I countered.

A few hours later, Dr. Deogaonkar, Dr. Bethoux, and a surgical resident came in the room. We began with the pleasantries and then Dr.. Bethoux said, "Alex has not been going through withdrawal as we had hoped. His blood pressure has been too unsteady. He still has his infection, but we are going to need to put an intrathecal baclofen lumbar line in, to help wean him off. This will greatly assist him with the process."

"I think it's a very good idea," I said.

"We will begin doing this a little later this evening," Dr. Deogaonkar added. "He will not be able to get another pump placed for at least six weeks, in order to make sure the infection is completely cleared up. I must add that there is a chance that even if a microbe of the infection is still in the body, it could exacerbate and become a problem. Even when we put the new pump in, there is no guarantee."

He was talking to and looking at Alex. "That is why you are going to be on IV antibiotics for the next six weeks. So we are going to keep you here for a while, Alex, until you are stabilized, and then you will go into a step-down unit. And from there you will have to go to rehab to get your strength back. You have several facilities to pick from."

"Thank you," I said. "I'll talk to Andrea and we will see which one best suits Alex when the time comes."

The next day they put an indwelling catheter in Alex as his heart rate and BP continued to climb into stroke range. The goal was stability, and to eventually wean Alex off the intrathecal baclofen and replace it with oral baclofen, Valium and Periactin. Keeping things balanced was a medical high wire act.

In the end, Dr. Deogaonkar would say that it was the second worst withdrawal from baclofen that he had ever witnessed, the first one being when he had a patient that temporarily ended up on a ventilator.

That night Danielle called again.

"Mom,"

"Hi honey, how is it going?"

"Mom, *please, please*, come home."

"What's going on?"

"He doesn't listen, he doesn't help me at all. I really appreciate you. I had no idea how hard this was. I will never take you for granted again. I promise. Just please come home."

That was oddly funny to me. "I will never take you for granted again." I heard the birds chirping in my ears. Flowers were blooming as the snow continued to pile up outside. A momentary pause in the pandemonium… But I knew that it was not something Danielle could stick to. She had broken the contract about the dog, saying she never signed anything. *Will you sign an affidavit?* I thought.

"Danielle, I will start working on it." If the weaning from the lumbar line helped to stabilize him, then maybe I could go home.

"Thank you, Mom, you are the best."

Moms are always best when they are out of town.

Andrea walked in to the kitchen as I was hanging up the phone. I looked up to see a smile on her face.

"I bought you a present today," she said.

"You did? Why?"

"Well, just consider it a birthday present."

"Really? What did you get me?"

"I ordered you a Vitamix."

"No."

"Yes."

"Noooo. It's too expensive!"

"Happy birthday!"

"No!"

"Yes, really."

"Oh my God, you didn't!"

"I did."

"Oh my God, oh my God, oh my God." I stood up and hugged her so tightly that I thought her skinny little body would flatten out. "Thank you so much. But I can't accept it."

"It's being sent to your house, so you don't really have a choice."

"I'm going to make kale shakes."

"Yum," she said sarcastically.

"This is so exciting! I can't believe you did that."

Robert and Fern had been calling regularly. And that evening I asked Robert if he wouldn't mind coming out for a few days so I could get home to the kids. He was amenable, and I was grateful. He made his reservations and I left the same day he came.

The snow pounded Cleveland that winter, especially around the time Alex was at the Clinic. One night Robert went to a restaurant that was affiliated with the hotel and, as he tells it, he was sitting down for dinner and watching the snow pile up outside. He began talking to a couple sitting across from him. They talked about being snowed in, and the gentleman asked him why he was there and how he liked it.

"My brother is here," he responded, "And I have to say he's been to a lot of hospitals, but this is the finest hospital he has ever been in. It's clean, the staff is very accommodating, and everyone is really on the ball. I am truly impressed."

"Well, thank you," the gentleman said. He introduced himself as Dr. Delos Cosgrove. "I'm the President and CEO of the Cleveland Clinic. It's nice to hear such glowing reviews. Here is my card. If you need anything just call my office."

"Wow, thank you," Robert responded. "That is very nice of you."

Within the five days that Robert was in Cleveland, Alex went from NICU to the step-down unit to rehab. The question remained whether or not he should come home or stay in Cleveland and wait for his next surgery. In the end, he came home to wait. That meant that he would continue to have a port, and have blood taken every several days, as well as take his baclofen orally. The hazy days of winter continued.

By the end of February, Alex went back to the Clinic with one of his male nurses to get his pump replaced. We called this nurse the captain, because this one was on his own ship. He was also the captain of complaining—nothing in his life was on course. He lay down whenever and wherever he could. I had caught him many times lying on the chaise lounge in my bedroom. The intrusion was bold and frightening. His boundaries were not well honed.

"Keep away from my wife," Alex had told him. She has a mean streak."

And maybe that is why he looked at me out of the corner of his eye all of the time. His presence made me a little fearful. He was a gun collector and loved to shoot. He talked about his guns all the time, and that scared me.

"How many guns do you have?" Alex asked.

"Oh, that doesn't matter," he said. "It's how many bullets that counts."

Alex's surgery went well, thanks to the doctors, the supporting staff at the Clinic, Gary, Andrea, Judy and Pedro. They all took turns visiting, while I stayed home to keep the kids on their schedules. I knew I was running out of fuel, and I could no longer use boxing to amp up my energy.

Alex returned home and the minute I saw him I asked, "What's wrong? Do you feel OK?"

"I feel fine, but the captain is an asshole," he said.

"What did he do?"

"First of all, he complained the whole time about his back, and how tired he was, and then he went to town at the hotel, with his meals. He gave me the bill at the end, and I thought 'This guy is really inconsiderate.' I haven't ever had someone think that my credit card was their carte blanche to spend whatever they wanted on food. And he complained the whole car ride home. I just pretended I was sleeping. Jesus, I'm the one with my life on the line. Can you imagine?"

"Look," I said. "He got you there, and he got you home, and you needed someone to do that. Please, just be glad for that."

"Where are my kids?" Alex asked.

"Adam is at Noah's and Danielle is at Jessica's with Ashley. Do you want me to call them to come home?"

"Yes, I need to see my kids."

I knew exactly what he meant. When things were not going well, our kids were our oxygen. We breathed them in and felt better.

I put Riley on Alex's lap and he began to lick his face. He was better than Xanax. I had learned quite a bit about medications, since

Alex took at least 20 pills a day. I had found an affinity for Ativan. I called it Ativan lite. It didn't leave me with that awful drug hangover the next day, and I could use it once every so often and not feel like an addict.

As time passed, we got used to the steadiness of Alex's new pump and I began to hope he was in the clear.

February was uneventful, and when March began, crew season was in full swing. Finally, for the first time in almost four years, Alex could watch the races in Philadelphia. His nurse drove him up in the van while I took a separate car. We had long ago learned that he might need to leave any function or event at any time. I had become a lone driver, not just because he might have to leave, but because I might have to run home to him or to a hospital where he had been taken.

He wheeled over to the white tent that the school had set up and surveyed tables laid out with salads, pasta salads, banana bread, homemade protein bars, and giant jugs of Gatorade. The BBQ was going.

"This is nice," he said. "Do they always get to eat like this?"

"Yeah, they're hungry when their races are over."

He asked for grilled chicken and macaroni salad and I got him a plate.

It was a rainy spring, where the skies literally grew dark day after day. As if in tandem, so did both of Alex's new and older catheter sites. Something was brewing, and it wasn't coffee. It had begun to turn red near his latest surgical site. He was on IV Cubicin, which was being monitored by Dr. Lucasti.

Dr. Graziani made a house call to check on him—not the first one, and not the last. She had driven down from Villanova and was at our house with in an hour. They called the redness a flank

352

erythema, and we told her that it had decreased about an inch. At night I would measure it and put ink spots at each end so the nurses and I could tell if had grown or shrunk. They did a urine culture and sensitivity and it turned out that he had an infection of E. Coli, which was sensitive to the antibiotic Macrodantin.

After she left, Dr. Graziani called Dr. Thomford, the infectious disease doctor at the Cleveland Clinic, and Dr. Deogaonkar, Alex's surgeon. Together they discussed the possibilities, concluding with the fact that because of the extreme difficulty Alex had with baclofen withdrawal, managing his spasticity, dysreflexia and oral medications, it would be best if the pump was not explanted. But if the infection got worse, the scenario would be different. In the interim he was to stay on the IV antibiotics, and slowly be weaned from his ITB (Intrathecal Baclofen) dose.

"How serious is this, Dr. G.?" I asked.

"It's very serious. Anytime an infection spreads to the blood or the spine it's serious. We can presume that this is MRSA, so we have the added pressure of it being resistant to antibiotics."

"Well, alrighty then. Do you want something to eat?" I had learned to change the subject with the greatest of ease, just like the kids.

36. APRIL REIGNS

Over the next few weeks we kept our eyes on the surgery site, and things seemed to be moving in the right direction. Danielle was turning 16, and I knew she wanted a party. But with all of the ups and downs there was nothing left in me to plan anything. She had learned long ago that we don't always get what we want, as did Adam. And no one in our family said, "That's not fair," when referring to ourselves.

"Danielle, how would you like to take a handful of your friends out to dinner for your birthday at your favorite restaurant?" I asked.

"Luke Palladino?" she inquired.

"Yes, Luke Palladino."

"How many?"

"A handful, that place is not cheap. Daddy isn't feeling well and I don't feel right going out without him. I will be your chauffer for the evening, I will get cake, and then you and the girls can come back to the house and eat cake."

"I love that restaurant, it reminds me of *Eat Pray Love*. Remember when we had that homemade fusilli with fresh pesto?"

"I do, it was exceptional."

"Thank you, Mom. Can you get that Death by Chocolate cake from Genardi's?"

"I'm on it."

Danielle's birthday was two days before Alex's, and that was a good thing. Those two sharing a birthday would have given me whiplash.

Forty-eight hours later I had decided to pick-up a tart cherry pie from Hammonton, which had a little bakery that was known for their pies. Since Hackett's had closed permanently, I could no longer shoot around the corner for a sweet, delicious, perfectly crusted pie made from freshly picked fruits. But this pie was pretty damn close.

When I left Alex his spirits were down, and when I returned with the pie he still wasn't smiling. He didn't care that I had driven an hour to pick it up, and all he could do was say. "It's not Hackett's."

"You OK?" I asked, not really caring. I thought I would shove the pie in his face, but then he would choke on it and I would go to jail for assault, and I hate orange.

"Not really," he responded. I felt his forehead. He was warm. "My head hurts, and my neck feels a little achy."

Karen was on that night. "Karen, can you take his temperature?"

Alex said, "I spoke to Dr. Graziani this morning. I told her I thought I might be getting a bladder infection because it feels uncomfortable in that area, plus I have some drainage. I saw Dr. Lucasti and he thought my pump area looked fine. He thought I might have a sinus infection."

Half an hour passed and he called Dr. Graziani again. She was concerned that his neck hurt, and thought that he might have to go to the emergency room because it might be his pump catheter. She wanted to make sure he didn't have meningitis or encephalitis. She told him to use Tylenol for the pain as it wouldn't mask any symptoms. His neck was starting to feel a little stiff.

"Is anything else bothering you?" I asked with concern. It was amazing: one minute I was pissed at him, and the next minute I was concerned. My mood was bouncing around like a kid on a trampoline. "I think you need to call Dr. Graziani back," I said.

After he got off the phone, he said, "She wants me to go to the emergency room."

"Which one?"

"I think this time, I'll go to Regional."

"Do you want to go to Philly?" I asked.

"I don't know. I'm not going back to Edison, Penn doesn't have what I need, and I'm afraid to go to Liberty."

"Why don't we start locally, and then go from there."

And so we were off to Regional. Another wonderful birthday celebration was on hand.

At Regional, we found a filled waiting room.

"Papers please!" Alex was pretending he was German Gestapo. "Vere are your papers?" We made our way to the desk and Karen helped get his insurance card and photo ID out of his man bag. It was 9 p.m. and within about a half an hour we were put in a room at the way, way back of the emergency unit.

Karen and I sat down and listened to a woman two rooms down carrying on. She had been arrested and wanted to leave, but she was so drugged they couldn't let her. "When you gonna let me outta here? I didn't do nothin' wrong," she kept repeating. "Come on, I gotta git home. I didn't do nothin'!"

One hour, two hours, went by. I felt like I was waiting for a bomb to go off.

Finally I went to the desk area and spoke to the doctor, "Excuse me, we've been waiting here two hours, how is that possible?"

"Ma'am, we are very busy."

"I know, but my husband does need to see someone."

"Someone will get to him as quickly as they are able."

I went back to the room, where Alex was being unusually patient. I guess somewhere along the line, his impatience had transferred into my body and my patience had transferred to his. Another hour passed, and I was getting pissed.

I got up, and did something I had never done in my entire life. Was it the boxing? Had it made me more forceful? Was there someone else in my body, taking over? I will never know. I walked over to the doctor sitting behind his computer, probably shopping for underwear, and ever so politely said,

"Excuse me."

"Yes?" he looked up from his keyboard.

"We have been waiting almost three-and-a-half hours. If you or someone else doesn't come in and look at my husband, I'm going to take you out."

"You're going to take me out?" he repeated.

"I box, and I've had it. So you better get someone in there," and I pointed to Alex's room.

I walked backed to the room, and within five minutes the doctor walked in. He took Alex's temperature, slapped a cuff around his arm and saw that his blood pressure was up, as was his heart rate. We called Dr. Graziani, and gave the phone to the ER doctor. She asked him to do a lumbar puncture because we were all worried about the possibility of meningitis, given the symptoms.

I will never forget that she had to talk the doctor through the procedure. We put her on speaker and she literally told the doctor what to do every step of the way. The results were an abnormal amount of white blood cells with a left shift, meaning that there were a high number of young, immature white blood cells, which could signify an infection or inflammation. Dr. Graziani was sure that given the symptoms—headache, fever, stiff neck—and the fact that Alex had recently had an infection with his pump catheter, treatment for meningitis was warranted.

By three in the morning, Alex had IV antibiotics and was sent home.

The next day he spoke with Dr. Graziani again. She implored him to go back to the hospital.

"Alex, you need the pump removed. From all of your symptoms, it sounds as if you have meningitis."

"I am not going back to the hospitals around here. They don't know what to do with me. If I go through withdrawal here, you may as well throw me in the ground. They don't have a clue as to what they should do with baclofen withdrawal. I called Dr. Deogaonkar and he agrees with you. He thinks it should be removed immediately."

"I'm not surprised," she responded. "I'm going to call Dr. Lucasti. I will call you back."

Within half an hour she returned the phone call. "Dr. Lucasti spoke with a neurosurgical resident at Liberty, who agreed you should be admitted. So, Liberty it is."

Alex hung up the phone and looked at me. "She wants me to go to Liberty Hospital."

"Then that's what we'll do." I picked up the phone to call Robert. "Robert, Alex has to go to the hospital. He is going to Liberty."

"I'll be right over."

Michael Daly was Alex's nurse on duty. He got Alex's things together, which always included the red plastic bookbinder with all of the nursing notes. They started to head up to Philadelphia as I waited for Robert and made plans for the kids.

"Danielle, you and Adam can order pizza for dinner."

"We always get pizza," she responded. "I want chicken katszu."

"Fine, you order chicken katszu and if Adam wants pizza order that for him. But please do me a favor and clean up."

"It is not me who makes the mess!"

"I don't care who makes the mess, just both of you clean up. We're going up to Liberty Hospital. I don't know when I'll be back. I think they are going to have to take out Daddy's pump again."

"OK, Mom."

"I'll call Adam on the phone and let him know," I said, which I did on the way to Philadelphia.

How many times had I left with Alex to go to the hospital? How many times had I told that to the kids? 30? 40? Too many to count, and so many that they didn't flinch when he went. When your kids take it so lightly, you know something is deeply wrong. I didn't worry what this would do to them emotionally, only because I didn't have the time or the energy. And I repeated my mother's words often, wherever I could—to myself, to friends, to anyone who would listen: "Worrying is like a rocking chair. It passes the time but it doesn't get you anywhere."

At Liberty we gave them our insurance card, and waited. The ER doctors and nurses were so nice that we both felt more relaxed. There were many memories in that ER, not all bad ones. I had given birth to Adam and Danielle there, and the gateway to the maternity ward was through the ER.

359

Alex was put in a room that had walls and a door. Mike D. Alex's nurse, Robert and I sat in the room with Alex. Dr. Graziani had spoken with the emergency room intake nurse and a different neurosurgical resident who was on call. She updated them with his medical history, his present condition and his past difficulties with baclofen withdrawal. She also recommended that they remove the pump and begin treating him with oral baclofen.

When the resident and a male nurse came in, Alex began to tell him his history, and how he had an infection, and how the previous night he was in Regional and the doctor there did a lumbar tap and it was positive for an infection. The nurse went to put an IV in, and Alex said,

"I'm a hard stick."

He responded with, "No need to worry. I've worked with preemies in the NICU and if I can hit their veins I think I can get yours."

Within seconds, Alex had his IV in. "You're good! You're really good. Most times I feel like a dartboard."

The nurse smiled.

The neurosurgical resident examined Alex. He had an elevated temperature and his blood pressure was on the rise. In my experience, this meant an infection was brewing.

"I have a headache and my neck is feeling very stiff," he said.

"Well, right now you have a low-grade fever, and with meningitis you would have a very high fever. You would also either have a rash, or you would be vomiting, and you would be very sleepy."

"He can't vomit," I interjected. "Also, he doesn't present like other patients. I know he may look OK, but he really knows his body."

Robert added, "He tested positive for an infection in Atlantic City."

"We've called and asked them for the reports. They have yet to fax them over. We are going to admit you, and hopefully when we get the reports, we can figure this out."

"Thank you," I said.

I'd said to Alex earlier, "You know some day Blue Cross is going to send out an assassin and kill you because you cost them so much money."

"I wouldn't doubt it," he'd responded.

Once again, Alex found himself in the neuro unit at Liberty. I hoped the slate had been wiped clean. The first nurse came in to check in on him. She finished hooking him up to the monitors and asked, "Mr. Kiejdan, is there anything else I can do for you?"

"No thank you, but I just want you to know that I was kicked out of here before." I looked at him, and thought, *Really? Why would you admit that to anyone! Can't we just move forward?* But I said nothing.

"Are you a bad boy?" she asked.

"It wasn't intentional. But obviously my doctor thought so."

I was looking at Alex, and I noted to myself that this was a very different man from the last time he was here. He knew what he was saying, and he didn't have the wild look in his eyes that had scared me twice before. But he still had his mouth...that wasn't going anywhere.

"Mr. Kiejdan—"

"You can call me Alex."

"OK, Alex, we still haven't received the tests they ran on you at Regional Hospital."

"I'll call my doctor there, maybe she can help with that." Dr. G.'s cell phone number was on speed dial and she was on top of things in minutes. She always had an efficient and immediate response to the problem at hand. How do you thank a doctor like that? Someone who has saved you over and over and over again?

After the nurse left, a neurosurgical resident came in. I sat at the end of Alex's bed. She asked him, "Sir, where did you have the pump put in originally?" He began the story of how he has had it for many years. But the infection started at Edison, where he got cellulitis. Then onto Cleveland, where they took it out, put him on the IVs, his port, waiting until it was OK to replace it, and up to why he was here at Liberty.

"Why didn't you go back to Edison?" she asked.

"Because that's where he got the infection," I interjected. "Why would anyone want to go back to a place that almost killed them?"

"I think you should go back to Edison," she continued.

"That's not happening," I said.

I looked over at Alex and the shock on his face was turning to anger. I hated anger. It didn't solve anything. But I had recently learned that on a very rare occasion, you needed it. It was survival anger, and survival anger was very acceptable in my book.

"OK," she responded, and left the room.

"What was that about?" Alex asked.

"I have no idea."

That night I got a phone call.

"Gail?" It was Alex.

"What's wrong?"

"They keep asking me why I didn't go back to Edison. Then they told me that the doctor here, who had put my pump in, was on vacation."

"So what! He's not the only one trained to remove a pump. I'm sure there is someone who could remove the pump."

"I think his partner is here, but I won't see him until tomorrow."

"Ok, just settle down, if you can. I'll be back tomorrow."

"I have to get this pump out. I spoke to Dr. Graziani and she spoke to Dr. Deogaonkar, and they both want this done ASAP."

"You have onset signs of meningitis…I don't know what the problem is."

"Are you coming in the morning?"

"Yes, after I get the kids off to school."

By the time I got there, I could see that he was overwrought with anxiety. "I saw another resident this morning. There must have been five different ones coming in and out."

"And?" I asked.

"He told me that 'they' don't think that I really need to take the pump out. But they would wait for the doctor to make the final decision."

"Did they get the lumbar test from Regional?"

"No, they keep calling there, but they never sent it over here."

"Can Dr. Graziani get it for them?" I asked.

"I spoke with her this morning. She's going to get a copy and have it faxed here."

"She's amazing. No ego. Just wants to do what's best for you. Thank God for her."

"But I spoke with Dr. Deogaonkar this morning and he said if they don't take it out, to get in the car and come to the Clinic and he will take it out. He will put me on the schedule, whenever I get there."

"Should we go back to Cleveland?"

"If they're not going to take it out here, we have no choice."

After the second night Alex said to the resident, "I am leaving, I am not staying here. This pump needs to be taken out, and if you're

363

not going to do it, then I'm going back to Cleveland, where someone will."

That afternoon, the doctor came in and told him that they would take the pump out, that he wasn't presenting like he had meningitis, and that they would take it out as a courtesy.

Alex called me that night. "They're taking it out tomorrow."

"Thank God. Do you have a surgery time yet?"

"It will be in the morning, probably around 11 a.m."

"I will try to be there by 10:30. I need to buy a wig while I'm there."

"What do you need a wig for?"

"Adam is a contestant in Mr. Mainland. And for his talent, he is doing an imitation of Christopher Walken."

"He's really good at that. When is the contest?"

"Friday night."

"I won't be there," he responded solemnly.

"I know," I said. "But I think it will be taped or someone is going to make a DVD, so you will get to see it."

"Please tell him I'm sorry."

"I will."

I went up to Philly by myself the day of the surgery. I was surprised to see Alex's sister Renee and his cousin Henny in the waiting room.

I sat down and asked, "Any news?"

"No. Nothing. He went in about 15 minutes ago."

"I have to buy a wig. I don't even know where to look," I said.

"There's a wig store two blocks from here," Renee said.

"Really? How do you know that?"

"I remember strange things."

"Wow. But a wig store? That's incredible. Well, once Alex is out, I'll shoot over to the wig store."

"What do you need a wig for?" she asked.

"It's for Adam, he's losing his hair."

"He's only 17!" she responded.

"I know. Actually, he is in the Mr. Mainland contest. And he needs one for his act."

"The store is not far, I can't remember the name of it but it is literally right around the corner," she said.

"I'll Google it," I responded. I loved Google. If I had a question in my head, Google could answer it. If I needed to prove something to someone, Google could prove it. Or disprove it. Either way, there were answers out there that I could pull up on my phone.

We sat there for about an hour. After we were notified that the surgery was over and that Alex was in recovery I went out and bought a wig. By the time I got back, Alex was in his room with his sister and Henny by his side. Renee had brought him something to eat, which sat unopened on the adjustable bedside table.

"What's in the bag?" he asked as I kissed him hello.

"It's a wig. Remember? Adam needs it for Mr. Mainland. Of course he waits until two days before to ask me."

"That's Adam," Alex responded.

"How are you feeling?"

"Relieved. I'm glad that thing is out of me."

"I'm going to call Ma and Edie and tell them everything is OK," Renee said.

"Thanks, Renee," he said.

After they left, I sat staring out the window. Alex had nodded off, so I texted Andrea, Robert, and Christina, to let them know that everything went well, then I texted Adam to tell him I found the wig.

The next morning Alex called me. "The doctor just left, and you know what?"

"What?"

"He said that I was right. That they found necrotic tissue at the base of the catheter, and that it's a Staph infection. I'm going to have to continue with an IV, but this time the antibiotic is Ancef, and it will be for about an eight-week period."

"You know your body. There's no denying that," I said.

Are you coming up today?" he asked.

"I don't know if I can. Adam has his contest tonight and I have to pick up his tux at the cleaners and do some errands for him."

"That's fine. Robert said he was going to come up and see me."

"Great. I will call you after Mr. Mainland and tell you how he did."

As I sat in the audience that night with Christina, I watched all the students and parents gather in the school auditorium. There was an excited buzz as the kids and their parents talked to each other. Emotionally, I was in transition. I had gone from real life purgatory to supposed 'enjoyment and entertainment' mode. The switch wasn't easy, and it was never automatic.

Over the years, I realized that I had become a person who spent most of the time in delay. Did it take longer to register what I had been through? Or had I, at some point, subconsciously realized that reacting immediately was a waste of time? Because you never have the facts immediately; things always need to play out. So why stress now, when you can still stress later? And the fact of the matter was that I had been living my life on hold since this injury first occurred. But I guess that's what you do when you have kids. You put yourself on a plane and circle the landing pad, or you run out of gas.

A friend of Adam's ran up to Christina and me and handed us a tongue depressor with a colored print of Adam's head on it.

"Thank you," I said.

"No problem, Mrs. Kiejdan. Adam has a cheering section over there, if you'd like to sit with us."

"Thanks," I said to Adam's friend. "I'll stay here and take a video." And off she went as the light began to dim. There were 10 contestants and there was a swimsuit competition, where he had to rip off his T-shirt by cutting it with scissors, and then there was a section where he had to wear a tux. He was escorted by a girl named Molly, who was one of his best friends. And then there was the talent competition, which he did without the wig.

There he was, the body and face of Adam, with the voice of Christopher Walken imitating Bella Swan from the Twilight Saga talking to Edward. He was so good he got a standing ovation. I was thrilled for him. I was looking at someone who had grown into a confident, funny, and focused young man. How the hell had that happened? And when? If I was a puzzle with scattered pieces, how did he have it all together?

When we walked out to the school lobby there were parents of his friends there to support him. Mark and Anne, Swarna, and a handful of others came up to congratulate me on Adam's second place win. I was dumbfounded. And as thrilled as I was for him, I knew he had done it all on his own. Most parents would think that was a great thing, but I knew in my heart I was missing out. It was like walking into your own surprise party, not having a clue as to what some of your closest friends and family had known all along.

By the time Alex got home, the excitement of Mr. Mainland had died down. Adam had decided to go to Tulane University in New Orleans the following year. And the discussion in the house was about whether Alex would be able to make the trip. He was on oral baclofen every four hours, and his rigidity and spasms were not bad, even though baclofen was more effective when it was being fed through an intrathecal catheter from the pump.

We watched as he spasmed, and at night he had such severe burning that he just wanted to be left alone. That never changed, there was no end to the pain, the burning, and the spasming. The only time he wanted company was when Riley came in bed. "Hey Riley?" he would say. "Fucky? Fucky?" When Alex's nurse rolled him over to help him get undressed, his arm would land in the perfect humping position. Riley learned that it was hump time, so he responded accordingly.

"Are you kidding me?" I would say. "What is your problem?"

"I know what he feels like. I just want to make him happy."

The dog learned many tricks that anyone in their right mind wouldn't teach a dog. He learned how to lick Alex's ear on command, how to lick his nipple, and how to offend his mother on a nightly basis.

Every night I would say, "You're disgusting!" And every night Alex would smile and laugh. Our poor dog was now a sex addict. I looked at the two of them, knowing that this was their nightly entertainment. I was just a spectator, a voyeur. It was how I felt when I was out in the world, as well. I had seen and experienced things that changed my core. We had many friends who took for granted that they could physically do whatever they wanted without restrictions. Once you have crossed that bridge, you can only look back at the other side and see how different that life is.

37. THE SUMMER OF 2014

The winter of 2014 had been brutal, even by southern New Jersey standards. Conversations were consumed by the debate over whether it was just another bad winter or it was global warming wreaking havoc. Much had changed, and would continue to do so. The kids were away at school, and the house was quiet except for the occasional barking from Riley. How many times had this dog saved our lives? He was a constant source of love, a loyal protector, and the center of our universe. After Danielle had left for Syracuse the previous fall, we had thought that we would have nothing to say to each other. The house was quiet, even with the nurses.

Initially, we did have nothing to say except, "When was the last time you talked to Danielle?" "Is she okay?" "Have you spoken to Adam?"

I knew the answer to that one. Adam didn't talk on the phone. He just texted, or if there was an emergency he would call and say, "Hi, I need money." Or, "Hi, I'm out of money." Other than that, he was doing great. Danielle just called to check in and say hello. We FaceTimed each other, and as long as we saw her sweet, beautiful face we were happy.

In February, Alex read an article on the Internet that motivated him to investigate an opportunity to bring joy back into his summers. He saw a video on YouTube of a man who was building all-wheel-drive wheelchairs to be driven on the beach by other wheelchair-dependent people. He was at once astonished and thrilled.

He had never gotten over not going to the beach. Spending his summers at Sam's Warehouse, or sitting in the kitchen when all of his friends were at the beach, brought a level of isolation that no one could possibly understand as they spent their days swimming, surfing, and sailing in the waters, congregating in their beach chairs, and enjoying the coastal views of the Atlantic City, Ventnor, Margate, and Longport beaches.

"You do not get the sand out of your shoes, even if your feet can no longer touch the ground," he would say. But through his computer he found a window on a world not yet broached, waiting to be discovered by someone just like him. Alex reached out to the man in the YouTube video, who lived in Boston.

This man didn't work on the plastic wheelchairs that you need to be pushed in, that didn't recline and gave you no independence. He worked on the electric chairs like Alex's. The builder's name was Dave Heim, and he, too, was in a wheelchair. And because he was an engineer, he knew that there was a way to adapt a chair so you could bring it to the beach and ride it through the sand.

Alex had an extra chair in the garage, which he used when his good chair broke down. Without hesitation, I agreed to him getting this chair adapted for the beach.

"Are you sure, Gail?" he asked me. "I don't know how much it's going to cost."

"Happy early birthday," I said. "Look, if this will make you happy, and we all know how difficult that is, then by all means do it."

So Alex picked up the phone to start his journey towards home. Dave lived on the outskirts of Boston. He had three young men working with him, two of whom were relatives. One of his sons came to pick up Alex's second wheelchair. He was tall with dark hair, and you could see by his hands that he had been working with them for some time.

"Thanks for doing this," Alex said.

As they wheeled the chair up the ramp and into the gold Chrysler handicap-accessible van, Alex turned around to me and smiled. It was an honest, from-the-heart kind of smile that I had rarely seen. He was excited, and he couldn't hide his happiness.

"How long will it take?" he asked.

"Maybe a month, maybe a little longer," the young man answered. "It depends on my dad's health."

"Well, I get that. Whatever it is, it is. I'd just like it before summer, if that's possible."

"That's not a problem. We have a couple of months to work on it."

"Okay, have a safe drive back. Tell your dad to call me if he needs anything."

Toward the end of spring, the gestation period ended and the wheelchair was delivered. As it rolled down the ramp from the van we could see the change... the pimped-up wheelchair was now in total road rage monster drive. It screamed, "Move out of the way!"

The only thing Dave had kept from the original wheelchair was the seating system and the motors. It had a new frame with new axles. The frame's width was increased for stability on the beach so it wouldn't tip over. There were four new tires as well.

"Why are the tires so big, Alex?" I asked.

"Large tires do not get stuck in mud or sand," he said. "This is now an all-wheel-drive vehicle, instead of just rear wheel drive. And the whole chair is higher, so hopefully I can navigate the beach with ease."

"I see he put a canopy on top. That was a great idea."

We smiled at each other. "How are you going to get it to the beach?" I asked.

"We're going to put it on John's big truck and he'll drive it down there. I'm going to get in my van with Joyce and meet him there."

John Ferrie had become one of Alex's closest friends and confidants over the past few years. He was a kind human being with a good soul and a twisted sense of humor. And that appealed to Alex even more.

He told me which beach they were going to and I arranged to meet them there. I did my errands, then headed over the causeway towards Margate. I parked in the Hamilton Beach lot, where they were selling beach badges for the summer. It dawned on me that this chair would need a beach badge, so I walked inside, where there were several older ladies seated, playing cards.

"Excuse me," I said. "Do you know where they sell the beach badges?"

"Oh, sure honey. Just go down the hallway and make a left. There's a young girl in the office selling them."

"Thank you so much."

"You're welcome, sweetheart."

I walked down the hallway as directed. I couldn't believe that after 18 years I was buying a beach badge for Alex. For the first time in eighteen years I enjoyed paying for the beach badge. For some, it was an expense that you had to pay to use the beaches every summer. To Alex, it would be a symbol of freedom.

As I walked outside into the bright sunshine, I could feel the late spring breeze whipping at my dress. It was one of those windy days at the beach. I looked over to the bulkhead to see the large red Fresh Cut truck pull in. Joyce was parking the van in the lot as I walked towards the truck. The ramp came down on the truck the same time the ramp came down on the van. John rolled the freedom chair down his ramp just as Alex was rolling over to meet him.

"Shall we give this baby a try?" John said. There was true joy on his face, excitement compounded by an endearing eagerness.

Joyce helped Alex transfer to the freedom chair. Alex got situated and turned it on, then adjusted the back and the legs to his preferred comfort level. He looked at me and smiled.

"I have a present for you," I said.

"Really?"

"Yep." I pulled the beach tag out of my bag. "Where should we put this?"

He beamed. "Wow, that's right, I need a beach tag. Pin it on the back of the chair." After I pinned the badge to his chair, he turned up the chair's power and started to roll towards the ocean. He zigzagged and spun around and then headed straight for the water. The tide was low, and you could see him pushing the speed stick and going faster and faster down the beach.

The three of us stood watching as he turned around, raised both his hands in the air with his fingers curled inward and his thumbs resting on the side of his pointer finger, and screamed, "I'm back!"

Epilogue

In 2017, the United States Lifesaving Association reported that beach attendance reached a little over 385 million visitors, with rescue totals reaching almost 76,000. The beaches and the businesses that thrive off of them in this country are no cottage industry. They amass 320 billion dollars annually, creating one of the largest and most significant forces driving the US economy.

Yet they are truly a throwback to another era. Technology has also taken a back seat here. There continues at this time to be no cell phone application that tells you of the ocean conditions in a specific location. There continues to be no signage in most areas to warn bathers of sandbars left from sand replenishment projects, no flags notifying swimmers that there are strong rip currents, and no information regarding the dangers of what lurk beneath the beautiful, majestic waters that ebb at our souls.

Acknowledgements

I would like to thank my husband Alex for teaching me that empowerment is a never -ending struggle. I would like to thank Adam and Danielle for giving me oxygen when I felt I could no longer breathe. I would like to thank the friends and family members who stayed to support us throughout this long interminable journey. I would like to thank Dr. Virginia Graziani for always being available and calm and a genuinely caring physician, even at the wee hours in the morning. And I would like to thank my editor Pat Dobie who helped me birth this baby. Without her insight, guidance and encouragement, this book would not have become what it is.

Made in the USA
Monee, IL
04 July 2022

99052971R00218